THE MARATHON

A TRUE STORY

KERRY SHEERAN

Ocean State Press
East Greenwich, RI

This book is non-fiction. Certain names of characters have been changed in order to protect their privacy. The timing and accuracy of specific events was written in accord with chronicle and the author's recollection. References used for research purposes are listed at the end.

Cover Photo by Kimberli DiIuro (www.kimberliphoto.com)

Senior Editor, Sandi Daine (www.sdaine.com)

Author Photo by Denise Lopez

Bubbly, Written by: Colbie Caillat & Jason Reeves.
© 2007 by SONY/ATV Music Publishing LLC, Cocomarie Music, Dancing Squirrel Music and Inafi Music. All rights administered by Sony/ATV Music Publishing LLC, 8 Music Square West, Nashville, TN 37203. All rights reserved. Used by permission.

Special thanks to all my family and friends who have helped me on this journey, specifically my: first draft consultant, Ann Sullivan; agent, Jennifer DesMarais Righi, online promotions manager, Jill Smith; public relations consultants, Greg Wind and Joy Weisbord; and my parents, Joseph and Donna Sullivan—for their dedication and support towards my completion of THE MARATHON.

ISBN: 978-0-9915097-0-6

For more information regarding THE MARATHON and its efforts towards assisting to fund prenatal and neonatal research and care, go to www.kerrysheeran.com.

The publisher is not responsible for websites (or their content) that are not owned by the publisher.

This book is dedicated to my children, the six miracles who refresh my spirit every day.

And to my husband, Tom, whose love keeps me running.

Contents

Promise me you'll always remember: You're braver than you believe,
and stronger than you seem, and smarter than you think.

Christopher Robin to Pooh (by A. A. Milne)

Chapter 1

THE LETTER

"ARE YOU SURE you have everything, babe?" She followed him around the house rattling off question after question. The more she asked, the more he panicked. *Why does she do this?* he wondered. Every time he was rushing to get out, no matter where he was going, she'd start in. Having been on hundreds of business trips and vacations, the world traveler in him bristled. After all, he'd made it to and from all of his destinations without any major catastrophes. He was a grown man, thirty-five years old and counting. *So for God sakes, why does she have to keep pressing?* "Did you make a list, hun?" she asked. *Arrrgh! Here we go*, he thought, *the LIST question*. If only she knew that some people had the mental capacity to remember what they need to pack without bullet points and sub categories. Lists were bush league.

She was talking to a guy who had spent the past nine months of his life preparing for this very day. Every step, every tear, every drop of sweat had landed him in this moment. And as usual, she was making him second-guess himself. Unzipping his bag, he furiously dug through it, hardly even paying attention to what he was looking for. His heart was beating faster and he knew if he didn't leave the house that very minute, things would begin to unravel. He zipped his bag closed.

The boys climbed on the couch, hoping to get the perfect Superman leap onto him. "Good luck, Daddy!" his older son giggled. "See you at the party!"

His wife hadn't stopped. She bustled around the kitchen, peering under stacks of newspapers and opening and slamming every drawer within reach. Time was running out; he had to go. The phone rang again.

1

Another good-luck wish going to voicemail, he assumed. Tom just couldn't talk to anyone else. It was time to get into the *zone.*

Peeling his sons off his back, he unzipped his bag for the last time. Rummaging through it, he took a final inventory: several tiny packets of GU energy gel, two pairs of socks, his favorite shorts, one long-sleeved shirt, one stick of Body Glide, four power bars, a water bottle, his wallet and his phone. *But wait?* His hands tapped his chest, then fumbled their way to the top of his head where they narrowly missed knocking off a brand new pair of polarized sunglasses. *Good,* he thought, *I have my shades.*

Returning to the big dig, he smiled when he got to the bottom of the bag and found his running sneakers. *There they are,* he thought. The only accessories he would really need for the next twelve hours. The two things that would carry him down the valleys, up the hills and past all of his inhibitions. His green eyes locked on the matching pair. When he finally blinked, he zipped up his bag with authority and threw it over his shoulder. *No more second-guessing,* he thought, *it's game time.*

After kissing his boys, he made his way over to his wife. She had finally stopped buzzing around and was ready to join him in his moment. "You know you can do this," she said, wrapping her arms around his neck. "*YOU* can do this." Her kiss was soft and a little longer then usual. Her eyes were honest. Their assurance was starting to rub off on him. He gave her one more squeeze. As he headed for the front door, he turned around to wave goodbye. "You can do this," she repeated, "but not without my help!"

His face dropped. Shaking his head, Tom let out a long, deep breath and walked across the room. He growled as he snatched his racing bib out of his wife's hands. Her smile was wicked. Few things gave her more pleasure then moments like this. *Why'd she have to do that? Today of all days?* he wondered. A smile cracked across his face as he shut the door.

It was a crisp Monday on April 20, 2009. The kind of day that could convince a person spring is right around the corner. Having been a New Englander for fifteen years, however, Tom knew better than to believe that. The wind was blowing slightly from the south. *Just enough,* he thought, *to get me through Wellesley.*

He pictured the entire route in his head again. It had been six weeks since his practice run and although he'd only gotten as far as mile 21, he had a pretty good idea about which parts would be the toughest. Telling himself to *stop*, he erased the course from his head and unrolled the window.

Downtown Providence was passing by on his right. Providence Place Mall, The Cheesecake Factory, the State House all standing tall— perhaps even saluting him as he made his way through the capitol city of Rhode Island in less than fifteen minutes. Making good time on the road always gave him an unnecessary high. *Sixty minutes to go*, he thought.

Tom was well acquainted with the ride to Boston. It was impossible not to think how his wife would always boast: *"I could do this drive in my sleep."* Luckily, it had never come to that. He thought about what a pleasure it was to be driving up there with happy anticipation, rather then ungodly dread. The fear of the unknown was absent from his head. The anxiety had untied its terrible grip from around his heart. *This day*, he thought, *is different. Today is about keeping promises. Today is for her.* His shoulders lifted and loosened up. He hung his arm out the window and felt the breeze.

Tom's phone rang. He remembered that the last time he saw it, it was buried among his necessities. His trip was coming to an end, and the fact that he hadn't picked it up or made one call in the last seventy-five minutes was bewildering. If anyone loved talking on the phone, it was Tom. He could be in the middle of a colonoscopy prep and he'd find someone interested enough to chat with him about it. Of course, he wasn't the only man with this gift. Mike, his college buddy, would dial him several times a week just to report the exact lengths and widths of his one-year-old's "turds".

Tom's wife had eventually learned there was no need to keep a journal, when instead she could listen to him entertain family and friends with stories of their recent adventures over and over and over. By his tenth retelling, it had been etched in her mind forever.

The fact that Tom had been *so* focused that he hadn't even *looked* at his mobile device the entire drive reaffirmed his commitment to the day's event. By the third ring he was shoulder-deep in his bag when he spotted the light from his phone underneath a white envelope. The letter wasn't something he'd noticed the last time he had rummaged through. He pulled it out and turned it over. On the front it read *'For you, Tom'*. His wife's handwriting was unmistakable. Beautiful and sharp, he often thought it could rival Palatino Linotype in a font-to-font challenge. He glanced at his phone as it rang for the fourth time. It was her.

"Are you there, yet?" she asked, sounding as nervous as he felt.

"I'm here," he answered. "What's in this envelope?"

"Oh, good. You found it. Don't read the whole thing yet. I wrote it for you," she said. He could hear her smiling. She hadn't done this in a long time. When they were first married, he'd find little love notes in his suitcase while away on business. But as the years rolled by, the frequency of the letters dwindled. To hold one in his hand was a rare treat. "Why can't I read the whole thing?" he wanted to know. "You'll see," she said. "Look for me later on, okay? I love you." Click. She was never really a phone person, which might explain why most calls made by Kerry left the recipient feeling important.

Finding his group was much easier then Tom had imagined it would be. Boston Children's Hospital had chosen a glaring yellow and blue-checkered print for its team's running attire. Hard to miss, a sea of similarly-clad runners stretched their legs and bounced around the parking lot in front of buses waiting to bring them to the starting line.

Suddenly things were becoming a lot more real. Tom was dressed like these folks. And just like them, he had raised thousands of dollars from family members, friends, and even clients. People hadn't simply made direct donations to the hospital; they had funded him and his cause. And not only had Tom asked for their sponsorship, he had guaranteed a final result: In return for their generosity he would run The Boston Marathon.

What was I thinking? he wondered. *Am I crazy? Seriously, how has it come to this?* Tom was so far in that the term "turning back" wasn't within the realm of possibility. Not to mention that most of his sponsors were going to want to know how long it took him to finish. So now, not only was it alarming that he'd committed himself to run 26.2 miles, but he also had to do it in a respectable amount of time. And regardless of what he had told people, Tom wanted a good time. His veins pulsated faster and faster. *Good*, he thought, *the adrenaline will carry me through the first ten.*

"Do you wanna borrow this, brother?" A bearded man handed him black chalk. It was customary for runners to write their bib number on one leg and their personal inspiration on the other. Having seen this in pictures and on television in years past, Tom looked forward to taking part in this particular ritual.

Gratefully, he accepted the chalk, then pulled the racing bib out of his bag and began to copy "25519" down his left shin. *That*, he thought, *looks cool.* He paused. A vision of her dark brown eyes invaded his thoughts. The rest of her face came into focus: her beautiful nose, her piercing dimples. Her delicate beauty consumed him. The scent of her hair somehow filled his nostrils. In an instant, he was relieved of the intense pressures he had felt only seconds before. With a swig of emotion he wrote the words *"Mighty Emma"* down his right shin. *THAT*, he thought, *looks angelic.*

Considering how many runners were on the bus, it was relatively quiet. *Finally*, he thought, *a chance to open the white envelope.* A lump swelled in his throat before he even read one word, as his eyes were drawn to the small picture at the top—a picture taken twelve months earlier when life was a lot different. He began to read:

My Dear Tom,

The marathon is finally here! Today's run will be painless when measured with the long journey your heart has endured. As you begin each mile, read and reflect on each of the challenges we've been faced with. Once that mile is complete, it might seem effortless in comparison.

He stopped. *"Mile One"* began the next line, and he wasn't about to spoil this newfound treasure. Much like Barbara Walters, Kerry had the gift of being able to tap into and wring out people's emotions. Especially his. And although it could be exhausting at times, for the most part he loved it.

The bus began to move slowly. It headed for the John Warren Lodge on Main Street in Hopkinton, a block from the starting line. Hundreds of buses packed the road. All filled with the same type of people—runners, about twenty-six thousand of them. Tom thought about the other runners who were there to support a charity and wondered just how many charities were involved in the marathon. He made a mental note to Google that question when he was finished.

He thought about the elite runners who had qualified, and how amazing it would be if he could run 26.2 miles in under three hours and ten minutes. He wondered where the Kenyan dudes were, who always seemed to be at the front of the pack at every marathon. *What are they doing at this very moment? What did they eat for breakfast? Will their families be in Copley Square to see them finish? How did they get to Hopkinton this morning?* His mind was going a mile a minute. So much so, he didn't notice the tall blond calling his name and waving to him from across this aisle.

"Tom! Hi! Feeling good today? How's your leg?" she asked. It was Jill, one of the nurses from the Neonatal ICU at Children's Hospital. It always took him a moment to place her face when she wasn't wearing her nursing scrubs. He had run into her a couple weeks earlier at the pre-race banquet and they'd exchanged stories about sore muscles, lost toenails and all of the aches and pains that come with marathon training.

"Did you get a good stretch in the parking lot?" Jill asked, seeming genuinely concerned. This was runners' talk. Tom had become well versed in this language over the past several months. Runners focus on five things: sneakers, pace, routes, injuries and stretching. And when they get together, they can talk for hours about each topic. Even more, they passionately *care* about every subject. Kerry never hesitated to remind Tom just how torturous it was for non-runners to have to listen to this back and forth chatter. *"I'd rather be water-boarded!"* she'd often admit.

"I did, I got a good stretch. It is what it is at this point," he assured her. In all honesty, he never really had much of a problem with his leg. But it gave him something to talk about during these types of encounters, so he just went with it. Jill looked down at Tom's shin, then up to his eyes and bit her lip. "This is a pretty big day, isn't it?" she asked, fully aware she was stating the obvious. Emma had left an impression on so many of the Children's Hospital staff, it was nearly impossible to run into someone who knew her without getting that same exact look. Tom nodded and bowed his head. "Is Kerry coming today?" Jill asked. She had already asked him that question when they'd spoke at the banquet, but Tom humored her. "She wouldn't miss it," he responded. "At least not on purpose!"

* * *

KERRY CAREFULLY PLACED the cake between two boxes, then slammed the trunk of her Honda Pilot and ran back around to the driver's seat. She pealed out of her driveway for the second time in five minutes. If she hadn't spent thirty minutes decorating the damn thing, she wouldn't have bothered coming back for it. Not her best work, by far, but the effort was there and she wanted a *little* credit for it.

The stick-figure man crossing the finish line rated about a four on her scale of ten. She had created some eights and nines over the past few years, having slowly defined herself as somewhat of a "cake artist". The haunted house for Thomas' fourth birthday was definitely her masterpiece. Not far behind was the Sponge Bob torte she had whipped up for Ryan. Tom's cake, however, while below par in appearance, represented something eminent. Across the top she had written ***"Congratulations Tom!"*** More then just a standard tag line, these words spoke volumes. In a way, this cake gave validation to every mile he had run over the last nine months.

Kerry was never the type to lavish excessive praise on somebody. If she was happy with her kids for cleaning up 4,695 Legos, she told them so, once. If a friend lost fifty pounds after months of intense diet and exercise, she'd mention how fantastic he or she looked, once. And if someone—whether he was her husband or not—trained unabatedly for just under a year's time to run his first marathon, she was going to let him know how impressed she was, once. In fact, she was going to hold off on telling him until the very day he ran it.

This was just the way she was. Drove Tom crazy. Having grown up in an environment where fusses were constantly being made, he craved a certain level of enthusiasm from his wife that didn't always exist. "You do realize you didn't marry your mother, right?" Kerry often reminded him. Her smile got her out of a lot of trouble. She was blunt, honest and unbelievably sarcastic. But most of all, Kerry did not like any expectations forced upon her. This aspect of her personality was both loved and hated. It certainly accounted for eighty percent of the clash between her and her mother-in-law, Jane.

Friction on both parts could be traced back as early as Tom and Kerry's wedding planning. Any person with half a brain could have calculated that:

> A Jersey Girl of Stoic Irish decent
> + A Brazen Italian Mother from Brooklyn
> = A Recipe for Sparks

Yet this kind of math was nearly incalculable for a love-struck 27-year-old with a diamond ring on her finger. When the happy couple had decided they had just enough in their budget to host two hundred guests at their August 2002 wedding, Kerry gave her fiancé the task of collecting a list of sixty invitees from his parents. They'd figured it out perfectly, inviting eighty friends themselves, then divvying up the remaining one hundred twenty invites between their two families. It made sense to be overly ample with their parents, considering they both came from big families. However, after six weeks of countless reminders, Tom seemed confused at Kerry's reaction to the list his mother had compiled for them:

"*What's this?*" Kerry had asked.

"*What do you mean? That's my mom's list,*" Tom had responded.

"*I mean, what's with one hundred and sixty people? It's one hundred people over our budget.*" Kerry had explained. Playing dumb wasn't in her repertoire.

"*I don't know, Ker, that's her list,*" Tom had said.

Kerry looked, but there was no fire in Tom's eyes. She could tell he had already conceded. And although she was still a little naïve, the bride-to-be was plenty aware of her role in this particular situation. After all, she'd seen countless episodes of *Everybody Loves Raymond*. Like Deborah, Kerry would have to be brave and confront her mother-in-law on her own. Unfortunately, Kerry's bravery had lacked experience. Which is why she sat speechless when the conversation ended with this explanation from Tom's mother, Jane:

"*That's just the way it has to be, Kerry. In our family, we always invite ALL the cousins. That's just the way we do it. You're going to have to understand.*"

Oh, Kerry had understood, all right. Apparently "*our family*" was going to take a little getting used to.

Glancing at the clock, Kerry couldn't believe it was already 10:45 a.m. She had just passed through Providence and was not at all pleased with the time she was making. This sat on her nerves for a good twenty minutes, until finally the sound of her ringing phone distracted her. She grinned as she picked it up. "Hello darling, it's me, Jackie," the voice on the other end announced. Kerry had to laugh. Not only was it the twenty-first century in the age of caller ID, but Jackie's voice needed no introduction. Her English accent was unmistakable. It rivaled the likes of Eliza Doolittle.

"Where are you, my dear?" Jackie asked.

"I'm just getting through Attleboro. I forgot the cake and had to go back, so I'm running behind," Kerry said.

"Oh, that's a stinker," Jackie sympathized. "Well, I'm just at the bar with some of my friends. Once we get a little buzz going we'll head out to Kenmore Square and watch the race from there." Kerry thought about the last time she had tailgated so early in the day. *Was it the Springsteen concert in 2003?* she wondered. Whatever it was, it had been a long while.

"I don't think it even occurred to me that people would be drinking," Kerry admitted.

"Are you serious? You should see Boston right now. The entire city is partying! Before I forget," Jackie continued, "I'm almost positive I saw Tom on the telly a few minutes ago. They showed him stretching with all the BCH folks."

"No way!" Kerry squealed.

She pictured Tom in her head. He looked embarrassed and was pretending not to notice the camera. She wanted to be there, to see him in person. Her morning had been so hectic with getting the boys off to pre-school and arranging their transportation to the after-party in Norfolk, Mass., it hadn't even occurred to her that the race was about to start. For a moment, she was excited. Then suddenly, it felt as though she were slapped on the back.

"I have to go, Jack. I'm passing through Norwood right now."

Kerry's voice was melancholy. The brightness in her eyes dimmed as she glanced at the patch of grass on the side of the road. The only stretch long enough to pull a car onto, just beyond the sign for Exit 11. Her breathing quickened. Her chest grew tight. Flashes started going off in her mind.

"Okay, honey. Take your time. Drive carefully and I'll meet you after the race. Keep your phone on you, okay? I love you, my dear," Jackie said.

They hung up. Kerry put her phone on the dash and plugged it into the charger. She glanced in her rearview mirror, then looked intensely ahead, barely blinking. *Just five more minutes*, she thought, *until the Route 95/93 split.*

Chapter 2

IT'S A GIRL

TOM LOOKED AROUND at the number of participants joining him on his quest to complete the arduous journey from Hopkinton, Massachusetts to Boston's Copley Square. People of all shapes and sizes. The young and the old. The iron men and the disabled. All willing to run, walk, wheel or crawl a total of twenty-six miles, three hundred and eighty-five yards.

His stomach wasn't craving anything in particular. Standing at the buffet line in the lodge, he remembered what his running coach had warned him:

> *"Keep your routine the same on the day of the race. Eat what you'd normally eat. Drink what you'd normally drink."*

Grabbing a bagel with peanut butter, he followed this advice to a tee as he filled up his coffee cup. Looking around as he ate, he couldn't help but notice all the traffic at the bathrooms. A woman in her mid-fifties had been speed walking back and forth on the same beaten path for the past thirty-five minutes. Her grayish-blond ponytail bounced in unison with her hurried feet. A classic case of the "pre-race jitters".

Tom was grateful he'd had a decent bowel movement before he'd left the house that morning. His urine output was picking up, though, which wasn't ideal. Looking at his coffee with hesitation, he took one last sip then dumped the rest in a nearby garbage can and headed for the bathroom. *I don't want to be one of those guys peeing in his pants mid-race,* he thought. He had come to find out through his extensive research that many folks don't want to take the time to make a pit stop. So without regard to anyone who may be getting splashed in their wake, they just let it flow. Thankfully this usually only happened with number ones.

There were dozens of occasions during Tom's training when he had to make a beeline into the woods for a number two. Shaky legs and all, he had to do what he had to do—sometimes in the shadows of a neighbor's back yard. After the first time it happened, he was sure to carry toilet paper in his pocket. Mother Nature seemed to work overtime during a long run. And much like a stealth bomber, she would sneak up on him even when he thought he was in the clear. Her bombs could be deadly and destructive. Tom learned over time that a clean drop could really make a person proud. A messy one, however, could damage one's pride for years.

Such an instance accounts for a certain section of town Tom has since avoided due to an encounter behind a maple tree with a woman in a green gardening hat, holding a shovel. *It wasn't my fault!* he would remind himself. *Her hat blended in with the bushes. Plus, who gardens at seven o'clock in the morning?* Unfortunately when one is forced to use the great outdoors as a rest stop, one learns quickly that privacy is never guaranteed.

Tom nearly collided with the pony-tailed woman as they exited their respective bathrooms. She excused herself and wiped the sweat from her brow. Lots of people in the lobby had moved on from breakfast and were now deep into their stretches. Tom found an area near the front window, grabbed his right leg and began pulling on his quadriceps. He leaned his forehead against the glass and felt a vibration from the crowd's eruption as the first group of wheelchair racers whizzed past. The hairs stood up on his arms. These people amazed him. Their upper body strength alone was something to behold.

He'd read that every year approximately thirty racers tackle the Boston course without a leg to stand on. For most, it is one of many marathons they will complete throughout the year. What was even more interesting was that wheelchair racers had to qualify just like everyone else. He thought about Bob Hall of Belmont, Massachusetts: the first person to ever attempt the Boston Marathon in a modified hospital wheelchair.

Back in 1975, Bob wasn't granted a number by the race director, but was promised a finisher's certificate if he could complete the world's oldest and most prestigious running race in less then three hours and thirty minutes. Two hours and fifty-eight exhilarating minutes later Mr. Hall wheeled across the finish line. His singular effort had led to widespread acceptance across the globe, legitimizing wheelchair racers as equal competitors in major races. Soon after his race, a formal division was established for these rollers. In fact, the Boston Marathon has been the base of thirteen men's and nine women's world records. A woman, Jean Driscoll, had set the current record of one hour, thirty-four minutes and twenty-two seconds back in 1994.

Tom had read about all of these folks. Every single one added to his inspiration. *How could I not want to challenge myself, knowing this group has just set out on their journey?* he wondered.

The roar of the crowd faded as the last wheelers passed, but the grin on Tom's face remained. He looked appreciatively at his own legs. They had become so lean and muscular. The minutes, hours and days that had made up the past nine months of training had molded his body into a new form. Different, even from his teenage years. His shoulders and arms were defined, his stomach tight. At home, his bedroom closet was filled with pants and shirts fit for a man thirty pounds heavier than Tom. Somehow even his head seemed smaller.

Most people he ran into these days went on and on about how terrific he looked. A couple friends from college said it looked like Tom had *"shrunk"*. One even told him he looked like Tom Hanks in *Philadelphia*. *"Gordo's just jealous that he can't lose any weight himself,"* Kerry would say.

Until he had lost the weight, Tom never even considered himself fat— although he did like to eat and hardly ever exercised. Kerry, on the other hand, would go on walks or short runs four to five times a week. A creature of habit, she was much like her father this way. There was just something about leaving the house and *"getting some air"* as she would call it. It was part of her regimen for sanity. Once in a blue moon she would convince Tom to come with her. *"How long do you want to keep going?"* he would inevitably ask after the first mile. If a jogger passed them, Tom would analyze their form. *"That guy's dragging his feet. Pick up your knees, dude!"* he'd mumble. Or, *"She may as well be walking at that pace, right?"* This grated on his wife, causing her to jump to the defense of her fellow athletes: *"Why don't you get your butt out here and actually do something yourself, one of these days? Then maybe you can comment on everyone else, okay?"* She'd be squinting her eyes and making a dumb-dumb smirk with her mouth.

"Maybe I will," he'd challenge. *"Maybe I'll run a marathon someday—then you can kiss my butt."*

"Sure, hun. Go for it," she'd laugh. *"I'll settle for another mile at this point."*

Continuing his stretch, another vibration radiated off the glass and into Tom's hand. This time the crowd was cheering on the real contenders— the elite runners who actually had a chance of winning the entire marathon. He heard the gun go off and stopped his stretch to get a glimpse of them heading out of the gates. *It's not every day you get to witness this sort of thing,* he reminded himself. The crowd made it impossible to see, but Tom imagined they were setting a quick pace from the get-go. Their bodies were trim. They were strong. Their feet barely touching the ground. Legs stretched long like gazelles. Tom pictured them focused, intense and covered in their sponsors' logos. The lodge quieted down momentarily, as most eyes were trying to get a peek of their own. Cheers filtered inside. Tom found himself clapping wildly and whistling right along. The excitement was bubbling up, and he wanted to be running alongside them.

Looking down at his number, Tom's stomach leapt to know it wouldn't be long before he could line up at the gates. Already suffering from dry-mouth, he reached into his pocket for one of the Tic-Tacs he remembered to bring with him. His eyes grew wide when his fingers came upon the letter from his wife. Having shoved it in there an hour earlier, it had gradually slipped from his mind. *Thank God,* he thought, *for that Tic-Tac. Kerry would have killed me if I forgot to read her letter.* Returning to where he'd left off, he read:

> *Mile 1: The beginning. We just found out that our baby has a problem. Bitter sweetly, however, we celebrate that....*

"IT'S A GIRL!" Kerry placed the piece of paper down on the counter. She and Tom embraced. The tighter they held each other, the harder they cried. The happy news on the little piece of paper was an answer to their dreams. They had already been blessed with two beautiful boys. Tom often described it as *hitting the jackpot.* One son? That was something special. But two sons? Why, that warranted a certain level of street cred. Kerry felt equally blessed. In fact, she welcomed the possibility of another boy, as long as she was guaranteed a girl by their fourth try. This was the deal she had made with God.

Early on in their marriage, Tom and Kerry agreed that they both wanted a big family. Having hailed from bountiful broods themselves, it was what they knew and loved. Kerry's ideal family included two boys and two girls. First, the boys, one after the other. This way, they'd be able to share a room, grow a strong bond and play on the same sports teams. Next, the girls. The boys would now be in the position to protect their sisters throughout their lives. The girls, too, would share a room, play sports together and grow up with an equally strong bond. Theirs would be built on many late night rap sessions, sharing secrets and clothes, and planning their careers and families—much like Kerry had done with her own sisters. Tom never thought about any of that, he just knew he wanted at least three, if not four, kids. A girl, he assumed, would eventually join them. Knowing this would be—brought them immeasurable happiness, despite the dark cloud lingering above.

That morning had started off relatively normal. The boys were finishing up their breakfast. Ryan sat comfortably in his highchair, carefully dropping one Cheerio on the floor at a time. His wispy hair was sticky with milk. Thomas quietly giggled as each one hit the ground. He wasn't about to ruin the show his little brother had been putting on for him. Tom walked into the kitchen and slipped on a matchbox car, knocking his head against the doorway. Too flustered to notice, Kerry was busy printing out MapQuest directions to her new OB-GYN's office. She had switched practices after her last check-up and was preparing for her first appointment with the nurse midwife her sister-in-law had recommended.

While most pregnant women wouldn't dare leave their doctor with three months to go, Kerry had decided she'd had enough. The same doctor who had so beautifully delivered Thomas had been blowing off her test results and acting dangerously nonchalant this time around. Little things had been popping up on ultrasounds. Choroid plexus cysts here, echogenic bowel there, an absent stomach bubble—all things that could possibly fall under the "normal variant" column. *But were they?* Kerry's OB-GYN was quite comfortable assuming this was so. She even went so far as to ignore suggestions, based on Kerry's level 2 ultrasound, that she should return for follow-up evaluations.

Kerry wanted to believe that her unborn child was just another victim of over-testing, but none of this had sat well with her. Her OB-GYN's practice was jam-packed with patients and had been treating her like someone holding a number on the deli line. Communication had become sloppy. The nurses made her feel like an over-bearing pest anytime she had called to follow up on her test results. *"I guess it must seem crazy, I know,"* Kerry explained to the last nurse she'd spoken to, *"but I'm actually interested in knowing the results of a test specifically run to rule out things like cystic fibrosis and toxoplasmosis for my baby. I'm just weird that way."* Things felt wrong. A voice in her head had been saying over and over:

> *"Don't trust these people, Kerry. This is important. You are this baby's mother. Protect your baby. This is important, Kerry."*

The voice spoke to her incessantly, until finally at her sixth-month appointment when Kerry told her OB-GYN that she was unhappy with her prenatal care and was leaving the practice effective immediately. Red-faced, she demanded her medical records be forwarded to her new practice. Then she signed a couple of papers and walked out the door, never turning back. The voice quieted down that very afternoon.

Tom picked up a rag. He shook his head from side to side when he saw Ryan's mess. "I could clean that up right now," he said turning towards Kerry, "OR you and I could run upstairs and take our clothes off?" The thought alone was getting him excited. "Come on, a quickie before we go?" he asked. Kerry was already shaking her head in disagreement. "Come on," Tom begged, "we'll put on Bob the Builder…it'll take fifteen minutes," he continued, pulling her close. "It would take ten minutes," Kerry said, "…and…no!" Her arms were unwrapping his. "Come on," she yelled, "we're gonna be late!"

Disappointed, Tom hung his head. He looked at his wife's swollen belly, then stubbed his toe on a Christmas toy that hadn't been taken out of the box yet. Glancing at his trouble-making boys, he thought: *My God, they're just babies themselves. How the hell are we going to be able to handle another?*

Ryan was eighteen months old. They had just installed a tent over his crib to keep him from climbing out. Thomas was three. He had just taught Ryan how to unzip and escape from the confines of the crib-tent. These two boys were as thick as thieves. Thomas was the ringleader. His enormous blue eyes melted the heart of anyone lucky enough to look into them. He was sensitive and demanding. Ryan was adorable. It took a lot to convince him to stop smiling. His stubbornness contended with his mother's, and Tom rarely missed an opportunity to compare the two.

Life was great for their sons. Thomas attended preschool Tuesday and Thursday mornings. The rest of the week was filled with playgroups, mass, music class, toddler sports and visits to the library. They were treated to McDonald's and Dunkin' Donuts on occasion, and loved watching movies with their mom and dad in bed. Tom missed them desperately when he traveled. Kerry read them books, said prayers and sang them songs every night before bed. The Sheeran boys were happy and much-loved. Things may not have been perfect, but they were damn near close.

"It's 8:15! We've gotta go!" Kerry announced. Her appointment was for 9 a.m. Tom stopped wiping the cereal from the floor, and gave a quick swipe to his boys' faces with the same cloth. The whole family jumped into the car and made it to Providence with three minutes to spare. "Not bad for rush hour," Tom and Kerry said in unison. In the waiting room, Tom played referee as the boys fought over who got to *"wake up the fishies"* in the tank. Another pregnant woman looked at them, then smiled sweetly at Kerry. "You're going to have your hands full," she said. "Do you know what you're having?" It seemed as though Kerry fielded this question at least once a day. So without hesitation, she smiled in Tom's direction, then gave her standard response: "No, we both really like to be surprised!"

The nurse opened the door and called Kerry's name. All four of them followed closely as she showed them to the exam room. Shortly after, the nurse midwife walked in and introduced herself. Her name was Ethel. Her glasses slipped down on her pudgy little nose, and she smiled each time she pushed them back up. Ethel wore heart-printed scrubs. Another pair of glasses poked out of her pocket. Tom made small talk with her about their impending trip to Florida in three weeks. He was worried, having booked the flight four months earlier, that this new practice might frown upon Kerry traveling at thirty-weeks pregnant. Ethel tapped his knee and assured him it was most likely not an issue. Kerry gave her a quick review of her medical history, along with an explanation as to why she had switched practices. Ethel seemed to take it all in, reading through Kerry's medical records while still occasionally smiling and maintaining eye contact.

Continuing on with her saga, Kerry noticed that Ethel's eyes hadn't looked up in a good twenty seconds. Their friendly chitchat had slowed down. Ethel's focus had flittered away and perched itself on Kerry's chart. "I'm sorry to interrupt," Ethel finally said, "but were you aware that you have placenta previa?"

Kerry's eyebrows flipped. *Placenta previa?* Her mother-in-law, Jane, had had it when she was pregnant with Tom's sister, and often spoke of the horrors of having a placenta that had covered her cervix. Kerry knew it was dangerous and could lead to things like hemorrhage and preterm labor. She also knew that pregnant women with placenta previa were put on strict bed rest. Another thing she knew: Nobody at the other practice had EVER told her she had placenta previa.

"What are you talking about?" Kerry asked "Are you sure that's **my** chart?"

Suddenly convinced she was in the presence of another deli-style medical practice, Kerry frowned. *This is just a silly blunder*, she thought, *the typical result of seeing too many patients at once.*

"It's right here on the records you had sent over from your OB-GYN," Ethel replied, turning the chart in her direction. As she read the notes, Kerry's eyebrows rose from the craters they had dug. She looked at Tom, hoping for some kind of logical explanation. Unfortunately, he seemed to be the most confused person in the room. Looking back at Ethel, she insisted: "My other doctor never once mentioned anything about placenta previa." Her face felt hot. Steam seeped from her nostrils. Ethel's playful tone was now a distant memory. "We'll have to put you on ultrasound immediately. And something tells me you might want to cancel those plane tickets," the new nurse midwife said, looking in Tom's direction.

Kerry lay down on the exam table and pulled up her shirt. This was going to be the third ultrasound of their baby. During her other pregnancies, the sound of surgilube squirting out made her giggle with Tom. The roll of the Doppler remote making its way to all sides of her abdomen filled her with exhilaration. The chance to see her baby in utero was a gift—something she looked forward to for months. In this moment, however, this was the last room she wanted to be in. She had plans later that morning to look at a rug she had found on Craigslist. It was for the baby's room. She was most likely going to buy it and bring it home. It was going to match the John Lennon-themed nursery she had kept intact since both her boys' stints as newborns. It was gender neutral as was the nursery. She would probably lose her chance to get it if she waited any longer. The woman was expecting her to pick it up that day. She wanted to be at that woman's house.

Tom was sitting in a chair behind the exam table with Thomas on one knee and Ryan on the other. He couldn't see Kerry's face. There was an ugly painting of a man fishing off a wharf in downtown Providence hanging crookedly on the wall. *That's stupid,* Tom thought, *nobody fishes off that wharf.* The ultrasound technician made no eye contact with any of them when she entered the room. She introduced herself, barely mumbling her name. As the warm lubricant jetted onto Kerry's belly, she arched her back. The tech moved the Doppler from side to side, giving them glimpses of the baby. "Is that its head?" Tom asked, pointing to the screen. The technician nodded, while periodically pausing to type. "Look guys, there's your little brother or sister. Whadda you think, huh?" Tom was trying to muster up some excitement, but even the boys knew better than to fall for that. "Can we go now?" Thomas asked.

"Is that the baby's heart?" Tom continued.

"I'm sorry sir," the technician snapped, "I can't keep interrupting the scan to answer questions." Her tone was more than a smidge condescending. "I'm taking measurements and entering them into the computer," she continued, "so I really need to be paying attention to what I'm doing." Tom slumped in his chair. "Your doctor will go over everything with you when I'm done," she assured him in a robotic tone. Tom was mildly apologetic. The room became quiet aside from the clicking keys on the keyboard. Kerry stared at the screen. It was at a weird angle, and she could hardly make out anything she saw. She thought about how they always seemed to get miserable technicians who never wanted to talk. How at the very least, the woman could tell them *what* she was measuring. *Why does everything have to be such a big secret? It's our baby!* Kerry thought. The technician continued to click and type...click and type...click and type. Ten minutes later, when the nine-hundred-pound gorilla was beating his chest, Kerry broke the silence:

"I'm sorry, but can you at least tell me if you can see the placenta?"

"It's right there," the technician said, pointing to the screen.

"Is it covering my cervix?" Kerry persisted.

"No, it's posterior. It's not anywhere near your cervix," she replied.

"So," Kerry concluded, "I don't have placenta previa?"

"I'm not seeing placenta previa," the technician answered.

"Okay, great. Thanks." *Geez,* Kerry thought, *was that so freaking hard?*

When they finished up twenty minutes later, the ultrasound technician opened the door and pointed them back in the direction of the midwife's office. Once they arrived, a nurse escorted them into a different room from the one they had been in earlier. Kerry sat on the exam table, hopeful things would be wrapping up fairly soon considering how long the ultrasound had taken. Minutes later the door opened and Ethel walked in. Kerry and Tom were both flashing smiles and tripping over their words. "I don't have placenta previa, do I?" Kerry demanded. They were anxious, yearning for the nurse midwife to return their happy gazes.

Ethel's eyes darted between them and the floor. Her voice sounded shaky. "You don't have placenta previa," she concurred, "but there were a few concerning things they *did* see on the ultrasound."

"Like what?" Tom quipped. He was trying to remain calm in front of the boys.

"I can't speak to it. I can no longer follow your pregnancy, unfortunately. Once a patient becomes high-risk we have to pair them up with an OB-GYN qualified to handle any potential complications," Ethel explained.

Kerry's mind went blank. *Is this woman really talking to me? If so, what in God's name is she talking about?* Her head was swimming with possibilities. *Is the baby's heart okay? Is it Downs? Is the baby even alive?* Kerry's breath escaped her. Her hands shook. Tom spoke the words Kerry's mouth couldn't formulate: "So you're going to pass us off without even telling us what they saw?" He was getting angry. Their friendly banter was a distant memory. "I'm so sorry," Ethel replied, genuinely. "The doctor is reading your report right now. Her office is across the hall. I can show you to the waiting room."

"Seriously?!" Kerry barked.

Ryan had fallen asleep in the stroller. Thomas was getting antsy in the waiting room—running back and forth from the bathroom door to the front desk. Other patients looked in Kerry's direction, wondering when she might tell him to *stop*, but she was too numb to even notice. *Please, God,* she prayed, *let this be another stupid mistake.* Tom put his arm around her shoulder. "I don't understand what's going on!" Kerry cried. Suddenly her hands moved across her stomach. She exhaled and squeezed Tom's hand. "I just felt the baby kick," she said.

The doctor opened the door and called Kerry and Tom into her office. Her wildly curly red hair seemed to match her flustered persona. She offered them a seat and didn't seem to mind that Thomas had taken up residence in hers.

"I know you're aware," the doctor began, "that a few concerning things popped up on your ultrasound today." The couple shook their heads in unison, waiting uneasily for her to continue. "What we'd like to do, before we jump to any conclusions, is have you seen on a Level 2 ultrasound at the Maternal Fetal Medicine office. Dr. Base is the expert on analyzing these kinds of markings."

"What markings?" Kerry asked, without a hint of pleasantness.

"I'd really rather not speak to anything until Dr. Base has a chance to look at you. That way, we're not jumping to any conclusions. For all we know this could be nothing, and if that's the case, we really don't want to head down any false roads," the doctor explained. Kerry looked at Tom, then returned her focus to the doctor. "What markings?" she repeated, quite clearly. Tom added: "With all due respect, Doctor, we're not walking out of this room until you tell us what you saw on that ultrasound."

Bowing her head, the disheveled doctor succumbed: "They saw a couple of things. One being the baby's clenched fists. This can sometimes be a marker for Down syndrome." *That's it,* Kerry thought. *I've been worried about this before, and here it is creeping up again. Why hadn't the blood tests shown any signs of this? How will I manage with two other young kids?* "They also saw fluid in the baby's abdomen," the doctor continued. "This could be a marker for any number of things, but I'm not going to go into any of them until Dr. Base sees you."

"Dr. Base just saw me six weeks ago," Kerry explained. "None of this was even an issue."

"That's good!" she assured them. "All the more reason to believe this is all nothing to be concerned about. I'll have my assistant call his office to schedule you an appointment."

The doctor excused herself and closed the door behind her. Tom was starting to feel a little bit better. Kerry felt like Alice, falling down the rabbit hole. One minute her biggest fear was paying a cancellation fee on a flight to Florida, the next it was an endless hollow of possibilities. Kerry was *so* fearful, not one tear fell from her eyes. This was good, considering Thomas hadn't taken his gaze off her in the last five minutes.

"It's probably nothing, Ker," Tom said. "You heard what the doctor said, don't jump to any conclusions. Let's wait and see what Dr. Base has to say." Tom wasn't sure what direction they were heading in with all of this, but was hopeful it was much ado about nothing. His feathers had been ruffled the last time Kerry was at Dr. Base's office, and all of those tests turned out to be negative. *Things like this probably happen all the time,* Tom thought. *Why should today be any different?*

> *Tom visualized himself in Dr. Base's office, laughing at all of the drama that had unfolded. Kerry was smiling and rolling her eyes. Dr. Base was shaking his hand and looking into Tom's eyes, assuring him there was nothing to worry about. Everything was fine.*

"I'm sorry," the doctor announced upon her return, "but Dr. Base's schedule is full for the next two days. We arranged an appointment for you at 10:30 a.m. on Wednesday." She was holding the door open with one hand and straightening her glasses with the other. "On the contrary," Tom said, scooping Thomas into his arms. "One way or another, he'll be seeing us today."

At four o'clock that afternoon, Kerry sat filling out paperwork in Dr. Base's waiting room. Tom was on the phone with Jane-Marie, his sister. She had come to their house to stay with the boys. The entire waiting room listened in as he carefully explained their foolproof methods of getting Thomas and Ryan to eat dinner. Kerry remembered the last time she was sitting in the very same chair. She had witnessed a pregnant woman being helped to her car. The woman was about six months along and hysterically crying. Genetic counselors were on both sides of her, trying to calm her down. *What had they seen?* Kerry wondered. *What ever happened to that woman and her baby?*

A nurse entered the waiting room and called her name. Kerry's shoes felt like they were glued to the floor. Dr. Base's office was anything but inviting. It was a place pregnant women came when something wasn't right. A place that could turn a family upside-down. Tom held on to Kerry's arm as they walked into the ultrasound room. Helping her up on the exam table, he put his hands across her legs to slow the trembling, but it was no use. He knew from past experience that once she began shaking, Kerry couldn't stop. It was difficult for Tom to see his wife in this state. The few other times he'd witnessed such distress, it was due to physical discomfort—like labor or kidney stones. Yet this time it was one hundred percent emotion. Feeling helpless, he took her hands and did the only reasonable thing he could think of. He prayed: "Dear God, please take away all of our worries and fears. Watch over our baby and let everything be okay with him or her. Please, God, just let everything be alright. Amen."

"Please, God," Kerry added.

Dr. Base walked into the room and Tom thanked him immediately for seeing them. He was a nice, older man with a soothing bedside manner. Kerry always thought he looked just like Mr. Keaton from *Family Ties*. Wasting no time, Dr. Base picked up the Doppler and began looking inside her womb. "The test results from my last exam in this office said that I had placenta previa," Kerry started. "Why was that?"

Uh oh, Tom thought. *Here we go!*

Dr. Base looked at her with sincerity. "That was a mistake. It was written accidentally on your report. You never had placenta previa. That was our fault," he admitted. *Okay*, Kerry thought, *at least I'm getting clarity on one portion of this confusing mess.* Tom let out a cleansing breath, then quickly inhaled and held it as Kerry continued: "So, this was written on my test results, along with a note that I should be seen for follow up ultrasounds…and these results were sent to my old OB-GYN?" Dr. Base was shaking his head in agreement. "She should have read this note and reacted to it, right?" Kerry pressed. Knowing obstetricians weren't in the business of ratting each other out, she took pleasure in having Dr. Base by the cojones just then. "Yes," he agreed, "she should have read that note and reacted to it immediately."

"Unbelievable," Kerry quipped.

Her cheeks flared up again. The neglect from her old OB-GYN had just shot to a crazy new level. Trust for any medical professional went flying out the window. Things shifted in Kerry's mind that very moment. Ignorance would never equal bliss, and she refused to believe otherwise. A new sheriff was in town, and she would be giving the orders from now on.

"We need to know what you're seeing, as you are seeing it," Kerry announced to Dr. Base. "We will not sit through another ultrasound, closed lip and unable to ask questions."

"We're borderline postal, Doc" Tom concurred.

Dr. Base seemed to understand. He turned the screen in their direction and began to explain. "First of all, I'm not concerned about how I'm seeing the baby clench its hands." He demonstrated the two different ways a baby could "clench" and apparently the way their baby was doing it was perfectly acceptable.

Tom squeezed Kerry's fingers and smiled. "What about the fluid in the baby's abdomen?" Kerry asked. Dr. Base took a good look, then shook his head and said: "It's not a tremendous amount of fluid. What I'm seeing could most likely be linked to some sort of an intestinal blockage. Sometimes," he continued, "babies swallow things like hair and blood when they're in utero, and the build-up of these things over time can plug their tiny intestines. Worst case scenario, your baby could require minor intestinal surgery at birth to correct this." Kerry looked at Tom. Her legs had stopped shaking. *Surgery* wasn't a word she was expecting to hear with regards to their baby when she'd woken up that morning. And yet, surprisingly, things didn't sound as dire as she had imagined. Tom's face bore the same reaction. He began to fire off questions about the surgery. *Where would it be done? What surgeon did he recommend? How long would the baby be in the hospital?* Dr. Base tried to answer as best he could, but encouraged them both to relax and try to adopt more of a *wait and see* mindset. "Nothing's going to change drastically, why don't you make an appointment to come back and see me in three weeks? We'll measure the ascites and make sure it is staying at an acceptable level," Dr. Base suggested.

"The ascites?" Kerry asked.

"The fluid in the baby's abdomen," Dr. Base said.

"What about our trip to Florida? We're supposed to fly out on January 27th?" Tom asked.

"Go on your trip. It will be good for you to relax a little after today's series of events!" He smiled and took Kerry's hand. "Go and enjoy," he insisted, "and when you get back we'll take another look at your prince or princess." Kerry forced a smile back at him. "By the way," Dr. Base added, "do you know what you're having?"

"No, we both like to be..." Their eyes met, and neither seemed capable of finishing their sentence.

"What do you think, Ker?" Tom asked. Kerry shook her head. "Let's find out," she said, "but not here, not right now. Let's ask the doctor to write it down for us and put it in an envelope. Then tonight, after the boys go to sleep, we can light a candle and read it in the privacy and peace of our own kitchen."

Chapter 3

A VOICE FROM WITHIN

OUT OF THE corner of his eye, Tom spotted Mike and Jeff, the Children's Hospital running coaches, enter the lobby. These two men were heroes in their own right, having helped shape countless non-athletes into fierce competitors in nine months flat. Smiling and shaking hands, they made their way to the center of the room. Mike used a megaphone to rally the crowd: "Okay, folks! This is it!" Tom's stomach jumped. "Miles for Miracles team members with numbers lower then 20,000 follow Jeff to Gate C. Those of you with numbers higher then 20,000, come with me to Gate D," Mike instructed. He passed the megaphone to Jeff. "Get ready! Get pumped! Let's hear some noise!" Jeff screamed, unleashing a wave of excitement. "You guys have worked really hard for this! Your patient partners and those whose memories we honor today are your inspirations! Let the idea of them invigorate you with each step. Do it for yourselves, do it for them. Just do it!" he screamed.

The lump in Tom's throat seemed to be rising up, but he kept his mouth tightly closed and bit the insides of his lips to make sure it didn't escape. As he looked around the room he saw watery eyes and massive grins. These checkered shirts were a proud bunch and *this* was their moment. Filing out the door with his team, Tom spotted Jill and flashed a heartfelt smile to her as they high-fived. Outside, the sidewalks were packed with news vans, photographers, banners and fans galore. Tom felt like all eyes were on him. Puffing out his chest, he soaked in every ounce of energy around him. He was there to race. Tom Sheeran was about to run a marathon.

Loving that he was a part of the mania, Tom filed into his gate and made one last attempt to loosen up. As he rolled his head in a circle, he recognized a Boston newscaster on the sidewalk, interviewing a man in his twenties wearing a jersey covered in pink ribbons. The young man explained that he was running in support of his mother who was battling breast cancer for the second time. Turning around, he proudly displayed his mom's picture on the back of his shirt. "This is for you, Ma!" he yelled into the camera, pumping his fist. A group of bystanders cheered.

Scenes like this were happening all over. So many people. So many stories. Tons of sentiment mixed with adrenaline. A powerful feeling came over the crowd, a feeling of invincibility—only possible with the innocence of not knowing that four years later, two men would set off bombs that would kill three spectators and injure more than 200 others.

Before Tom knew it, he was moving. At first, his steps were stuttered. Pretty soon he was able to walk without tripping. Then once he was able to space himself from the tight crowd, his stride began to lengthen. He remembered what his buddy, Mike, had told him (in his wicked-good New England accent) about his own "Bahston" Marathon mistake two years earlier:

> *"Dude, I busted out of the gates and was flyin—I mean fahst for the first ten miles. My adrenaline was in ovahdrive and I felt like it would cahry me the entiyah race. I completely left my two running pahtners in the gawd damn dust aftah hahven trained with them fah months. I blew my entiyah plan, and paid fah it the lahst sixteen miles. Dude, be cahful. Do naught do whaht I did."*

Tom truly didn't want to make that mistake. He knew he had to set a good pace from the beginning. As he crossed the starting line, he pressed the *start* button on his watch and began to jog.

The spectators watched with glee as the giant herd of humans moved past them down Route 135. It was difficult to separate from the sardines crowding him, but somehow around the half-mile point, Tom managed to break free. Eventually he could see the 1st mile marker. A crowd of fans was chanting. At first he couldn't make out what they were saying, but as he got closer he heard: "One down! Twenty-five-point-two to go!" *That's much funnier than it is helpful,* Tom thought. He looked at his watch. Eight minutes and twenty-five seconds had passed as he crossed the mile marker. *Good,* he thought, *not too slow and not too fast.* This was the pace he wanted to keep. If his body came equipped with a cruise control button, he would have pressed it that very second. Unfortunately it didn't, and he was all too aware that this was just the beginning. Having done everything he could to prepare for this marathon, he knew the run was going to play out its own way. *If I can just keep from rolling an ankle,* he thought, *I should be okay.* This kind of thinking was starting to stress Tom out. He reached into his pocket and pulled out Kerry's letter. It was the perfect time refocus, and so he read:

> *Mile 2: Our first trip to Boston in search of the most important second opinion of our lives....*

"NOT AGAIN!" TOM screamed. Another red light. Traffic had been backed up for miles, and just when they thought they were moving...bam. Stopped in their tracks. "Where are we right now? Are you sure you're going the right way?" Kerry asked.

Anytime she'd driven into Boston from Rhode Island she'd always taken Route 93. But this morning they had to drop the boys off with Tom's brother and sister-in-law in Norfolk, Massachusetts. Sean and Danielle had given them back-road directions to Brigham & Women's Hospital, and warned them if they tried to go any other route at rush hour, they'd pay dearly. This would have worked out great, time-wise, if Tom hadn't been stopped for a speeding ticket on his way through Westwood. The extra twenty minutes and $115 hadn't been factored into their morning commute.

"I thought we went this way to avoid traffic?" Kerry snapped. "What road are we on right now?"

"VFW Parkway, and I think we're getting close. But keep your eyes peeled for a D&D or Starbucks," Tom suggested. Kerry furrowed her brow. "We're NOT stopping for coffee, Tom! My appointment is in fifteen minutes and we don't even know how far the parking garage is from the hospital, never mind how far the hospital is from here. No way!" she snapped.

"Ker, I've been on the road since 5:30 a.m. I NEED another coffee. So what if we're late to the appointment? I don't even know why we're going here anyways. Dr. Base told us to sit tight until we get home from Florida, and you're freaking out—making me drive all over kingdom come for a second opinion. We already know what they're going to say...for God sakes, we already met with the surgeon in Providence...I am so sick of sitting in doctors' offices... I'd say we've covered our bases pretty well, so I think we can afford to go three minutes out of our way to get coffee so that I can actually get through this morning," Tom countered.

"We are NOT stopping!" Kerry repeated in a loud tone. Tom was obviously going deaf. "WE ARE NOT STOPPING!" They didn't stop. The next twenty minutes were filled with a silence that lasted until the moment they pulled up to the entrance of the hospital, already eight minutes late.

Two days earlier, they had met with Dr. Phillipe Rousseau, a renowned surgeon in Rhode Island. Upon further deliberation, the worried couple wasn't satisfied with the short version of the *What to Expect When you Expect your Child Might Need Surgery* explanation they'd received from Dr. Base. They wanted the entire scenario detailed for them blow-by-blow. And they wanted it from the person that might actually be doing the surgery. So on January 15th, a cold, wet morning, Tom and Kerry had once again scrambled to get Jane to watch the boys and had headed up to Providence with their ultrasound reports....

In the waiting room, Kerry busily filled out paperwork. Tom was on his phone. He was working on a project for one of his biggest clients, Merrill Lynch. They wanted to build a generous sized command center in their Singapore location, and Tom wanted his company to handle the project. Sales had been pretty good in 2007, but the new year had just begun and with another baby on the way, he yearned for the commission this job would provide. He chatted without much regard to the volume of his voice or the sign on the wall requesting cell phones not be used in the waiting room.

Kerry grabbed onto the arms of the chair and pushed herself up. Her belly was getting bigger by the day, and the third trimester waddle had started to set in. Handing the clipboard to the receptionist, she let out a sigh and shook her cramped-up hand as she returned to her seat. *The paperwork*, she thought, *is starting to get really annoying.*

Another couple walked into the waiting room and checked in with the receptionist. Tom continued his discussion of audiovisual monitors in their presence, until Kerry poked his side and pointed to the sign. As he exited into the hall, the couple turned around and made their way to their seats. Kerry looked down. This wasn't the kind of place where one smiled and made eye contact with strangers. This was the waiting room of a pediatric surgeon. There was nothing happy or exciting about this room. If someone were sitting in it, most likely his or her child were going to be operated on. Kerry looked around. The walls were cluttered with Sesame Street characters. Cookie Monster and Big Bird served as a terrible reminder of how small and helpless her little girl would be. No, there was nothing cute about the waiting room *or* the prospect of handing her newborn child over to a stranger and having him slice into her little body.

Kerry's chest grew tight as she glanced at her watch. Forty-five minutes had already passed since they'd arrived. *Jane is going to kill me*, she thought. Her mother-in-law had agreed to watch the boys, but was leaving for a three-month stint in Florida with Tom's father the next day. Jane had tons of packing to do, and the longer this appointment dragged out, the more of a burden Kerry became. At least, that's how she felt.

"Mrs. Sheeran?" the receptionist called. *Thank God*, Kerry thought as she once again pushed herself up. "I just have to get my husband, he's in the hall," she explained.

"Mrs. Sheeran," the receptionist continued, "we have you down for an appointment with Dr. Rousseau on Friday at 8:30 a.m.? Not today. We're sorry, but he is booked for today, so you're going to have to come back on Friday."

Kerry's face heated up immediately as she countered: "That's impossible. I just made the appointment last Friday and I am positive it is for today. I spoke to Judy." Her assuredness lacked effect.

"I'm sorry," the receptionist replied, without an ounce of sympathy, "but we have you down for Friday. Dr. Rousseau can't meet with you today."

The door opened and Tom shut his phone off as he snuck back into the waiting room. Kerry glanced back at him. He couldn't help but notice the ruddy shade of her complexion and the pulsating flare of her nostrils. She turned back around and squinted her eyes at the receptionist. Speaking slowly and enunciating her words, Kerry explained:

"I spoke to Judy last Friday. She made the appointment for us for today, Tuesday, at 8:30 a.m. I wouldn't have made an appointment for Friday at 8:30 a.m. because I don't have anyone to watch my kids that morning. So, if JUDY wrote it down incorrectly in YOUR appointment calendar, that was HER mistake. NOT mine. OUR appointment was for today. I arranged babysitting for my two young boys so that we could be here, TODAY, to meet with Dr. Rousseau. That is what we plan to do. We did not just sit in your waiting room for forty-five minutes to be sent home. So please figure out how you're going to fix JUDY's mistake, and please do it fast because my husband needs to get to his office and I need to get home to my children."

Wide-eyed, the receptionist quietly got off her chair and walked through a door leading to the surgeons' offices. "What's wrong?" Tom asked. He looked over at the couple, who seemed to return his same look of bewilderment. Before Kerry could answer, the door leading to the offices opened, and the receptionist made eye-contact with the carpet as she announced: "Mr. and Mrs. Sheeran, Dr. Rousseau will see you now."

Dr. Rousseau spoke to Tom and Kerry for thirty minutes or more, carefully explaining how their daughter's potential surgery would go down. He concurred the diagnosis was likely an intestinal blockage, based on the ultrasound's findings. His French accent was thick, and Kerry was not shy about asking him to repeat whatever it was she didn't understand. He talked about the possibility of a colostomy for their daughter. This was something Tom and Kerry were not familiar with.

Dr. Rousseau explained that if there were a complication with her intestinal tract, the baby would have to have a way of eliminating poop. "If ze bowels aren't excreted, ze body will become toxic," he said. Essentially, he explained, this meant bringing a portion of her large intestine to the surface of her abdomen. Their baby would then be able to excrete into a plastic bag that attached around her colostomy. "Instead of changing ze diaper, you will change ze bag periodically," he said matter-of-factly. Kerry tried to process what she was hearing. *Oh okay, so I'll be buying bags instead of diapers. Do they sell them at Babies R Us?* Her cheeks flushed. Perhaps this was routine for a surgeon of his stature, but to her there was nothing commonplace about cutting a hole in her baby's abdomen and pulling her guts out. Tom was in shock.

"Is this something you'll create immediately?" Kerry questioned.

"Yes, if X-rays convince us zat ze bowel iz blocked and we aren't able to unblock it manually, we will have to do ze colostomy surgery immediately," he answered.

"How long will she be in the hospital?" Tom asked.

"Most likely a couple of weeks," he replied.

"So she'll come home from the hospital *with* the colostomy?" Kerry wanted to be clear. Suddenly things were getting even more complicated then she had anticipated.

"Yes, she will come home with ze colostomy and she will have it until we are able to perform ze surgery to repair ze blockage," Dr. Rousseau said. Tom opened his mouth, but before he was able to ask, Dr. Rousseau answered: "I cannot tell you, now, when *zat* surgery would take place. It all depends on ze location of ze blockage, ze magnitude of ze surgery etc. Zere's a lot we're not going to know until ze baby iz born, so we need to just wait and see and hope for ze best. You never know, you could go back for your next ultrasound and zere may be no signs of a blockage. Sometimes zese zings repair zemselves in utero and ze babies are born perfectly fine." Tom squeezed Kerry's hand. His eyes flickered with hope. Kerry could not return the same look. Her hope was out of reach at the moment.

Fear had started to take over, and it was inviolable. Kerry's eyes glazed as she and Tom thanked Dr. Rousseau for his time. She remained in a fog the entire way back to the parking garage. Tom wanted to talk about how the meeting had gone, but was interrupted by a phone call from his office. Kerry replayed Dr. Rousseau's words in her head, over and over. First the part about the colostomy surgery, then the words *"sometimes ze babies are born perfectly fine."* She tried to listen to the second part, but couldn't help but picture events unfolding for their baby as he had described in the first scenario.

Her heart ached at the thought of not being able to take her baby home after she was born. The beautiful room she'd been preparing for months would be empty. Kerry silently panicked over how she would care for her boys while her newborn daughter recovered from surgery in Providence for two weeks.

Please, God, she prayed, *just let everything be okay. Please, God. Thank you for giving us a baby girl, but please don't let her have to go through this. Please, God—let everything be okay. I'm begging you, God.* Kerry's prayer started seeing red. *You'd be taking the most joyful part of having a baby and ruining it. I should be able to hold her and feed her and bring her home to our family, and I'm not going to be able to do any of this. It's not fair. It's cruel.* These were the things that Kerry would miss the most. These were the things she had pictured continuously ever since she found out she was pregnant. These were the things only a mother could understand.

Somewhere in the midst of her prayer-gone-angry, a voice started speaking to her. This voice was familiar and consuming. It repeated the same thing over and over, until Kerry could no longer deny that she heard it. *What more can I do?* she wondered. *What am I missing?* A tear streamed down her cheek as she listened to its instructions:

> *"Keep looking, Kerry. You still haven't found the answer you need to hear.*
> *Your daughter needs you to keep looking, Kerry."*

Her head was in overdrive, trying to understand everything she'd been told by Dr. Base and now Dr. Rousseau. She couldn't seem to wrap her mind around it all, and Tom was too busy with the Singapore project to discuss any of it further. So when she got home, Kerry did what she always did when she needed help: Kerry called her sister, Jean. Jean, a mother of three, was ten years her senior *and* a nurse. So not only was she qualified to give her medical opinion, Jean had thrived on telling her little sister what to do and how to do it since the day Kerry was born. "Come to New York, get someone at Colombia Presbyterian to look at you. You can live with me. Hell, you could even deliver the baby down here and I'll take care of your boys while she gets her surgery," Jean said. This sounded out of the question for Kerry. And yet, the fact that Jean was offering it convinced her that she needed a second opinion one way or another. "Thanks Jean, I'll think about it," Kerry said.

"Okay," Jean replied. "Well on a positive note, it's pretty awesome that you're having a girl." Jean was trying so hard to sound excited, but Kerry knew that the nature of their conversation was more bitter than sweet. "Stop! Now you're just trying to make me cry!" Kerry said.

Kerry thought about what it would be like to uproot her family and deliver the baby so far from home. Thomas would miss school and Ryan would miss his crib. They had moved Ryan into Thomas' room two weeks before, and he was just now starting to get used to his new surroundings and his brother. Tom and Kerry were familiar with the hospitals in Providence. They'd just gone through tons of testing. They had even gone so far as to meet with Dr. Rousseau. They were covering all their bases and acting like responsible parents. *Aren't we?* she wondered. Kerry recalled the voice's instructions:

"Keep looking."

Now she'd heard it from Jean too. Kerry knew what she had to do, but believed there had to be another way. *Boston,* she thought, *is only an hour away. And Harvard sure does breed a lot of medical geniuses.* She remembered this from her days working in sales for the medical insurance company, Blue Cross Blue Shield of Rhode Island. Most of her clients insisted their insurance cover out-of-state doctors so that if need be they could head up to Boston for their medical care. It wasn't a slap in Rhode Island's face, just a fact. Boston was home to some of the top hospitals in the country. Bigger fish, bigger pond.

Kerry's wheels turned faster. She started thinking of all the people she might know with connections in Boston. She made a list of friends who had delivered their babies there. She wrote down the names of women she knew whose children had had surgeries in Boston. Then, she turned on her computer and sent emails to every single person on her list, asking for guidance and pleading to be put in touch with their doctors. Friends and friends of friends wrote back to her almost immediately. There was no waiting around, the emails came pouring in. Within hours, she had the name and number of Dr. Louise Wilkins-Haug, the department head of Maternal Fetal Medicine at Brigham and Women's Hospital. She'd heard from two other friends that Brigham and Women's was where she needed to go based on its direct connection to Boston Children's Hospital. The level of help and support Kerry was receiving was overwhelming, partly because of the kindness people were showing, and partly because it was becoming glaringly obvious that she needed this kind of help. Her new mission was coming into focus. Something felt very right as she spoke to Dr. Wilkin-Haug's assistant, who was kind enough to squeeze Kerry in because of the good word a friend of a friend put in for her.

* * *

The waiting room for ultrasounds at Brigham and Women's Maternal

Fetal Medicine department was jam-packed. Tom and Kerry's coffee-run argument was still fresh, so she didn't mind that he stood in the hallway, chatting away on his phone about projectors, monitors and consoles. Tom truly had a gift when it came to being able to carry out business regardless of his surroundings. Kerry was grateful for this ability yet couldn't conceive of being able to think (never mind talk) about anything besides the state of their unborn baby's health. *What will they see when they look inside my womb today? What are they going to tell us about our little girl? Will it be worse then I've imagined? Better? Will the doctor be annoyed with me for making this appointment when nothing's even wrong?* she wondered.

Kerry looked around the waiting room. The place was all business. There were no cutesy decals on the walls. The ultrasound technicians came in and out, calling patients' names, wielding a serious yet friendly demeanor. The patients ranged from very pregnant to unnoticeably with-child. All of them seemed to have their spouse, partner, friend or mother with them. *This is the kind of place,* she guessed, *where a woman doesn't want to be alone.* Kerry did her best not to make eye contact with anyone, and instead picked up the December issue of a pregnancy magazine on a nearby coffee table. A famous soap star graced the cover. Kerry recognized her face. Her body was slim, aside from the perfectly round belly she cradled in her arms. She wore a form fitting red sweater with white trim. Her long blond hair fell loosely around her shoulders. The teasers read: "*Eating Healthy for You and Your Baby During the Holiday Season*" and "*Top Ten Gifts for a Mom-to-Be*". The issue reeked of holiday celebration.

Kerry thought back to a few weeks prior when she had been celebrating Christmas with Tom, the boys, and Tom's family. They were happy and carefree. Her biggest concern had been whether or not Santa delivered what the boys really wanted. She'd spent the last few hours of Christmas lying on the couch because her varicose veins were throbbing. Jane and Jane-Marie catered to her; sympathized over her tired legs; lamented how busy she'd be next year at Christmastime. The kind of attention a pregnant woman ate up with a spoon. Now the attention Kerry was receiving had turned sour. *Worry* wasn't fun or pretty. It wasn't exciting. *That soap star doesn't look worried,* Kerry thought. *She's probably having a perfectly smooth pregnancy. Her biggest concern is most likely how she'll be able to fit a prenatal yoga class into her busy acting schedule. She probably has her perfect little house with a perfect little nursery and maybe even plans on delivering her perfect little baby drug-free. She probably drinks healthy protein shakes every morning and sings to her belly every night.* Kerry dropped the magazine on the table. *How totally insensitive,* she thought, *to have this in THIS waiting room.* It took every ounce of her restraint not to tear it into a million pieces.

A thin woman in a white coat with dark hair entered the waiting room. "Kerry Sheeran?" she asked. Kerry popped up like a cork, held up her finger, then made her way to the hallway and called out to Tom. The woman smiled patiently and held the door open until the nervous couple passed through the threshold into the unknown.

"My name is Dr. Benson and this is Anne," she said, pointing to another woman-in-white. "We'll be conducting your ultrasound exam. Can we talk a little bit about why you're here today?" Dr. Benson hadn't wasted any time, carefully placing the towel over Kerry's lap and squirting the warm surgilube on her twenty-eight-week pregnant belly. It had been about a week since the horrible experience at the midwife's office, and the sting of it was still fresh. Kerry and Tom did their best to fill her in on the details of the pregnancy to date, while the doctor went to work with her exam. Both Anne and Dr. Benson were listening, periodically pausing to take a measurement and speak softly to each other. After a few minutes of retelling their confusing story, Kerry couldn't help but jump to the obvious question: "So, based on what you're seeing, would you say it's an intestinal blockage?" Kerry expected to be reprimanded for asking questions, but didn't care. "No," Dr. Benson replied, "I'm not seeing that at all."

The happy couple's eyes lit up. *Ahhhh, peace. Thank you God! Thank you!* Kerry thought. These words brought comfort, relief…the answer to their prayers. *No intestinal blockage. So glad we came! God is good! We'll be home in time to get the boys for lunch. Maybe we'll go out to celebrate. Everything is going to be okay!* she silently cheered.

"Unfortunately, what I'm seeing is a lot more serious then a blockage. The baby's intestines don't follow all the way through. It's called intestinal atresia. I'm also seeing signs of hydronephrosis in her kidneys which could be linked to a blockage or swelling in her ureters. This can be damaging. Her intestines will require surgery, but can hopefully be repaired and your daughter…." Dr. Benson stuttered, "…uhh, you knew you were having a girl, right?" Tom and Kerry cautiously nodded their heads, *yes.*

"…Anyway, your daughter will most likely be okay, running around playing soccer one day and having a productive life." Kerry looked at Tom for some kind of understanding. She'd heard the words *damaging, surgery* and *playing soccer,* but wasn't sure whether she should smile or cry. Tom was equally confused, nervously stroking Kerry's hair, attempting to provide some comfort.

"What's concerning to us right now," Dr. Benson continued, "is the level of ascites we're seeing in the baby." Ascites—that word, again. This was the word they had been introduced to a week prior. *The fluid in their baby's abdomen.*

"Last week, Dr. Base wasn't concerned with the level. He told us to come back in a few weeks to get it measured," Tom explained in a cracked voice.

Dr. Benson's face didn't change expression, and yet her words were alarming: "The amount of ascites we're seeing in your daughter is extremely dangerous. The fluid is pressing on her diaphragm, lungs and heart. Any more could cause cardiac failure or a number of problems to her other organs." Kerry's heart sank. Tom thought he was going to be sick. "Not to mention," Dr. Benson added, "the amount of excess fluid you're carrying could put you into pre-term labor at any moment. We'll have to do an emergency procedure to remove the fluid from you both."

Tom and Kerry were in complete shock. Speechless and helpless, their only ability to communicate was by squeezing each other's hands.

Dr. Wilkins-Haug introduced herself shortly after the ultrasound. She was a serious woman, mid-forties, with a short bob and no time to waste. Her expert advice was that Kerry and Tom sign the consent for the procedure immediately. She answered all of their questions with sharp wisdom and total competency. The only question Dr. Wilkins-Haug wasn't able to answer was: "Why hadn't someone already caught this?"

Dr. Wilkins-Haug explained that she and Dr. Benson were going to have to "tap" the excessive fluid from both Kerry and the baby by using the same type of syringe used for amniocentesis. The trick was to pierce through Kerry's abdomen, through her uterine wall and into the baby's abdomen. The doctor had to be precise with the needle. Any misstep could be life threatening. Risks included puncturing the baby's organs, rupturing Kerry's uterus, or the most likely of all: premature labor. So not only did the doctor need a steady hand, but the baby had to remain unbelievably still during the course of the procedure. *That sounds impossible,* Kerry feared.

The words of the medical team began swirling in a tornado-like cloud through Tom and Kerry's minds. The whites of their eyes exposed their fright: tears dripped from Tom's, while Kerry's remained locked in a state of panic. Neither of them had imagined anyone would be saying the things *these* people were saying. What happened to the *"Everything's fine!"* or *"Yes, we concur with your doctors in Rhode Island"* responses they had envisioned earlier? Nothing was going as they expected. *This can't be! How could things have gotten so dire over the course of a week that they have to stick a foot-long needle into our baby's abdomen? What if they miss? What if they mess up? What if these people are wrong and everything's really okay?* Tom squeezed Kerry's hand with each question that raced through his head. Kerry did the same. She took her eyes off Tom since it wasn't helping to see how terrified he'd become. Instead, Kerry stared at the ceiling. The stucco, white, ugly ceiling. *How did we end up in this damn room?* she wondered. *In this hellish situation? How have I become the person pregnant women fear most of becoming?* Kerry bit her bottom lip. *How could you, God?* she thought, glaring through the ceiling. *How could you do this to us?*

Kerry took the pen from Dr. Wilkins-Haug and put her signature on the consent form. It felt like she just signed over custody of her unborn daughter to a room full of strangers. Moments later, things began happening. The pinch of the needle didn't faze Kerry. Her eyes were locked on the ultrasound screen. Tom was rubbing her head, but she asked him to stop, for fear it would somehow shift her around and cause the doctors to mess up. Dr. Wilkins-Haug wanted to remove the baby's fluid first since she seemed to be in a good position for access. Dr. Benson worked the ultrasound. It suddenly occurred to Kerry that she forgot to ask the doctors how often they performed this procedure. It may have comforted her to know that this was something they did every day. *Why didn't I ask that question?* she thought. It was too late, now. Kerry kept her eyes on the needle as it passed through her uterus and into her daughter's belly.

Amid their panic, it was hard not to be amazed as Tom and Kerry watched the syringe pull 160 ccs from their unborn daughter's abdomen. The black fluid on ultrasound was slowly disappearing from the screen, and reappearing in the syringe. Dr. Wilkins-Haug's hands were steady and her voice was calming. She reassured them that the baby was cooperating—staying nice and still, and that all was going well, so far. A minute later, she announced that she was finished with the fetus and moving on to the second portion of fluid removal. Almost immediately,

Kerry felt a jolt within her womb. They watched on the screen as the baby flipped over, away from the needle and up against the left side of her stomach.

"Well, that was good timing!" Dr. Wilkins-Haug joked. "And now we have this nice pocket of fluid to work with on the right," Dr. Benson added. Kerry looked at Tom and attempted to smile. If the doctors were happy, that was good. They squeezed each other's hands as Dr. Wilkins-Haug removed 450 ccs of amniotic fluid from Kerry. Tom and Kerry silently prayed their baby wouldn't roll back towards the needle. Thankfully she didn't. When the doctor was finished, she removed the syringe and handed it to one of her colleagues.

The room was full of medical staff, busily bottling all the fluid and getting it ready to send off to the lab for analysis. Kerry looked around and wondered, *When did all these people come into the room?* She had no idea they'd been there the entire time. An older nurse, probably in her late fifties, walked over to them and took Kerry's hand. She rubbed the top of it with her other hand.

"How are you doing, honey?" she asked. "That was a lot."

"A lot of fluid?" Tom asked. "It looks like a lot of fluid."

"Fluid? Yes, that's a good amount of fluid from both of them," she responded. "But that's not what I meant." The nurse moved her hand up to Kerry's face and brushed the hair away from her eyes. "That was a lot for you to just go through. Are you okay, honey?"

Kerry looked at Tom, then back at the nurse. Her eyes spontaneously filled with tears as she erupted into uncontrollable weeping. Tom followed suit. The three of them held each other as the rest of the crew exited the room. Compassionately, the nurse reassured them it was over, and that it had gone as well as it could have. All of Kerry's emotion from the entire day poured out with each sob. "Deep breaths now, honey. I know. It's okay. Deep breaths. We don't want you going into labor now. Deep breaths and calm down...it's okay...it's over...good thing you came here today...you did a good job...your baby is okay...deep breaths...you need to calm down and relax...it's all over," the nurse said.

Chapter 4

THE BAPTISM

TOM'S PACE FELT good. The kinks were slowly working themselves out, and his body was loose. The crowd of runners hadn't broken up entirely, but he was making his way to open ground. A wave of emotion passed through his core and his eyes watered. *THIS IS HAPPENING! I'm running a freaking marathon right now,* he thought. *I AM RUNNING A FREAKING MARATHON!* It was like the days Thomas and Ryan were born. He knew they were coming. He planned months in advance for their arrival. Yet the days his sons actually made their entrance into the world, it was inconceivable to him that such a thing could take place. *What a feeling!* He beamed. This was one of those days he was going to remember for the rest of his life. The bends of the road, the cheers from the crowd, the rush of being a part of something so big and meaningful— this felt **INCREDIBLE!**

He looked to his left. A woman twice his size was checking her watch and keeping a steady pace. She wore a belt around her waist with little compartments to hold her water, energy boosters, iPod and tissues. Her pouch looked heavy as it bounced in unison with each step she took, but she didn't seem to mind at all. She looked determined and focused. To his right, a skinny young man in his twenties was blowing snot rockets every ten seconds. He just couldn't seem to clear his nose. *Maybe he should borrow one of the lady's tissues,* Tom thought. *Never mind,* he decided, *not getting involved.*

With Hopkinton behind him, Tom was happily making his way through Ashland. Passing a party at TJs Food and Spirits, he couldn't help but sing along with AC/DC's *"Highway to Hell"* as it blared from two giant speakers.

Up ahead, he was picturing the Mile 3 marker. Thinking back, he remembered when he was first able to run three miles without stopping. It was the first route he'd ever created within his neighborhood, and it was hilly. Tom had told himself with each telephone pole he passed, that he just had to make it to the next one. Somehow he managed to trick himself into running the entire three miles at a respectable pace. *Not bad for a guy who hates to exercise,* he had thought. *Now that I know I can do this, I'm gonna do it again.* It felt like progress to Tom. It felt like something he could do. He enjoyed the idea of challenging himself to the next mile or the faster pace. It felt good and Tom liked feeling good. He'd had his fair share of feeling crappy in his recent past, so this new feeling of control and potential was appealing. *I'm gonna do this,* he had thought.

The same thought rang through his mind as he wiped the sweat that was already dripping from his forehead. He mopped his brow, then reached his damp hand back into his shorts, uncrumpled the paper and read:

Mile 3: Emma is born. We hear her cry. She is tiny. You baptize her.

"Reading and running? That's impressive, brother!" Tom looked to his left. The woman with the sports belt had moved up a few notches and was replaced by a bearded man who looked kind of familiar. He chuckled and nodded his head in such a way that Tom couldn't know if he was genuinely in awe, or totally making an ass out of him. He wore a Miles for Miracles jersey. Within seconds, Tom had him placed.

"You're the guy from the bus. With the chalk," he announced with a smile.

"That's me!" the bearded smartass replied. "You can call me Joe, from Needham."

"Hey, Joe. Tom, from Rhode Island." He gave Joe a salute. He wasn't really sure why he did this, but it wasn't like he was going to shake hands with the guy while they were running. Plus they were sort of on the same team, so a salute felt respectable.

"It's mile three and I'm starting to get bored already. What are you reading about?" Joe inquired.

Tom wasn't sure he really wanted to get into his private business with Joe

Schmo from the bus. Besides, do I want to strike up a conversation with someone this early on? What if I get stuck talking to this guy for twenty-three more miles? What if his pace screws mine up? What if all the chitchat messes up my breathing? Tom wondered.

"Just reading about the day my daughter was born," Tom offered up.

"Oh yeah?" Joe asked. "Was she born in Rhode Island?"

"Oh, no," Tom answered. "She was born at Brigham and Womens." He looked ahead as he finished his answer. "In Boston."

* * *

TOM SQUEEZED KERRY'S hand as the words came out of Dr. Wilkins-Haug's mouth: "I'm afraid we're going to have to deliver her today. There's just no way we can continue to keep up with all the fluid."

Even though the past two weeks had been laden with multiple panic-stricken trips to the hospital, Kerry still felt blind-sided by her words. Even though she and the baby had undergone two additional "taps" since that initial life-changing appointment, her jaw still dropped in shock at the thought. And even though Dr. Wilkins-Haug had admitted Kerry to the hospital forty hours earlier for "close watch," it seemingly hadn't crossed her mind that childbirth was even a possibility for at least another month. Kerry had just come to terms with the fact that she was going to have to depend on Tom's parents to care for her boys while she was on bed rest. It was going to be difficult, but doable. Kerry had accepted this. But now, in an instant, everything was changing.

"I'm only thirty weeks pregnant! She's not ready to come out yet!" Kerry shuddered.

"It's what we have to do to give her the best chance at surviving," Dr. Wilkins-Haug responded. Her head was shaking up and down. Kerry looked at Tom. He was shaking his head too—as if it were some sort of a conspiracy. Kerry's breathing quickened and she felt her own head start to shake up and down, then drop in a defeated slump. From the sound of it, her womb had just been condemned. No longer did it serve as a secure encasement for her growing baby, but rather was a death trap. Kerry had failed as a protector. Her child was better off without her, and the sooner the better. *Why is this happening?* she wondered.

Kerry hesitated before picking up the phone to call her mother. For some reason, if she were going to call her mom and tell her everything that was about to happen, then maybe it was all really going to happen. She dialed the number.

"Mom? It's me, Kerry," she muttered.

"What's wrong? You don't sound good," Donna said anxiously.

"They have to do an emergency C-section today. The fluid is too much to keep up with anymore," Kerry explained. *There,* she thought, *I said it.*

"Oh, my God, honey, oh, my God…how will the baby even survive being born this early? What kind of a chance are they saying she has? Oh, Kerry, we'll start packing immediately…we'll get on the road as soon as possible…oh, Kerry, how can this be?" Donna cried. She was now officially in a "state."

"Can you please call the rest of the family for me? I can't have this conversation over and over. Please, just tell them what's going on—and to say some prayers." Kerry heard the words she was saying, and yet didn't believe any of them. She didn't *really* need anyone's prayers. This was all a weird mistake and it was only a matter of time before Dr. Wilkins-Haug would walk back in and call the whole thing off.

"I've gotta go, Mom. Somebody just walked in." Kerry hung up the phone and said hello to the friendly-faced young woman with long blond hair standing at the foot of her bed.

The woman introduced herself to Tom and Kerry as Dr. Scanlon, a fellow from the Neonatal Intensive Care Unit. She smiled throughout her entire spiel regarding *What to Expect When Your Child is Born Way Too Early.* She talked about bradycardia spells and how preemies' tiny brains forget to tell their lungs to keep breathing, and their heart to keep beating. She spoke at length about the life-long damage their underdeveloped lungs can suffer from being forced to breathe air months before they are ready. She talked about their nervous systems being immature, and the extreme sensitivity they have to light, sound, and even touch. Tom shrunk lower and lower into his chair with each topic covered. Dr. Scanlon went on to describe the hemorrhages that take place in many premature infants' brains and how potentially harmful or deadly they can be. Once Kerry heard this, she was too distracted to pay attention to any more of the discussion. She missed the part about the tears in the intestines and holes in the hearts. *This is all too much. Those poor little babies...and their parents,* Kerry thought. *But why bother listening? Our baby isn't going to have to go through any of this. Everything is going to be fine. As soon as Dr. Wilkins-Haug comes in, she is going to reassure us that this is all unnecessary.*

"So I think it would be a good idea for you to come take a quick tour of the NICU with me now," Dr. Scanlon suggested while nodding her head. Kerry hadn't really heard what she'd just said. But she knew from her short experience in this hospital that when someone was nodding their head at her, it meant she should do whatever they were telling her to do.

Kerry turned to Tom for guidance, but he looked like he'd just seen a ghost, so she turned back to Dr. Scanlon.

"I'm sorry, Doctor, what did you just say?" Kerry asked.

"I said I think that you and your husband should come take a tour of the Neo-Natal ICU...the NICU...with me...right now...so you are somewhat prepared with the logistics you will be experiencing once your baby is born." Her sweet voice had hardened, her smile had faded.

"Awesome," Tom quipped. "Sounds great. Just where I want to go right now."

"We'll go," Kerry interrupted, "but can we have a couple of minutes to talk?"

"I'd love to say *yes*—but your surgery is scheduled for 1 p.m. today, so our time is limited," Dr. Scanlon informed them. Kerry's face turned white.

Forty-five minutes later, Tom pushed Kerry in a wheelchair back to her depressing hospital room. They remained in a state of shock over what they'd just seen and spoken to the NICU nurses about. Kerry couldn't get over the sizes of the babies she'd gotten a glimpse of. Tom couldn't believe how beaten down the parents looked. The only positive moment of the entire tour was when a NICU nurse poo-pooed the idea that ten weeks premature was a big deal. *"Oh, honey, that's old compared to some of the peanuts we take care of in here,"* she had said. *At least that's something,* Kerry thought. *It could be worse.*

Tom and Kerry didn't even have a chance to use the bathroom, before two more people were simultaneously knocking on and walking through the door. If Kerry's eyes could talk, they would have been growling the words: *Good God, WHAT NOW?*

"I'm sorry to interrupt, but my name is Isabelle Arnold and this is one of our chaplains, Andrew Williams," announced the woman in a buttoned red sweater.

"I'm sorry, but this really isn't a good time," Tom informed them.

"I know," Isabelle quickly agreed, "but the reason we are here is that I'm one of the hospital's social workers, and your patient profile mentions you are both Catholic and that you're interested in the spiritual services our hospital provides for times like this."

Kerry glared at Tom. She'd given him all the paperwork to fill out when they were admitting her two days prior. Kerry was thinking along the lines of social security numbers, addresses and such—things her brain couldn't be bothered with at that moment. *How has religion worked its way into this scenario?* she wondered. *And what exactly does this woman mean by "times like this?" What the hell is that suppose to mean?* Tom took the reigns:

"So are you the Catholic chaplain?" Tom asked.

"Actually I am Christian, but not Catholic," Andrew admitted. He was a clean-cut man in his late forties. He wore a tweed jacket and khaki pants, and probably had an extra twenty-five pounds on him. He looked like the kind of guy who carried a pipe in his jacket pocket. While his head remained mostly bowed, he did make the occasional eye contact.

Kerry's eyes darted back at Tom's. "What?" Tom defended. "I checked off the box that asked if we practice a religion. Geez, sorry!" Without hesitation, Kerry spoke: "So I don't get it, did my husband check off the wrong box? What religion are you, Andrew?"

Andrew's eyes met quickly with Kerry's, then locked in place on one of the floor's blue speckled tiles. "I'm Lutheran," he said.

"So how is this going to help us?" Kerry lashed. "What do you mean by 'times like this'? Just tell me why you're here right now."

"I'm here to offer you some spiritual support. To pray with you," Andrew explained.

Tom looked at both of them apologetically. He wanted to make Kerry stop talking. He knew why Andrew and Isabelle were there—they'd just walked through the scariest hospital bay he'd ever been in. He saw baby after baby hooked up to machines that were keeping them alive. He saw human beings that were smaller then he ever imagined a human being could be. He saw the faces of the parents who were holding vigil next to their isolettes and cribs. Tom saw all of this. He knew why they were there.

"Isn't there a Catholic chaplain in this hospital? Can we get a Catholic guy? Do you have priests?" Kerry continued. She thought for a moment. "I wouldn't mind saying some prayers with a priest or a nun. Maybe they could do a special blessing before the surgery. We want the baby baptized immediately. Can we get a Catholic?"

"I'm sorry, but our Catholic chaplain isn't available right now, which is why I brought Andrew here," Isabelle explained.

"The baby can still be baptized. Plus, I'm pretty sure that in God's eyes, we are all his children no matter the differences in our religion," Andrew suggested. He glanced at Kerry, ever so gingerly. She returned his glance. Again her eyes spoke volumes. Only this time they were saying: *Are you freaking kidding me right now?* Her husband caught a glimpse of this and interjected.

"That's true, and we would love a prayer," Tom said. "Thank you."

The woman in the red sweater took a few steps back as Andrew walked forward and began his prayer. Tom and Andrew closed their eyes. Kerry left hers opened. Her mind wandered off after his opening line, and began its own private conversation: *Times like THIS, God? Are you really about to let THIS happen?*

The prayer was finished, and just as Tom was thanking Andrew, Kerry's nurse walked into the room with a look of authority. "It's time to head down to pre-op," she said. Turning to Tom she added, "Make sure you have all of her belongings because we're not sure if she'll be coming back."

"Excuse me?" Kerry squealed.

"I mean, to this exact room," the nurse clarified.

Tom kissed Kerry's head. "Game on," he whispered.

The door to the operating room opened, and the nurse put her hand up to Tom and Andrew. "I'm sorry, but you can't come in with us just yet," she said.

"But, I'm...." Tom began.

"I know. After her spinal is in and the room is prepped, you can come right in," the nurse assured him. Tom let go of Kerry's hand. She hadn't spoken since they began rolling her gurney. Her teeth had been clenched; her eyes glazed over as they passed through the hospital's halls. Some rooms were tinged with solemn faces, but others overflowed with flowers, helium balloons and happiness. *Why do those people get to be happy?* Kerry wondered. *Everyone's probably standing around talking about how perfect their babies are. Those women are in that euphoric state after childbirth where you want to immediately get pregnant again so that you can experience it all over.* Each time they had passed one of these rooms, Kerry's shoulders cringed and she clenched even harder.

"I love you," Tom quivered.

"I love you, too," she managed.

The door shut and the smell of alcohol filled Kerry's nose. A few people dressed in blue scrubs with O.R. caps worked busily around the room. She didn't look at any of their faces. A pair of eyes with glasses pulled down his mask and introduced himself as the anesthesiologist. He said his name, but Kerry didn't catch it.

"You okay?" he asked. Kerry nodded. Her chest was heaving, her blood-shot eyes were darting all over the room—the monitors, scalpels, scale, baby cart, ultrasound machine, needles. Her heart felt like it was trying to break through her chest. "I'm going to ask you to sit up and hang your legs off the side of the bed," the mask with glasses said.

"Just lean forward and hang on to me," some blue eyes insisted.

"I'm going to need you to stay very still," the mask with glasses warned. "Can you do that for me?"

Kerry wanted to say *yes*. Usually she was very cooperative, but her body had a mind of it's own. And in that moment, it trembled uncontrollably. Her legs shook so hard the bed moved. Her hands shook so hard the woman she was hanging onto juddered. The more they assured Kerry she was okay, the worse she trembled. *Oh, my God,* Kerry realized, *they're going to stick a needle in my spine and numb the crap out of me so that they can slice open my uterus and rip my little girl out of my body.* She felt the baby kicking. *And once they take her, I don't even know if she's going to be okay! What if she's better off inside of me? How do they know?*

"I need you to take some slow deep breaths and try to calm down, Kerry," the blue eyes said slowly. "Deep breath in, and exhale." The nurse did this ten or fifteen times, and then carefully nodded to the pair of glasses. "Nice and still, Kerry," he said. "You're going to feel a little pinch and then some pressure." Kerry didn't feel anything. Her body had surrendered. Things were at the point of no return and she knew it. The blue eyes squeezed Kerry's arms and exhaled. "It's all over, honey. You can lay back now," she said. "It's all over." *No it's not,* Kerry thought. *It hasn't even begun.*

Tom walked into the room, dressed from head to toe in scrubs. He looked ridiculous. For some reason the other five or six people in the room who were dressed in the same exact get-up looked completely normal. But Tom looked like he was wearing a Halloween costume. It was hardly the time to crack jokes, however, so Kerry decided to remain in her solemn state.

"You okay, babe?" he asked. Tom was shifting around and trying to take in the scene. His heart raced, but he didn't dare show it. "Everything's going to be okay, babe. You're in good hands right now," he insisted. Behind Tom, a pair of brown eyes clenched a bible and agreed with every word he said. Kerry looked at Tom. "Is that...?" she began.

"Yes," Tom explained. "Andrew has some holy water so I thought he should go ahead and baptize her as soon as she comes out."

"Oh, I can't baptize her since I'm not Catholic," Andrew corrected Tom. "I can do a special blessing on her, though, if you'd like." His brown eyes nervously smiled at the couple.

"So we can't even baptize her?" Kerry quipped. "Now our daughter's not going to be baptized after all this because the Catholic person isn't working today? Freaking unbelievable! I guess God's just going to have to understand since this is all HIS doing," she lashed. "I guess if our baby dies, he's going to have to give her a pass on the whole *going to purgatory* thing since this is how HE decided things were going to go."

"Ker?" Tom interjected. "Babe?"

"You can baptize her, Tom," Andrew said. "Any confirmed Catholic can baptize someone."

"Really?" Tom asked. "Okay, what do I do?" Andrew gave him the prayer to recite while pouring the water over the baby. Then he handed the holy water to Tom.

"So we're all good then?" Kerry asked. "Is that all he needs to do?"

"That's all he need to do," Andrew said.

"Okay, great. Because things are starting to get pretty intense around here and if Tom's going to do the baptism…." she began.

"Say no more. You are all in my prayers. God bless," Andrew said as he quickly and happily turned around and walked out of the room. Tom looked at Kerry and shook his head in disapproval. "He needed to go," Kerry informed him. "It was time for Andrew to go."

Within minutes, Dr. Wilkins-Haug arrived and was ready to perform the last tap into the baby's abdomen before delivering her. She was snippy with the ultrasound operator; he couldn't seem to do anything right. Once he finally got a clear shot of the baby, Dr. Wilkins-Haug pierced through Kerry's uterus and into a big pocket of fluid in the baby's stomach. "Hold it there," she insisted. "Keep it there…you're moving…hold it there until I'm out." Seconds later she finished. "Table down," was her next instruction. She looked at Kerry and Tom. "Did you give her a name yet?" Dr. Wilkins-Haug asked.

"Emma," Kerry said with great difficulty.

"Emma Ann," Tom concurred with pride.

"Okay," Dr. Wilkins-Haug said. "And I understand you're going to baptize Emma immediately, Tom?" He shook his head. "Okay then everyone, let's get ready to welcome Emma." Her eyes smiled and winked at the petrified couple. Tom watched as she sliced a sharp, thin line along the bottom of Kerry's stomach. His eyes widened as she pried his wife open, through layers of tissue. "Lots of pressure, Kerry," Dr. Wilkins-Haug warned. Kerry didn't feel anything. The curtain was blocking her view; all she could see was the terrified expression on Tom's face.

"Here she comes, babe," Tom declared. "I can see her, she's almost...she's out! Babe, she's out." Emma let out the tiniest cry her parents had ever heard. "She's beautiful, Ker! She's bigger then I thought! She's so beautiful!" Tom cried. Dr. Wilkins-Haug whisked Emma off to the side of the room where a team of doctors and nurses began their assessments. Kerry looked over, but all she could see were little arms and legs flailing.

"Is she okay!? Is she okay!? Emma, my baby, my baby! Oh, my God, is she breathing? God, please let her be okay! Is she alright!?" Kerry pleaded.

"She's okay," Dr. Wilkins-Haug said, "but she needs some help. Tom, why don't you...." Tom rushed to the side of the room and looked right into the eyes of his precious, beautiful baby girl. He started to weep. There she was, his three-pound, eight-ounce daughter. She was real. She was alive. His tears dripped on her perfect little head. "I love you, Emma. I love you so much, honey," Tom cried. He gently kissed her three times. Then he cupped his hand and poured some holy water into it. It seemed redundant to pour it over her tiny forehead, since she was the most sacred thing he'd ever laid eyes on. But as he did, Tom proudly proclaimed: "I baptize you, Emma Ann, in the name of the Father, and of the Son, and of the Holy Spirit, Amen."

Chapter 5

EVERYTHING CHANGES

"WOW," JOE FROM Needham sniffed. "That's some birthday." He shook his head at Tom. "Reminds me of my Gracie's, sorta." Tom and Joe had spent the last mile together. They were at a steady eight-minute and thirty-seconds pace, which was pretty impressive. Mile 3 continued through Ashland, where the scenery was mostly residential. Given the waning excitement of the first couple miles, Tom found it pleasant to be running with his new friend. Conversation was a big distraction and it didn't seem to be taking too much of a toll on his breathing. Tom smiled to know that mile 4 was fast approaching, having recognized the surroundings from his practice run.

"Did Gracie have complications?" Tom asked. *Duh*, he thought, as soon as the words escaped his mouth, *we are running on the Children's Hospital team.* Not to mention the picture of the little girl Joe had taped onto his back.

"She did," Joe answered. But she wasn't born super early like Emma. We knew before Gracie was born that her heart wasn't right. Problems with the pulmonary valve, really complicated. Anyhow, your story reminds me of the day she was born."

"At Brigham and Womens?" Tom asked.

"No, we had her at Mass General, but they moved her to Boston Children's the day after she was born."

"What a hospital, huh?" Tom insisted.

"They saved Gracie's life five times," Joe said shaking his head.

"Anyhow, I'm feeling the wind at my back right now. Great talking to you, brother." With a burst of energy, Joe took off into the crowd, weaving through runners until he was barely visible. Leaving Tom alone with his thoughts.

Up ahead Tom got a visual of the mile marker. Four miles wasn't really anything to sneeze at, again reminding him of the twenty-two point two that still remained. The water stop seemed like a good idea, even though he wasn't terribly thirsty. *Too soon*, he decided, *for a GU.* A group of people cheered as he quickly chugged a cup of water then tossed it to the side—a few feet shy of the garbage can. *Boy*, he thought, *runners make some mess. God Bless the poor folks that clean this all up.* It was the only socially acceptable form of littering that he could think of. *If only Kerry was so accepting of the way I toss my shoes around the house,* he thought.

Ahh, Kerry, where are you right now? Tom wondered. He imagined the traffic into Beantown *had* to be terrible. *Will she even make it into the city in time?* His brother Timmy and friend Brad planned on camping out near the finish line. His other brother, Sean, said he'd be there with his daughter somewhere in Wellesley. Mike planned on surprising him. His parents were going to squeeze in somewhere on Heartbreak Hill, but couldn't say for sure exactly where they'd be. Rest assured Tom would hear them as he ran past, knowing his mother had the ability to project her voice further and louder then any human he'd ever known. Jane would take down whomever she had to in order to give "her Tommy" a kiss, then snap ten to fifteen photos. But Kerry, Tom wasn't sure about. Although her kiss seemed genuine earlier that morning, he still found himself wondering: *Was she even impressed? Will she be here to support me? Does she still resent everything I had to give to this race in order to achieve all 26.2 miles of it?* If he had to guess, the answers to all of his questions were *yes.* He was 99% sure of it. Which is why he couldn't say for certain.

Thinking about his wife prompted Tom to take out her letter. He felt a pit in his stomach as he read the next line:

Mile 4: Everything changes....

THE RECOVERY ROOM wasn't far from the operating room and the nurse taking care of Kerry was as sweet as pie. She called down to the NICU to get an update for them and was proud to announce that Emma's APGAR score was a six, which was pretty good considering her gestation and abdominal complications. Tom kissed Kerry. This was better then they had expected. Things were going to be okay. Tom looked at his phone. "Jean called, she's coming in a couple of hours," he announced.

"What? I thought she was in Vermont?" Kerry asked.

"She was but she left. She just left me a message that she'll be here around 3:30 or 4 p.m.," Tom reported. This was good. Jean was the exact person Kerry needed. She was calm and collected. Nothing fazed her. Jean had seen a lot as a nurse, and had a good sense about what was *nothing big*, and what was *something worth getting hysterical about*. In Kerry's opinion, Jean would assess this particular situation as medium to low on the drama meter. Emma was small but alive and her APGAR score was relatively good. *Maybe I'll even get to hold her, so that when Jean walks in, she can see for herself just how good everything actually is*, Kerry thought. *She might even regret having left her ski vacation for what's turned out to be a nonemergency. And Emma. I'll get to tell her what we named our beautiful daughter: Emma Ann Sheeran.* The day was turning around. Kerry closed her eyes and smiled, not expecting her happy daydream to be interrupted.

"My mom's downstairs and wants to come up," Tom announced without so much as a glance in Kerry's direction.

"Right now? When did she get here?" Kerry asked.

"I don't know, babe! My phone was off during the delivery. She must have just gotten in the car after the last time we spoke. Anyway she's here and she's coming up." Tom was using his *I'm not going to argue about this* voice.

"No, not right now! I'm not ready right now. Please! I just got out of surgery and I haven't even seen Emma. Not yet!" Kerry pleaded.

"Oh, it's alright for Jean to come, but it's not alright for my mom to? That's not fair at all and you know it! What do you want me to say to her? Glad you drove all the way here, but sorry—we're not ready to see you yet?" Tom fired back.

"I want her to come! I love your mom and want to see her! But can't I at least see my baby first?" Kerry begged. The fact of the matter was Kerry needed to mentally prepare for her mother-in-law's presence. It wasn't as if Jane were going to slip into the room and quietly observe. A wallflower she was not. Knowing how deep her passion for her grandchildren ran, Kerry was certain Jane's anxiety would shoot through the roof the moment she stepped foot in her recovery room. And given the way their day had been unfolding thus far, any additional hysteria could quite possibly send the young mother into a complete tailspin. Which is why she just wasn't ready. And yet that didn't matter one bit. Because seconds later the door to the recovery room swung open like a scene out of *Gone With the Wind*, and in walked Emma's grandmother.

"How's my baby?!?! I'm worried sick! Where is she?!?!" Jane shrieked. Kerry closed her eyes and exhaled.

"Did they take her right to the ICU?" Jane asked. "They probably need to take them right to the ICU when they're that premature, I'm sure. Was she breathing okay? Did they have to intubate?" Her Brooklyn accent was always more pronounced during stressful situations.

"She's okay, Ma," Tom assured her. He waved his hand up and down in a calming motion. "Yes, she's in the NICU right now, but I saw her and she's beautiful. Bigger then I expected."

"How big?" Jane served.

"Three pounds, eight ounces," he returned.

"Oh, my God! That's tiny, Tommy! When I had you and Timmy you were only five pounds—give or take a few ounces—and THAT was really small. I'll never forget it. Three pounds? My God, she must be a peanut!" Jane said.

"It's not *that* small, considering everything," Kerry interrupted. "We were worried she'd be much smaller."

"Oh, my God, Kerry. How are you doing, honey?" Jane asked, spinning towards her. "You must still be coming off anesthesia? What did they give you? A spinal? I remember when I had my twins, they gave me Demerol and it made me crazy! I was standing on my bed screaming at all the nurses. I'll never forget it!" Kerry wasn't sure if she was supposed to still answer the question. "Where's your nurse?" Jane continued. "I don't know," Kerry responded. "She was just here a minute ago." The room was spinning. It was hard for Kerry to focus. Their dialog felt like a game of Ping-Pong.

"I'll find her. Where'd she go? We need an update!" Jane insisted. "Did you name her yet?"

"We named her Emma. Emma Ann," Tom proudly answered.

"Oh, Emma Ann—what a beautiful name! What made you pick it? Is someone in your family named Emma? Your dad's mom?" Jane prodded, looking at her daughter-in-law. Kerry was too dizzy to answer. "We just liked the name Emma. And Ann is Kerry's middle name," Tom responded. At this point he knew he'd have to field all the questions. Kerry had officially checked out. Her light was on, but Tom could tell nobody was home.

"Where's this nurse? We need an update on my Emma," Jane repeated.

"She was just here, Mom," Tom pleaded. "She gave us an update. She said Emma was in the NICU and that her APGAR score was pretty good, considering everything."

"Yes, APGARs. The newborn assessments of heart rate, respiration, muscle tone, skin color, and I believe the last one is how they respond to stimuli," Jane confirmed. "The highest score is a ten, right?" she asked.

"Yeah, I forget exactly, but something like that," Tom assured her. The door opened and in walked Kerry's nurse. She held a water pitcher and some cups, and quietly said hello to the new face in the room. The poor thing had no idea she was about to be interrogated. Within seconds, Jane unleashed. "Hello, I'm Jane. What's your name?" she began.

"Holly," The nurse said with a smile.

"And Holly, what exactly was Emma's APGAR score?" Jane asked.

"She scored a six on the APGAR scale, I believe," Holly responded with the same kind smile.

"So a six out of ten. Okay. What was she lacking in?" Jane pressed. The barrage continued. Holly was defenseless. "I don't know for sure," Holly admitted, "but a six is pretty good for a 30-weeker." Holly's smile was back. She filled a cup with ice water and handed it to Kerry. "Are you ready for a sip? Or are you still feeling nauseous?" she asked. Kerry shook her head *no*. "Okay, just wait until you're ready. We can probably get you something for the nausea. In the meantime...." Holly began.

"Are they going to let you see her?" Jane asked, looking directly at Kerry. "How long ago did you deliver?" she added. Kerry shrugged her shoulders. She didn't want to admit it, but it *had* been a while since the delivery and she *was* dying to get a look at her daughter. Jane turned back towards Holly. "When can they see Emma?" she barked. "It's a little nerve-wracking not to be able to see your baby, you understand." Kerry perked up. Suddenly Jane's tenacity was just what the doctor ordered.

"I'm not sure exactly, but don't worry. If anything were wrong, there would be a team of surgeons standing in this room, reporting to you directly," Holly said. Kerry, Tom and Jane all took a collective deep breath and enjoyed the safe feeling Holly had just given them. Everything was going to be okay. This was all just part of the standard premature infant-care that a top-rate hospital like Brigham and Women's gave. If Tom and Kerry had learned anything over the last month, it was that they had to be patient with healthcare providers. The truth of the matter was that Emma was just *one* of the *hundreds* of patients in the hospital. Things take time.

The four of them joked about how the nurses were probably doing her footprints and handprints on their official forms. Most likely, they guessed, Emma *did* need some oxygen. They probably had to do blood work and such. All of this takes time, they concurred. Holly wasn't worried in the least; and as a result, neither were Tom, Kerry and Jane. Patience was what they needed. And this was okay because they knew that if anything were wrong, there would be a team of surgeons standing in the recovery room reporting to them directly. And there wasn't. Until two minutes later when the door creaked open. Three attending surgeons and two surgical fellows filed in and stood at the foot of Kerry's hospital bed. They were not smiling.

"My name is Dr. Russell Jennings, I'm the attending general surgeon, these are my associates: Dr. Buchmiller—GC, Dr. Borer—Director of Urology, and our surgical fellows," said the man with the mustache and green scrubs. "I'm sorry but your daughter is in trouble."

That was how he opened. The air was sucked out of everyone in the room, even Holly. Tom felt like he had just been punched in his gut. He literally could not breathe. Jane's eyes were as wide as saucers and she let out a terribly loud gasp. Kerry wasn't sure what was happening. She wondered why these people were standing in her room, introducing themselves. *Clearly they are in the wrong room. Director of Urology? GC? What does any of this mean? This is a bad mistake. They have the wrong patient. My daughter is doing fine with an incredibly good APGAR score. So move along, people,* she thought. Kerry glanced at Jane's horrified expression. *There is no need for drama, this is all a mistake,* Kerry thought. She meant to roll her eyes but was so dizzy she forgot.

"My God! What is it? What's wrong?" Jane screamed. The surgeon directed his response towards the young couple. "We've diagnosed your daughter with what's called tracheal esophageal fistula and atresia." Dr. Jennings began. "Basically her trachea has a fistula, a hole, in it. Her esophagus isn't connected. It ends approximately one inch below her throat, near her clavicle. The bottom portion of her esophagus unfortunately routes into her lower trachea, which of course leads to her lungs. Her connections are all wrong."

"Oh, my God! This is terrible! This is awful!" Jane shrieked. The quiet man with glasses interjected over the noise: "This of course," he began, "is in addition to the issues we already knew about with her intestinal atresia and urinary complications. She also appears to be experiencing renal failure. One of her kidneys is considerably smaller than the other. And she has quite a bit of hydronephrosis."

"Oh, no! Oh, God! Oh, Tommy! Oh, my God, Kerry. This is terrible!" Jane screamed. Her eyes were officially popping out of her head. Tom covered his ears with his hands. It was as if they were speaking another language and he only understood every fifth word. Their morose tone, however, suggested things were not good. Kerry felt the same way. She covered her mouth. Dr. Borer had shattered her hopes that these people were in the wrong room when he mentioned Emma's intestinal atresia. Kerry needed to hear these doctors; she needed to understand them. But the room was spinning, and Jane kept gasping. It was impossible to focus on the news they were delivering.

"But nobody saw this trachea or esophagus problem on ultrasound! How can this be? What does this mean?" Kerry begged.

"Unfortunately this particular complication doesn't often show on pre-natal ultrasound. What it means is that we'll have to do an emergency surgery to tie off the fistula and dorsal esophagus," Dr. Jennings said.

"Oh, my God!" Jane gasped.

Kerry turned towards Jane and pleaded: "Mom?! They're talking... I can't hear what they're saying...please!" Suddenly things were becoming *too* clear. She looked at Tom, then back at the doctors.

"When do we have to decide if we want to go through with the surgery?" Kerry asked. This seemed to be a legitimate question, but Dr. Jennings furrowed his brow and quickly retorted: "You don't really decide one way or another. If she doesn't have this surgery, she could vomit—flood her lungs—then die." Kerry and Tom were still very fuzzy on the logistics of Emma's imperfections, but they certainly understood the words "vomit" and "die". Grabbing each other's arms, they felt the horror thrashing through their veins. The heaviest of all weights had been dropped on their already fragile shoulders, and their minds couldn't keep up with all their questions. *What happened to our dreams of having a little girl? Of the family we imagined? How could they be describing the beautiful baby we just baptized an hour ago? One little spit-up and she could be taken away from us?* "Just do the surgery, please!" they pleaded in unison. The surgeons all shook their heads. "Right now!" Kerry added.

"We've already scheduled her for 7 o'clock tonight," Dr. Buchmiller announced. "They've got her stable in the ICU as we speak."

"But what if she vomits?" Tom shook.

"They can control that for now. She'll be okay until the surgery," Dr. Jennings assured them. He seemed confident; intelligent; believable. Tom and Kerry's broken hearts crashed on the cold floor of the recovery room. They looked at each other with mouths agape. Seeing this, Jane ended her silent streak: "They need to see Emma now," she demanded. "Someone needs to bring them in to see her RIGHT NOW." Jane looked over at Holly, who was visibly shaken. "Right away," Holly agreed, "I'll call up to the NICU."

Drenched in tears, Tom held the door open as two nurses pushed Kerry's hospital bed through the doorway. "Oh, my God, Kerry" was all he could say while squeezing his wife's hand. Rolling down the long halls, Kerry didn't cry. She didn't speak. She made no eye contact with anyone. Nothing made sense. Everything was unfolding in front of her, yet nothing seemed real. Apparently God's plans for Emma were completely different then hers and Tom's. She was crushed. Abandoned. Tricked. Everything had changed in that recovery room. Everything she knew to be true, wasn't anymore. The direction in which things were headed was becoming clear. Fear made her question just how desperate she really was to see the baby who had been taken from her body.

A month ago it was Christmas. She was lying on her couch, feeling kicks and rolls in her womb. She was daydreaming about their next Christmas. About possibly having a girl. About names and dresses and pink. All of those dreams were gone now. Snatched away in an instant the moment they reached in and took Emma.

"Baby Sheeran?" Holly asked as they rolled Kerry past the NICU nurses' station. "We have Baby Sheeran's parents here to see her," she announced.

"Bay 8," another nurse answered. "But not for long. We have orders to transfer her over to Children's, STAT."

"We'll be quick," Holly assured her. Tom was pushing Kerry's hospital bed faster then anyone should ever push a hospital bed. His eyes scanned the walls and ceiling for the number eight. "Is this it?" he asked, stopping short every ten feet. There were so many monitors, so many isolettes. And all the same, it looked completely different from the NICU he had taken a tour of four hours earlier. A girl in her twenties with freckles and light brown hair peeked out from behind a computer screen. "Are you Emma Sheeran's parents?" she asked with a gentle smile. "I'm Kristin. Emma's doing okay, she's nice and stable now." Kristin helped to roll Kerry's bed into place. "Congratulations" she said softly. Kerry squeezed her eyes shut. That word tore right through her heart.

Kerry looked at her daughter. She stared at her fuzzy black-haired head. She gazed at her scrawny arms and legs. Emma's skin hung off of her. Kerry looked at her tiny face. It was perfect, aside from the tubes coming out of her mouth. She was beautiful and peaceful and helpless…and hers. Kerry's heart swelled. "Can I touch her?" she asked. It felt so unnatural to be asking another person if she could touch her own baby. "Of course you can," Kristin said. She put the side of Emma's isolette down and pushed the bed as close as she could. Kerry reached her arm out and touched her daughter. Her swollen heart was now sitting in her throat. Emma's hand frantically jerked up, then landed on top of Kerry's. The fragile infant opened up her tiny fist and clenched down on her mother's finger. "It's me, baby. It's Mommy. I love you, baby," Kerry whispered. "I love you, Emma."

Tom was crying. "She's so beautiful, isn't she, Ker?" he said. He just couldn't get over his little girl's beauty. "Isn't her hair so cute? I didn't think she'd even have hair this early," he admitted, wiping away his tears. "Can I kiss her?" Tom asked.

"Sure," Kristin smiled, "It might be a little hard but you can try." His head was too big to fit through the side of the isolette, so he kissed his hand, then gently cupped the top of Emma's head. "It's Daddy, Emma. Daddy loves you, honey."

"I hate to interrupt," a tall, thin nurse apologized, "but we have to get Emma over to Children's right now." Kerry gasped. "Children's Hospital?" she asked.

"Yes," The nurse said.

"Is that where they're doing the surgery?" Kerry asked. She already knew the answer was *yes*, but felt the need to ask questions. Kristin nodded her head. Everything was happening so fast. Decisions were being made left and right. It seemed like she should be double checking things. It felt like the motherly thing to do. This was *her* baby, after all.

The tall nurse lifted the side of the isolette and impatiently waited for Kerry to take her hand out of it. After a few seconds she sympathized: "I'm so sorry you have to say goodbye for now. But it takes time to admit a new patient and they need to start the process." She gave the couple a warm smile, though neither of them had been looking at her to see it. "I'm so sorry," she tried again. "I have to close the side of Emma's isolette for safe travels." This time she added a light-hearted giggle. Still no movement from Tom and Kerry. The tall nurse's glare darted in Holly's direction. She opened her eyelids as far as they could open. Finally Holly spoke: "Kerry, you have to let go of Emma's hand so they can put the side up." Holly looked at Tom: "You need to take your hand off her head now, so they can close the bed." Tom snapped backed into reality and took his hand away. He quickly kissed it one last time, touched Emma's hair, then stepped back two steps. Kerry didn't move. She stared at Emma. Her fingers were so small and skinny. She scanned her chest and abdomen. It looked tiny but perfect. "Ker," Tom said. He reached for her arm, and slowly tugged. "They're taking her, Ker."

"HOW DO THEY KNOW?!" Kerry snapped. She looked at all the nurses. "How do they know all these things are wrong with her body? How can they know? How can they be so sure, so fast?"

"They scanned her from top to bottom right after she was born. They knew from the start when they couldn't insert the tubes the proper way, something wasn't right," Kristin answered.

"But how can they even do surgery on such a tiny thing? How will she ever survive it?" Kerry pleaded. Her face looked gray and pathetic. She was shaking.

"They do them every day and a lot are on babies even smaller then Emma," the thin nurse said. Tom tugged at Kerry's arm again, until she finally let go. She quickly kissed her hand and reached back for Emma's, but Emma had moved hers away. The thin nurse flipped the side of the isolette up and snapped two locks into place, quick as a whip. Holly moved to the top of Kerry's bed and started pushing. Tom couldn't control his tears. He shook his head from side to side, trying to prevent his emotion. Then he reached down for Kerry's hand. "I love you, Emma!" Kerry called out. Her voice sadly shook. "We love you so much!" Tom added in between sobs. He looked back at the thin nurse. "I'm coming with you," he demanded. Unfazed by the drama, the thin nurse shook her head in agreement as she quickly pushed Emma's isolette in the opposite direction. "Don't let anything happen to our baby girl," Kerry yelled as she watched Tom and Emma disappear around the corner. Her heart was so high in her throat, she feared it would project out as she vomited into a pink plastic bin. An utterly sickening goodbye.

It was already 4:30 p.m. by the time Kerry was settled in her new room. She was alone and throwing up every fifteen minutes or so. It should have been painful, considering the fresh wound from the C-section, but Kerry didn't feel a thing. She flashed-back to the moment after Emma's delivery when Dr. Wilkins-Haug announced she had done the incision in such a way that a VBAC (vaginal birth after Cesarean) would be possible, should she and Tom decide to have any more children. *Was that some kind of a sick joke?* Kerry wondered. *How unbelievably inconsiderate to even mention something so twisted.* In all her thirty-three years on earth, she'd never experienced anything so terrifying. Kerry felt like she was in a never-ending horror movie. Each new moment scarier than the last. *Why would anyone ever want to go through what we're going through, again?* It wasn't even worth debating—her reproductive days were officially over.

Even though she was adamant about this, it saddened Kerry immensely. The beautiful experiences she'd had giving birth to Thomas and Ryan were now capped off with the single most frightening birth she could ever have imagined. In fact, she had a hard time even referring to what just happened with Emma as a *birth*. It felt more like a robbery. Armed with knives and drugs, her daughter was sliced from her uterus. And Kerry was powerless to these thieves who now wanted to cut their knives into Emma. She sat up again and vomited bile into her bin.

Jane was at Children's Hospital with Tom. Kerry was happy her husband had some company and insisted he only call her hospital room if something were wrong. Cell phone calls were not permitted inside either hospital, and the time it would take for him to go outside on the street to call her was too precious. She preferred he stay by Emma's side, and Tom promised to comply. Jane was happy to offer her support. She felt so helpless. Her son was in pain and there was nothing she could do to fix it. Jane couldn't help her reaction in the recovery room—everything those surgeons were saying *was* horrible. *It was awful!* Having been a nurse for thirty years, she knew that sometimes things go terribly wrong. But nothing like this had ever happened to any of her children. And until today, it hadn't happened to any of her grandchildren either. This was bad. Perhaps the worst part was having to watch *her* baby experience the nightmare.

The phone next to Kerry's bed rang loudly. It startled her. *Something happened!* she thought, spilling her vomit bin all over the bed as she reached to answer it.

"Hello?" she quivered.

"You have a visitor. Can we send her in?" the voice on the other end of the line asked.

Kerry exhaled. "Yes," she answered. It was hard to think who this visitor could possibly be. She assumed it was a nurse, doctor or some other hospital worker. *Is it Dr. Wilkins-Haug?* she wondered. *Is she here to deliver the bad news in person? Oh, my God, that's probably who it is!* Luckily Kerry didn't have to wonder for too long. Seconds later her sister walked in.

"Oh, my God, you just made me knock my barf all over myself!" Kerry snapped.

"It's great to see you, too!" Jean said, looking disgusted.

"I thought you were my doctor with bad news!" Kerry explained. She felt dizzy again, but was so relieved to see her big sister. "It's bad, Jean. The baby's in really bad shape," she said. Sitting up, Kerry retched more bile just as her nurse walked in. There was nothing in her stomach at this point, but that made the straining worse. She was itchy too. Everything itched: her arms, chest and legs. She clawed at herself in between retches. "What's wrong with me?" Kerry asked. "I can't stop throwing up and I want to crawl out of my skin!"

"It's the anesthesia," the nurse answered, "Some people have a bad reaction."

"Can you give her something for the nausea?" Jean asked. "It can't be good for her to be vomiting so much with all those stitches." The nurse shook her head and agreed to have the doctor write an order, then quietly slipped out of the room. Jean kissed Kerry on the head before sitting down in the chair next to the window. "What's her name?" Jean asked. For the first time all day, Kerry started to cry. Tears poured from her eyes as she recounted all the events that had led up to that very moment. Jean sat in shock and listened to her sister describe every complication from top to bottom of her fragile niece. She did her best not to appear horrified, calmly shaking her head as Kerry spoke. Somehow Jean managed to hide every worry that raced through her mind. She smiled when Kerry finally told her Emma's name.

When the nurse came back in to administer the anti-nausea medicine, she seemed a bit concerned over the state of Kerry's hysteria. But Jean carefully diffused any intervention by reminding her that the medication was probably going to knock her sister out. Jean was so calm. So collected.

Once the nurse left again, Jean crawled into the bed and held onto her. She listened as Kerry described her brief moment with Emma in the NICU. The moment, she feared, might be her only. Kerry sobbed and sobbed and sobbed. And she might have stopped sooner, if Jean hadn't begun crying herself. "There's nothing worse," Jean wept. "I'm so sorry,

Kooks. There's nothing worse." *Jean's crying?* Kerry thought. *It's official—this is seriously a big, bad deal.*

Kerry woke up at 6:55 p.m. and reached down to feel her flat, tender stomach. Emma wasn't there anymore. Jean was on her cell phone; it sounded like her call was coming to an end. Outside the window it was pitch black. Kerry closed her eyes and tried to return to the world where nothing had happened, but it was too late. Reality had already set in. Jean hung up and smiled at her.

"So, it wasn't all a bad dream?" Kerry asked.

"I wish," Jean pouted. "That was Mom. They're already in North Carolina, so they should be here by tomorrow afternoon."

"You're not supposed to use your phone in here," Kerry warned.

"As if I care," Jean replied. "What are they gonna do? Anyway, I talked to Diane, and Mom's calling Janet, Joe and Danny."

"I can't talk to anyone right now," Kerry informed her.

"You don't have to talk to anyone. Everyone knows Emma was born and they're all praying for her," Jean said. Kerry looked down. *Prayers don't work,* she thought. *Shit happens and then more shit happens—and just when you think it can't get any worse—MORE SHIT HAPPENS! And prayers can't do anything about it.*

"Oh, my God, What time is it?" Kerry screamed. She looked at the big clock to the right of her bed. "Oh, shit! It's 7 o'clock. Oh shit! They're starting the surgery right now! Oh, my God, my baby! My baby! Please God, let her be okay!" Jean got up and sat back down in the bed. Kerry started to hyperventilate. Her uncontrollable sobs were back in full force. Jean wrapped her arms around her and gently rocked back and forth. "I...didn't...even...get...to...hold...her yet," Kerry said with whatever breath she could capture. "Oh...my God, please...don't let...her die!" Kerry wanted to tear out her IVs and run down the halls. She wanted to kiss her baby's tiny black-haired head and hold her hand. If only she could take Emma and run away from all of this. Run away from the hospital and everyone in it. But she couldn't. Instead she was being held prisoner, with no say in anything that was happening. She couldn't even get up and go to the bathroom, never mind run the halls. Snot ran down her face. Her eyes were so swollen, she could hardly see. Jean kept silent, but continued to rock her sister.

The door opened and a friendly-faced woman in her forties with blond hair walked in. She was plain clothed and unfamiliar. "Kerry Sheeran?" she asked.

Kerry peered at her through bloodshot eyes. Blotches splattered across her face as she addressed the stranger: "PLEASE...TELL ME... YOU'RE NOT A...SOCIAL WORKER!" Kerry bellowed. Jean stifled a burst of laughter. She gave the woman a sympathetic look, knowing there was more to come. The woman shook her head *no* and attempted to explain her purpose (something about hospital records), but Kerry quickly cut her off. "IT'S...NOT...REALLY A...GOOD...TIME... RIGHT NOW!" Kerry yelled. "I'M...KINDA...HAVING...A... MENTAL...BREAKDOWN!"

The poor woman was speechless. Kerry looked possessed. "SO, IF YOU...CAN DO ME A FAVOR...AND JUST LET ME HAVE MY BREAKDOWN...AND NOT TELL MY NURSE OR THE SOCIAL WORKER OR THE CHAPLAIN ABOUT IT...BECAUSE I THINK...I'M ENTITLED TO THIS RIGHT NOW...I'D REALLY APPRECIATE IT!" Kerry sat up tall and pointed to the exit. She had finished her tirade. Jean couldn't wipe the smirk off her face and was doing everything in her power to keep her eyes straight down in her lap. The blonde woman turned around and made a beeline for the door. It was the last time she was ever seen.

Kerry looked at Jean and they both burst out laughing. The situation had reached a new level of lunacy. "How much can a human take?" Kerry asked.

"At least you've stopped barfing," Jean pointed out.

"And itching," Kerry added. "That was bad."

"How's your incision?" Jean asked.

"I don't even know," Kerry answered.

"Let me see it," Jean insisted. Kerry lay back and let her sister pull down her dressing to expose what looked to be a six inch slice that had been stapled shut. "They didn't stitch you, they stapled you!" Jean said. "Did you know that?" Kerry shook her head *no*. They could have sawed her in half, then nailed her back together for all she knew. She looked down at her stomach. The staples looked barbaric. *Appropriate*, she thought, considering how she felt about everything.

The phone rang. Hairs on the backs of their necks stood up. Kerry looked to Jean, who had no comfort to offer at the moment. "Hello" she whimpered.

"Hi babe, it's me," Tom announced.

"What's wrong?!" Kerry quivered.

"Nothing's wrong—she's okay," he assured her. "They're pushing the surgery to tomorrow morning."

"What? Why? She's not in surgery right now?" Kerry asked.

"They had another emergency case, so she got bumped. And they're certain they can keep her stable until the morning. They're going to do it tomorrow at 7:30 a.m.," Tom explained.

"So I can see her again?" Kerry asked. That was all she cared about. This was good news, sort of. Although she'd have to experience the stress of sending her baby off to surgery once more, it was worth it if it meant she could see Emma. "How is she, babe? Is she okay?" Kerry asked. Tom was confident that Emma was in great hands, and that she was sufficiently stable. He'd had the chance to speak to one of the attendings in the NICU, who took the time to sketch out exactly what was wrong with Emma and what needed to be fixed. It made so much more sense to Tom, now that he could see it. Tom also discovered that her tracheal and esophageal complications were more common than he'd imagined. *Common* being a relative term, considering she was in one of the top three children's hospitals in the country. Tom sounded okay, and this sounded good to Kerry. "She's adorable, babe. She's so cute. I love her so much," he cooed.

"Tell my baby I love her too," Kerry cried. "Tell her I'm coming to see her as soon as I can!"

Chapter 6

Twelve Long Hours

TOM'S LEGS FELT strong. He'd been running on an upward slope for at least half a mile or so, and remembered that this was the marathon route's transition into Framingham. Goodbye country, hello city. Framingham, he recalled, was lined with office buildings, factories and stores. It would give him something to look at, which was good, although he preferred the more rural landscapes. Hopkinton and Ashland had been fairly flat and pleasant. It was a nice way to start the race. Like easing into the shallow end of a pool instead of jumping cold turkey off the diving board. Framingham, however, was a reminder that the Boston Marathon was no joke. It was going to be a hilly, windy, tough race. Tom gave himself an imaginary pat on the back. *Not bad*, he thought, *for a guy's first marathon.*

Crowds lined the street as he crossed into Mile 5 territory. His eyes took notice of the countless Red Sox hats. *This is worse than being at Fenway Park*, he thought. Tom's allegiance to the Yankees was so true, his eyeballs burned a little every time they looked at a Red Sox logo. In fact, before Emma was born, he did his best to avoid Boston as a whole, being that the fans were such colossal pains in the ass. It didn't help that he enticed more drama by wearing his Yankees hat every time he stepped foot into the state of Massachusetts. Something inside of him thrived on the deep seeded rivalry between these teams.

Once, Tom even convinced Kerry to go to a Yankees/Red Sox game at Fenway with their 10-month old, Thomas. The kicker was, Thomas was dressed in an A-Rod shirt and a baby-sized Yankees hat. *This is the true test*, he had thought, *to see just how bad Sox fans can be.* As expected, they held true to their reputation. *"Your parents dress you so ugly,"* a grown man had snarled on the T. *"Poor thing, he has no idea how ridiculous he looks,"* a mother of four had jabbed while waiting in line at the gate.

And of course, they were met with countless *"Yankees Suck!"* everywhere in between. Grandparents said it. Little boys said it. Little GIRLS said it. There was no escaping these foul-mouthed, angry people. The topper was the drunk guy that poured half of his beer on Tom in the 9th when A-Rod shellacked a homer off Curt Schilling to win it. Tom was standing next to Kerry, who was holding a baby, and that asshole wanted to fight. And Tom would have fought him tooth and nail, had Kerry not stepped in. *"We're leaving right this second, and don't even think about punching that guy! Your son is in danger!"* she had scolded. With that, they were on the next T out of Boston. Of course the Sox fans had to eat crow the whole train ride home, which was amazing.

The extent of Tom's hatred for the Red Sox and their fans, however, had waned a bit over the last couple of years. While he still detested the team itself, he had a new soft spot for the people of Boston. The doctors, nurses, janitors, technicians, EMTs, policemen—all of these people were his heroes. And regardless of everything that happened, they all did their best for his daughter. He was indebted to these folks for life. Without them, he never would have gotten the chance to even meet his beautiful Emma.

New England Patriots fans, Tom believed, sucked too, yet for some reason they seemed slightly more tolerable. The rivalry between the Patriots and his home team, the New York Giants, was heated but not *as* hot—until recently of course. It just so happened that when Emma was born on January 27, 2008, the Pats and the Giants were gearing up for their ultimate match on Super Bowl Sunday the following week. This was during the golden era of the Patriots, when Tom Brady could do no wrong. Every time Tom turned around, Brady was wearing another Super Bowl ring on his hand. Gisele Bundchen was already on the scene, which added to his superstar status, of course.

Tom recalled happily his wherewithal to pack his Giants hat when they were leaving for the hospital two days before Emma was born. If he were going to be in Boston, then he was going to serve up a side of *snarky* while he was there. Tom Brady was going down and his perfect little football team was too. Bill Belichick was going to suck it. The sooner Boston knew this, the better. So he wore that hat everywhere he could, and only took it off when he absolutely had to (in the operating room, for instance). Just because Tom had a newfound respect for Boston, didn't mean he was going to stifle his own pride for New York. He was softer, not crazy.

Halfway through Mile 5, Tom passed by a fellow New York fan. He was cheering on the runners alongside his young daughter, who also wore a Yankees baseball cap. Grinning coyly at the duo, Tom pulled out the letter and held it up to his eyes. He made sure nobody was directly in front of him as he read the next line:

Mile 5: Our 10 week premature baby undergoes a 12-hour operation….

TOM HAD SPENT the entire night with his newborn daughter. Jane was with him until 9 p.m., but had to drive back to Rhode Island to relieve Jane-Marie, who was taking care of Thomas and Ryan. Luckily Tom's parents had returned from Florida once things started going downhill for Kerry's pregnancy. They stuck around Rhode Island to help out with the boys during all of the doctor's appointments and hospital visits. Tom and Kerry were indebted, as it would have been next to impossible to care for their kids during the last couple of weeks without help. Now that baby number three took center stage, the boys were automatically shuffled into the back seat. And regardless of how guilty it made their parents feel, it just *had* to be like that. Thomas and Ryan were young, clueless and happy. Of course they missed their mom and dad, but Tom's family members were pros at keeping them happily distracted—and this made everyone feel a little bit better.

Kerry's night was filled with bad dreams and little sleep. She longed to be with her children. It seemed like forever since she'd nuzzled Ryan. She missed his pouty lips, his chubby cheeks. Ryan was just a baby himself. He didn't deserve to be taken away from his mother for days on end. He *needed* her, and so did Thomas. Everyone in Thomas' pre-school class knew that he was going to be a big brother for the second time. He'd made it a point to remind them every morning at circle time. He had even agreed to let Ryan move in with him, so that the baby could have her own room. And now, Kerry didn't know if he was ever going to get to meet Emma. She had no idea how they were going to explain any of this to them. If Emma didn't make it, it would affect her boys for the rest of their lives. *Thomas is only three years old. This isn't something a toddler should have to suffer through,* Kerry thought. He'd be "the boy whose baby sister died" at school. It would follow him and he'd feel the loss. None of this was fair. *It's cruel,* Kerry thought. *It's just plain cruel.*

The nurse came in at 6:15 a.m. and removed Kerry's catheter. This provided some relief and allowed Kerry the ability to get up and walk to the bathroom when needed. It was nice to get up. The feeling of being chained to the bed was gone, and this made her even more anxious to visit Emma before her surgery. Jean was sound asleep in the chair next to her. Minutes later, Tom snuck into the room pushing an empty wheelchair. He smiled at his wife as he eased her into the seat, quietly springing her from her prison cell. Rolling down the halls, her heart raced at the thought of seeing Emma. "So, this is really happening at seven-thirty?" Kerry asked. "They're not going to cancel again?"

"It's really happening, honey." Tom said. He'd done a great job of learning his way around both hospitals. First, he took Kerry to the second floor of Brigham and Women's *Connors Center*, then showed her the signs pointing to the "Pike". This was the bridge that connected Brigham and Women's to Boston Children's Hospital. It was totally encased, crossing over one of Boston's side streets. All that separated the two hospitals was a sliding glass door. "This is how we brought her to Children's last night," Tom whispered. Once they were in Children's, Tom maneuvered the wheelchair down a few corridors, into an elevator, then pressed the number seven. When the doors opened, he checked to his right, then to his left. He swung her towards the left and headed straight for 7 North— the NICU. Kerry was impressed. She had no idea how Tom remembered the course between both places. *There's no way,* Kerry feared, *I'll be able to retrace my steps if I have to.* Her sense of direction was terrible on a good day. And this was not a good day.

The NICU was a little different then the one at Brigham and Women's. It was the same concept—open units with four to six beds per bay. The hand-washing station was almost identical. Yet the level of intensity at Boston Children's Hospital was quadrupled. They could see it, smell it and feel it. It made them want to keep their heads down. It was scary. Kerry stared at her lap until Tom turned left into Bay 6. Her little black-haired angel was right on the end as they turned the corner. Emma's nurse had just finished taking her temperature. "Is she okay?" Kerry asked. "She's okay," her nurse answered. "We just need to take her temperature periodically. It's totally routine."

"You can stand over here and reach in for a minute," Tom told Kerry. "But not for too long, otherwise an alarm will go off." Kerry was disgusted. "A timer?" she asked. "No, an alarm," Tom corrected her. "Her isolette needs to stay at a certain temperature. If it gets too cold it means she's working too hard to stay warm." Kerry shook her head. It was obvious that she had a lot to learn. Everything was so intimidating. Everywhere she looked there were tubes, monitors and machines. People hurried around. Curtains hung closed in between a few of the babies' beds, but most were pulled open. *Ding Ding Ding.* Alarms sounded off in every direction. Some at a slow pace, others at a loud, panicky pace. *Beep Beep Beep. Beep Beep Beep.* So much of the beeping seemed to go unanswered. And just when one set of beeps stopped, she could hear another lingering in the background. At Emma's station, the nurse busily worked the touch screen that monitored oxygen, vitals and IVs. Kerry didn't understand what any of it meant. *Tom's a whole day ahead of me,* she thought. *He really seems to know what the hell is going on.* It felt as though her mind were being swallowed by her surroundings. *This is becoming an all too familiar feeling,* she lamented.

Kerry's hand reached inside Emma's isolette and touched her daughter's head. "Hail Mary, full of grace," she prayed, "the Lord is with thee. Blessed art thou among women. And blessed is the fruit of thy womb, Jesus." *Mary was a mother,* she thought, *she would understand how I'm feeling right now.* "Holy Mary, mother of God, pray for us sinners, now and at the hour of our death, Amen," Kerry finished. *Is Emma's hour of death coming?* she wondered. The words of that prayer never meant as much as they did in that moment. Tom reached in on the other side and held Emma's hand. "Our Father, who art in heaven, hallowed be thy name," he began. Kerry blocked Tom out. She was done praying to God. Tom could if he wanted to, but as far as she was concerned He was nothing but a huge disappointment. Kerry decided she was going to stick to Mary from now on and see how that worked out. *Of course, if God really is listening to any of this,* Kerry thought, *I assume he'll take Emma's side and not hold her mother accountable for any bad thoughts.*

The isolette alarm sounded. Kerry jerked her hand out and closed the little plastic portal to the crib. Tom did the same. As much as they wanted to touch her, it wasn't worth the toll it would take on her fragile body. The last thing Emma needed was to work extra to stay alive. Plus, they were both so happy just to be in the same room with her. Kerry carefully lowered herself down to a sitting position. "Talk to her, Mom," the nurse said. "She's been listening to your voice for the last seven months or so, right? I'm sure it would sound good to her." Kerry looked at Tom, who was nodding his head. For a moment, she felt strange. It was one thing to sit in a rocking chair with her newborn cradled in her arms, while she whispered in her ear. It was another to sit in a wheelchair and talk in a baby voice through a thick wall of plastic. Suddenly the voice in her head insisted:

"Do it. Who cares what you look or sound like?
Emma wants to hear your voice. Say something she would like to hear.
You're her mother. Be her mother right now!"

Kerry thought about the voice. It was always so bossy. And yet, it had a pretty good track record. So she spoke to her daughter. She told Emma all about her brothers, cousins, grandparents, aunts and uncles. She described their house from top to bottom and gave vivid details about the nursery. She explained to Emma how very badly she wanted to hold, hug and kiss her. Kerry told her over and over and over that she loved her. She begged Emma to be strong so that she could someday meet her family. Kerry said a lot to her daughter in those twenty minutes. It felt incredible to say these things. Something in her soul felt deeply intimate. As if Emma heard and understood everything she said. It was a beautiful, unexpected connection.

A woman in a hospital robe was pushed in a wheelchair past Emma's station. She held two little bottles of milk in her hands. Kerry watched as the woman handed these bottles to her own baby's nurse. Turning to Emma's nurse, Kerry asked: "Can babies this small drink breast milk? I didn't think they could nurse when they were this small."

"They usually can't breastfeed when they're as little as Emma. But that doesn't stop us from feeding them," the nurse explained. "Some moms pump and we feed the babies their breast milk through nasal-gastric tubes." Tom and Kerry looked confused. "We call them NGs. It's a little tube that's inserted up their nose and down into their tummies. It's hard for these little babies with underdeveloped bodies to learn how to drink. Breathing and swallowing at the same time is harder than you'd think. So we give them a little help, until they're ready," the nurse explained. Tom and Kerry shook their heads to signal their understanding.

"Of course," the nurse added, "it's different for Emma. Since her esophagus doesn't attach to her stomach, there's no way to put a nasal gastric tube in." Again, Tom and Kerry shook their heads. "I believe they're planning to give Emma a g-tube as part of her surgery today. A g-tube is a little tube that goes directly into her stomach. It has a button called a "mickey" that opens and closes for feeding," the nurse continued. This time Emma's parents weren't shaking their heads. "It's not a big deal," she assured them. "It's what she needs to be able to get nutrition and grow." Tom and Kerry slowly began to nod. They were trying to wrap their heads around the idea that a hole was about to be cut straight through to Emma's stomach.

"Kids get them all the time. It doesn't mean it's a permanent thing. But if you want us to give her your breast milk, or anything else for that matter, it's the only way," the nurse said. These were the things Tom and Kerry hadn't thought through. They understood why Emma needed a colostomy—that made sense. But the issue with her trachea and esophagus was still so fresh and complicated. "Emma can't swallow," Kerry said, as if an epiphany had just taken place.

The nurse excused herself to take a quick phone call. When she hung up she announced: "They're ready for Emma." Tom and Kerry's hearts sank. Opening up their respective sides of the isolette, they reached through to touch their baby's beautiful, uncut body for the last time. Within a minute, part of the surgical team appeared at Emma's bedside and introduced themselves. Kerry's bottom lip quivered. Her face turned blotchy. Tom got one look at Kerry and started to lose it himself. "Please," Kerry said, "don't let anything happen to her. PLEASE?!" A pretty young nurse smiled at Kerry. "I'm going to be with her the entire time. I promise we'll take good care of her," she said.

"Please?!" Kerry begged.

"I promise," the nurse repeated. Tom held on to Kerry for support. "Please keep her safe," he wept. He was looking at the four other people ready to take Emma away. "She's my only daughter. Please," Tom cried. The four of them collectively nodded and smiled at the frightened parents. Following Emma and the team down the service elevator, Tom pushed his wife through the halls, all the way to the swinging doors of the operating room. They kissed Emma one more time and said goodbye. Then the doors swung shut and the team was gone. Emma was gone, again. Their pain was all-consuming. It was fierce. Tom and Kerry had just willingly handed their daughter over. Nothing they had ever felt in their lives could compare with the desperation that paralyzed them in that moment. It was contrary to nature. All they could do was weep.

Tom wheeled Kerry back to her hospital room, leaving her in Jean's hands while he rushed back to Children's. It was understood that he would spend the day in the surgical waiting room on the 2nd floor. Tom wouldn't have it any other way. He even had his computer with him, so he would be able to work. Of course Kerry couldn't comprehend how Tom could possibly concentrate on work. Not that she second-guessed his level of concern for their daughter, but rather marveled at his ability to focus on something outside of the bubble they were trapped in. Tom, of course, operated from a different perspective. He was a father. A provider. He had three children. His littlest was just born with head-to-toe complications. The hospital wasn't free. Emma's surgery wasn't free. His job required him to make sales in order to make money. And in order to keep the job that paid for his insurance, which in turn paid for the hospital and the surgery, he needed to sell command centers. Not to mention, it was all a welcome distraction from the absolute hell he was living through. Therefore, did it make sense for him to return some emails and make some phone calls while he sat in a waiting room all day? *Yes.* Was it crucial that this Merrill Lynch deal in Singapore go through? *Yes.* Did he give a crap what anyone else thought about any of this? *Hell no.*

Tom set up shop in the corner of the waiting area. A liaison nurse named Sandy gave him a nametag and told him she'd be checking in every ninety minutes. Emma's surgery was supposed to take anywhere from ten to twelve hours. This was a long time for anyone to be under anesthesia, never mind a three-pound baby. Tom knew this because he had spoken to the anesthesiologist earlier that morning. He had signed a piece of paper saying that it was okay for them to pump Emma full of anesthesia for twelve hours or more if need be. They told him there was a chance she could have a bad reaction to it, which could lead to brain damage or death and he *still* signed the paper. Tom had also met with the general surgeons and the urologist. He had signed off on all of their procedures too: tying off the tracheal/esophageal fistula; surgically placing a catheter to help reduce some of the fluid on her kidneys; creating a colostomy; creating a g-tube. In all honesty, Tom had totally forgotten about the g-tube until the nurse brought it up in front of Kerry.

The surgeons were also going to place a chest tube in her right lung to make access to the fistula possible. They would have to collapse her lung to do this. This is what they told Tom they would *have* to do in order to give Emma a chance at life. They'd explained it to him as if he had no other choice. So Tom signed all the papers himself. He didn't bother talking to Kerry about the risks. *What is the point?* he wondered. In his opinion, the less she had to worry about, the better. Clearly Kerry was turning into a basket case. *She'd been so strong up until the last hour*, he thought. Originally, Tom had planned on telling her everything after they saw Emma off. Yet when Kerry fell apart outside of the operating room, her primal sobbing changed his mind. Yes, Tom had taken the responsibility of knowing *everything* that could possibly happen to Emma over the next ten to twelve hours. And it weighed heavily.

Back in her hospital room, Kerry wasn't clueless by any means. She understood the gist of what was going on, but still had a million unanswered questions. The vibe she had gotten from Emma's doctors and nurses, however, was: *Let's first get through this critical part of Emma's quest for survival. If all goes well, then we can talk about her quality of life and future.* Nobody actually said this. It just *was*. Even Jean refused to entertain any conversations with Kerry about the future. Of course she was curious herself, but now was not the time. Jean was there to support Kerry. "I need you to be my brain for me," Kerry said with pathetic eyes. "I need you to listen to these updates and repeat them back to me. I need you to ask the questions I'm supposed to ask and remember all the answers. My brain isn't working right," she explained. Jean shook her head. "You got it," she agreed.

At 10:30 a.m., the surgery was three hours underway and all that had really taken place was line placement, scopes and intubation. All was going well, as far as Tom had been told. He sat with his heart in his mouth every time Sandy walked in his direction, even though seventy-five percent of the time she wasn't even looking for him. Sandy's job was to call into the operating rooms every hour and a half to get an update from the nurses. She would jot down the information and walk it to the anxious family members, then recite it to them in person. There were four or five of these liaison nurses walking around, from what Tom had seen. Sandy was a thin, blond woman in her fifties. Her hair looked like she'd stuck her finger in an electrical socket. She wore glasses and a white jacket with her name stitched across it. She smiled a lot. *Too much*, Tom thought.

The waiting room was filling up. The more Tom looked around, the more he saw faces with the same expression as his. Fathers riddled with panic. Mothers in pain. Some were crying, others were laughing. Some were alone, others carried huge entourages with them—like the Middle

Eastern family sitting in the semi-private room. They were all eating a ton of food. Tom watched them as they passed dishes to one another. A giant blue cooler on wheels doubled as their dining table. He had to wonder how *anyone* could eat *anything* just then, never mind a four-course meal. He continued to scan the room. The man to Tom's right looked angry. Tom stared as he open and closed the lid to his coffee incessantly. Each time the man tried to take a sip, it was too hot. The young woman to Tom's left looked spacey. So did the older woman with her, who appeared to be her mother. Their eyes were heavy. *Maybe that's just genetic,* Tom thought. *Or, maybe they're snowed.* That seemed to make more sense to him. He looked around some more. *I wonder if half the people in here are on Xanax,* Tom thought. He shook his head. It seemed like a great idea.

Looking at his watch, Tom saw that it was 12:10 p.m. Over four hours had passed since Emma's operation began. Sandy was late. He waited for his 12 p.m. update. The last two times, she'd been very punctual. Another nurse walked up to the couple two chairs down from him. They seemed grateful to hear what she was saying. The waiting room had undergone a turnover. The Middle-Eastern family was gone. The spacey mother/daughter duo had left about an hour earlier. Their child's surgery was a success, from what Tom had gathered. The fact that the women were hugging the surgeons and smiling incessantly led him to believe this. Tom noticed that the surgeons themselves always made an appearance at the end of every surgery. They came out, sat down and talked to the families in person. Tom longed for this part of the day. It seemed unattainable at the point he was at. The idea that Emma's surgery wasn't even half over was completely disheartening.

The angry man to Tom's right walked past him and sat down. He reeked of cigarettes, and was holding another cup of coffee. This was his fourth. Tom couldn't judge him, seeing as how he'd been to Starbucks three times himself. He thought about the days when he used to smoke, then pictured himself going outside to smoke a butt. The smell filled his senses. It relaxed him. It gave him something to do. He pictured himself lighting another cigarette with the first one. Tom looked outside. There were lots of people smoking. Nobody was really talking to anyone else, just pacing around with their cigarettes. It looked like there was a hospital entrance across the street as well. Tom assumed this was Brigham and Women's, but he wasn't certain.

Nurses were smoking. Doctors were smoking. Tom had to wonder: *Why aren't I?* All he had to do was ask the angry guy for one cigarette. *This is one of those times in life when it is totally acceptable*, he thought. He'd run downstairs, get a light from one of the people outside, smoke, and run back up. In fact, he'd seen a CVS around the corner. *Forget asking anyone for a cigarette. I'm a grown man*, he thought. Tom would go to CVS, buy his own pack of Marlboro Mediums and a lighter, and he'd be all set. While he was there, he'd even buy some mouthwash and gum. Tom hadn't smoked in over four years. He owed this to himself. There was no need to even justify it. The last two weeks of his life already did that for him.

He looked at his watch. It was now 12:15 p.m., and no Sandy in sight. *Something's wrong*, Tom thought. He stood up and looked all around. He looked at his watch again. 12:16 p.m. Tom grabbed his wallet off the table and headed for the nurses station. When he got to the glass window, there were three nurses sitting behind the counter: Two brunettes and one with grey hair. The grey-haired nurse was on the phone. She looked at Tom's nametag, then gave him a nod and held her pointer finger up. Her conversation went on. The two brunettes didn't look in his direction. *Something's wrong*, Tom's mind repeated. He knocked on the glass. All three nurses looked up, stunned. The grey-haired nurse jotted down a couple more notes, then hung up the phone. She took her glasses off and looked at Tom: "Mr. Sheeran?" she asked.

"It's 12:16 and I haven't gotten an update on my daughter. Where is my nurse? I haven't seen her since 10:30. Please!" Tom pleaded.

"Mr. Sheeran," the grey-haired nurse continued, "that was Emma's O.R. nurse I was just speaking to." Her voiced cracked. She apologized and cleared her throat. Tom was ready to launch himself through the glass. Luckily, she slid the window open just in time. "Everything's fine," she said. "It's quite an involved procedure, so they were trying to be thorough with their report."

"But she's okay? She's doing okay?" Tom begged.

"Yes," she assured him. "Emma's doing well. She's tolerating the anesthesia and so far everything is going as expected." Tom exhaled. His shoulders dropped. Tears filled his eyes. "Thank God," he said. "Where is the nurse who was giving me updates?" he asked, raising one eyebrow. "Where's Sandy?"

"She's on a lunch break," the grey haired nurse explained. "I'm sorry you had to wait a few extra minutes. We're covering each other's cases and are still catching up on the 12 o'clocks," she smiled. "Anytime you want to, though, you can come down here. We'll let you know what we can," she said. Tom listened as she went on to explain that Emma's chest-tube was in, and that they were working on her tracheal-esophageal fistula. She explained that this was going to take a while. The surgeons had to detach the bottom portion of her esophagus from her trachea and close the holes. It would not be easy. Tom pictured their giant hands in Emma's little body. The whole thing seemed impossible. He swallowed the acid that had bubbled up into his throat. Then he thanked the nurse and walked away.

Tom called Kerry from the sidewalk in front of the hospital. She and Jean put the phone on speaker and listened to his update. They squeezed each other once the words 'she's okay' were spoken. Tom told them about the waiting room: the people; the stress; the nurses who kept him guessing. He mentioned that he hadn't eaten all day and was going on his fourth cup of coffee. Kerry heard an ambulance siren in the background. "Where are you?" she asked.

"I'm just heading to CVS," he explained, "to…get something…to eat." Kerry laughed. She'd been married to Tom for five years and had known him since kindergarten. He was a food snob through and through. If Tom was going to put something into his body for the first time in twelve hours, it wasn't going to be a bag of chips from CVS. "You're not buying cigarettes, are you?" she asked. It was hard to hear anything over the sound of the crickets chirping. "Tom, you'd better not be buying cigarettes right now," Kerry quipped. Jean smirked and backed away from the phone. "I'm not kidding," she continued, "I will reach through this phone and choke you if you put one cigarette in your mouth." She glared over at Jean who was now in a full on chuckle. The cat still seemed to have Tom's tongue. "Tom, turn around, walk the other way and go get yourself something to eat at Au Bon Pain," she instructed. "If you start smoking during this, you'll never stop. And if I can't smoke through this, then nobody can!" she insisted. Kerry was serious. She said goodbye to Tom, then slammed the phone down and looked at Jean. "I'm going to need for you to repeat everything he just said to me," she announced. "And give me one of your cigarettes," she added. "I know you have Merit Ultra Lights on you."

"I don't know what you're talking about," Jean laughed.

At two o'clock, Jean put the finishing touches on her mascara, then closed her compact and put it in her purse. She walked over to the bedside table and picked up the lunch tray. Kerry had hardly eaten anything, but Jean wasn't about to get on her case for that. She could hardly stomach her own food. After tossing everything in the trash, Jean sat back down and opened the top of her coffee cup. She took a swig. It was cold and stale. Her phone rang. "It's Mom and Dad," she told Kerry. "They're about an hour away." It amazed Kerry and Jean, how fast their parents had packed up everything in Florida and headed north. Their father, Joe, was seventy-two years old and famous for taking naps. New Jersey to Boynton Beach was usually a three-day trip for them. Joe was not normally a fast-mover. Their mom, Donna, was sixty-six and famous for operating on little to no sleep whatsoever. She, too, was a nurse. Kerry and Jean agreed that Donna was pushing Joe to drive almost the entire east coast in thirty hours. It was a massive undertaking. And although she was touched, it scared the hell out of Kerry that such an effort was being made for her and her family.

"Are they driving all the way here because they think Emma's going to die?" Kerry asked. Jean shrugged her shoulders and took another sip of her coffee. "Is that why *you* came?" Kerry added. "Just tell me. I don't know what I'm supposed to be thinking right now." Kerry put her hands on her head and tugged at her hair. If only she knew what to expect, it would be so much easier to prepare herself. She could talk about the funeral. She could ask Jean questions, like: *How do I find a burial site? Where would I buy a coffin? Would I shield the boys from the loss or involve them in it?* There were so many things to consider. "Is that why you're here?" Kerry demanded.

"Kooks, nobody knows what's going to happen," Jean said. "I'm here because I love you. I hate to have to tell you that," she smiled. The look on Jean's face affirmed what she was saying. "Emma might be okay. She might not. But nobody in this entire hospital can tell you either way," Jean explained. Kerry bit her lip. "Don't start crying again, please!" Jean begged. "You're gonna get me started and I just fixed all my makeup." Jean wrapped her arms around her little sister. "Oh, I forgot to tell you," she added, "Diane's on her way too. She should be here by 3:15." She chuckled a little and squeezed Kerry even tighter.

A new nurse walked into the room and introduced herself to Kerry. "Nice to meet you," the nurse said. Turning towards Jean, she reached out her hand and asked: "Are you her mother?" Kerry immediately stopped crying and let out a HUGE, insensitive laugh. Jean shot daggers out of her eyes—first at Kerry, then right through the nurse.

"I can't believe you just said that," Jean said shaking her head. "I hate you."

The nurse dropped her hand to her side. Her face flushed beet red. She stuttered and tried to explain herself, but Kerry saved her. "Don't apologize," she insisted, "Jean's my sister…and thanks. I was in desperate need of a laugh just now." Kerry carefully sat up and handed her arm over to the nurse. The poor woman did everything she could to avoid making eye contact with Jean as she wrapped the blood pressure cuff around her patient's arm. Jean sat back down in her chair and took out her compact. Looking over, Kerry flashed her a devilish grin. It felt good to smile. The air she'd been breathing for the last two days had been so damn heavy. It felt lighter for a second. *Maybe I can smile a little*, she thought. *Maybe I can get through this. Maybe **Emma** can get through this.* She imagined the surgery was more then half way over at this point. *That's probably a good sign*, she thought. *If anything bad were going to happen, it probably already would have.* This is what Kerry told herself. It made her feel okay. She let out a deep breath. *Am I right, God? Is there a chance she's going to be alright? Oh, wait*, she stopped. *I forgot. We're not speaking.*

Moments later, Kerry felt a tingle in her breasts. It was a familiar sensation, yet one she wasn't expecting. She reached across her chest. Her boobs felt fuller. Not totally full, but heavier. Kerry looked at her nurse. "Is my milk going to come in?" she asked. Her nurse was happy for the change of subject. She took off the blood pressure cuff and smiled. "I don't see why it wouldn't," she answered. Kerry shot her a puzzled look. She assumed this nurse wasn't familiar with what was going on. "Mine wasn't your average C-section," Kerry explained. "They took my baby out ten weeks early. How is my body supposed to produce milk for a baby that shouldn't even be here for another two-and-a-half months?"

"You'd be surprised at what your body can do," the nurse replied. She looked at Jean in an attempt to involve her in the conversation, but Jean remained consumed in re-applying her mascara. "It's all about hormones," she continued. "Your body knows you're not pregnant anymore, even if your mind still wishes you were." Kerry winced. That last comment stung a little. She thought about the mother she'd seen in the NICU, who seemed tired yet proud to be handing her "liquid gold" over to her baby's nurse. Kerry remembered her conversation with

Emma's nurse. Then suddenly, the voice spoke to her:

"You have no control over anything else, Kerry. The least you can do is feed your child."

That, Kerry thought, *would require pumping.* She hated pumping. Luckily she'd only had to do it a handful of times since Thomas and Ryan were both great nursers. In her opinion, breastfeeding was the ultimate joy. It was beautiful. Kerry loved it *so* much that she nursed Thomas for an entire year, only stopping because she was pregnant with Ryan. She nursed Ryan for fifteen months, only stopping because she was pregnant with Emma. She endured yeast infections, bloody cracked nipples and an excruciating case of mastitis that landed her in the hospital for four days, and still Kerry continued nursing her babies. It was a private, sacred bond between her and them. It was one of her favorite things about being a mother. And in this moment, Kerry realized it was never going to happen with Emma. *How could a baby who can't even swallow, ever nurse from her mother?* she wondered. She closed her eyes and bowed her head. Yet another simple joy being ripped to shreds and thrown back in her face. Stiffening her lip, she looked up at her nurse. "Do you have a pump I could use?" Kerry asked.

"I'll get you one right now," her nurse answered.

The suction on her nipples hurt, but Kerry didn't care. The physical pain gave her something new to feel. Minutes went by as the pump pulled and pulled at her, yet nothing came out. Kerry looked at her nurse, then at Jean. Neither woman had anything to offer. She reached over to the gauge and switched it higher. The pump pulled faster and faster, harder and harder. But no milk came out. Kerry was failing. First she'd failed at keeping her baby safe inside of her, and now she couldn't even provide food for her. She pressed the cups to her breasts as hard as she could. Her nipples were turning purple. She switched the pump to the highest setting. Jean reached for the cups. "Why don't you just try later, Kooks? Maybe it's too soon," she suggested. Kerry pulled away.

"I'm doing this," she said.

"Your nipples don't look so great," the nurse added.

"I'm doing this," Kerry repeated. "You don't have to watch if you don't want to!" Jean and the nurse looked at each other with wide eyes. They *didn't* want to watch. It was sad, not to mention gross. The pump kept pulling. It sounded *so* mechanical. Kerry looked at the clock. It had been about five minutes since she'd started. She closed her eyes and grit her teeth. Another minute went by. The nurse left the room, while Jean sat flipping through the hospital's dinner menu. Kerry looked at the clock again. Another two minutes went by. Her nipples were so dark with blood, it was even starting to frighten her.

She looked at the clock. It was 2:43 p.m. *At 2:45 I'll stop*, she thought. *But I'm not giving up. You think you're going to steal this from me too, huh? You think you're just going to take everything I love? What the hell did I ever do to deserve this? Why are you punishing me? Why me? WHY ME?* Kerry was *so* angry, she didn't notice the liquid squirting from her left breast. It sprayed against the side of the bottle and trickled to the bottom. Jean put the menu down and gasped as she pointed to the milk spraying out from Kerry's right nipple. "It's working!" Jean cheered. Kerry's breasts started spraying in unison. The bottles slowly filled. Kerry laughed. "It's totally working," she bragged.

It's so yellow!" Jean said. "I've never seen it so yellow."

"It's the colostrum," Kerry said. "This is what comes out first. The real milk doesn't come in for a few days. But this is supposed to be the important stuff. Chock full of antibodies and immunity and all of that." Kerry was smiling. Emma *needed* this milk, and she had produced it for her. She imagined that when Emma was back in the NICU, she could hand it to her nurse and they would feed it to her through her new g-tube. Perhaps all of the nutrients would be super healing to her tiny body. "This will help her," Kerry said. "It's something."

"Good job," Jean said. Kerry smiled again. The voice in her head chimed in:

"I knew you could do it."

At 3:15 p.m. the phone rang. Kerry's heart sank as she answered. "You have visitors. Can I let them in?" the voice on the other end asked. Kerry let out a deep breath and agreed to the visitors, then hung up the phone. Even Jean fought back tears as she watched her exhausted parents walk over to Kerry's bed and embrace her. Donna and Joe held on for a good forty to fifty seconds, until snot was dripping from all three of their noses. So much that they had to let go. Jean sniffled. "Just so you know, you're not allowed to make us cry. It's a rule in here," she informed her parents.

All four of them blew their noses in unison. Sullivans were loud blowers, and four of them at once could be likened to an elephant's trumpet. They all giggled at the sounds they were making. Jean decided it was time for her to join Tom in the waiting room, considering he'd been alone since 7:30 a.m. on the most stressful day of his life. She assumed he could use the company. The timing was perfect since Jean really couldn't handle the emotion her parents had brought into Kerry's hospital room. This was all new to them, but she'd been living it for twenty-four hours already. So Jean happily passed the torch to Donna and Joe, assuring Kerry that somehow she'd find her way across the bridge to Children's Hospital.

"Call me after the next update!" Kerry yelled as the door was closing.

"I will," Jean yelled back.

It took Kerry about forty minutes to catch her parents up on everything that had taken place. Reliving the horror of finding out about Emma's complications was tough. It was still raw and seemingly unreal. Kerry had to subconsciously remind herself that what she was saying was actually true, not some crazy story that had happened to someone else. Donna interrupted her every few seconds to ask questions, which didn't help. Kerry wanted to be finished talking about it, not interrogated. But Donna was in shock and asking questions was her way of understanding the situation. Perhaps, even, of accepting it. Joe was barely able to mutter "Oh, my God" every now and then. It pained him to see his daughter suffering. The entire situation was beyond his realm of comprehension.

"What are they saying her chances are?" Donna asked.

"They're not saying," Kerry answered.

"How bad are her kidneys?" Donna asked.

"I don't even know," Kerry said.

"How far down does her esophagus go before it stops?" Donna asked.

"I don't know exactly—a couple of inches, I think," Kerry said.

"Where are they creating the colostomy? Is it an ileostomy or a colostomy?" Donna asked.

"A colostomy, I think. I don't even know what an ileostomy is." Kerry said. She shifted around in her bed.

"What are they saying caused this to happen? Is it chromosomal? Why does this sort of thing happen?" Donna asked.

Kerry closed her eyes. *That's it,* she thought. That last question was the killer. Things had been so frantic and fast that Kerry hadn't even had a chance to ask anyone the obvious question: *Why?* The problem was, she was afraid to know the answer. Having retraced her footsteps a million times over the last couple of weeks, she had tried to pinpoint what exactly she could have done to cause Emma's problems. She recalled all the way back to the moment she found out she was pregnant while on a camping trip in Vermont. From then on, she didn't drink alcohol, there were no X-rays performed and she didn't take any unauthorized medications. She had been diligent about checking with her doctor before she even popped a Tylenol. Which meant she had narrowed it down to two possibilities:

1. The DEET bug spray they had used on the camping trip.
Or
2. Inadvertently standing in front of the microwave.

These were the only two things she could come up with. Surely Kerry wondered why all of Emma's complications happened. Of course she worried it was something she'd done. But Kerry hadn't asked that question yet. So it wasn't fair that Donna had.

"I don't know, Mom," she answered. "Why don't you write all your questions down and hand them to the doctor the next time she comes in?"

"I'm sorry, honey." Donna cried. "I can't even imagine how hard this is for you." Joe was crying, too. The Spanish Inquisition was over, which was good considering how heavy the atmosphere had become. *Boy, did Jean pick a good time to scoot out,* Kerry thought.

Luckily, the phone rang shortly after, shifting everyone's focus. It was Tom with an update. Emma was continuing to do well and the surgeons had successfully tied off the fistula. They were now moving on to creating her g-tube. Afterwards they would finish up with her colostomy. They estimated needing another four hours or so to complete things. Tom sounded positive and was happy that Jean had come to join him. He was also pleased that his brother, Sean, would be coming to sit with him soon. The past eight hours alone had been harrowing for him.

It crushed Kerry when he admitted this. She'd been so consumed by her own torture, it hadn't occurred to her that being alone would be even tougher. *At least now*, she thought, *Tom sounds okay*. This made Kerry feel all right, which in turn had the same effect on her parents. She told him to ask Jean to stay with him, at least until Sean arrived. "Please call me as soon as you know anything else," Kerry begged, then she hung up the phone.

Donna, Joe and Kerry rejoiced over the news of Emma's endurance. It was hard for any of them to imagine such a tiny human being going through *so* much in one day. They tried to focus on all the positives: Emma was alive; she was beautiful; she was theirs. Donna was especially happy to hear that she was baptized, and moved that Tom was able to do it himself. "So many people are praying for her," Donna said. "Dad and I said the rosary at least ten times on the way up." Kerry thanked them. "We've got to have faith that God will take care of her," Donna continued. "Have faith in God, Kerry."

Kerry shook her head in agreement because there was no reason her parents needed to know she had nothing of the sort. *Faith* didn't make sense. The word itself sounded like a hoax. Ever since she was a little girl, she thought she had *it*. She said her prayers, went to church, received all of her sacraments and lived her life as a model Catholic for the most part. Kerry did everything she was supposed to. She thought she had faith. Yet it was clear to her now, she never really did. *If I had faith, I'd believe that God was going to take care of Emma.* But she didn't believe that. *Why should I?* Kerry wondered.

Diane arrived around 4:45 p.m. She had her ten-month old son, Adam, with her. He was still nursing and refused to take a bottle, so she couldn't leave him at home. Diane told the receptionist that Adam was Kerry's son, since hospital policy only allowed children who were siblings to visit.

"And they believed you?" Kerry asked. "Yeah, they must think you're some kind of a baby-making freak show," Diane laughed. "Oh, they think I'm a freak-show, alright!" Kerry assured her. "I've turned the corner on my ability to freak!"

Baby Adam smiled at his aunt. Kerry reached out her arms and kissed his face. His bright blue eyes reminded her of Thomas', and his baby smell had her longing for Ryan. Diane placed Adam next to her on the bed and Kerry soaked him in. He was happy to sit there, smiling and cooing as his aunt held on to him. Kerry was in awe at how lucky Adam was to be ignorant of the sorrow and fear that lingered around them. She yearned for his innocence, for a fraction of his happiness.

"Hand me my phone, please," Kerry said to Donna.

"But you can't make phone calls in here," Donna contested, pointing to the sign on the wall.

"Jean's been doing it for the last two days, it's fine," Kerry said.

"Just because Jean's been doing it doesn't..." Donna started.

"Mom, you're kidding me, right? Please give me my phone." Kerry couldn't go another second without talking to her boys. Donna reluctantly handed her flip phone over and Kerry proceeded to call her mother-in-law. Jane was grateful to receive the recent update on Emma. Kerry had prepped herself for any hysteria that may have ensued, yet Jane delivered a much calmer, albeit desperately concerned response than she'd anticipated. It helped to be slightly removed from the black hole that the hospital had become. Plus, she had the distraction of two toddlers to help diffuse her stress. *Thank God for Jane*, Kerry thought. *What would I do without her right now?*

When the boys got on the line, it felt like a warm blanket had been wrapped around Kerry's body. She stroked Adam's hair as Thomas rambled about his yucky banana and papier mâché turtle. He asked Kerry where she was and when she was coming home three or four times. He started to cry when she didn't give him a straight answer, but Kerry changed the subject and told him she'd bake him cookies when she was back. He bragged about having a sleepover at Ga-Ga's and Pop Pop's. Thomas sounded pretty good. Kerry told him she loved him five or six times, each time squeezing Adam's leg a little harder. When Ryan got on the phone, Jane coached him to say "Hi, Mama." After that, all she could really hear was the sound of him breathing, drooling and smiling into the phone. It sounded heavenly. Kerry told Ryan she loved him and made kissing sounds. Adam giggled at his aunt's noises, and she playfully tickled his belly. When she finally hung up, Kerry smiled. She pulled Adam closer to her and kissed his head. He didn't seem to mind her affection at all.

At 7:15 p.m., Tom sat in the waiting room, gazing out the window at the darkness. Every other family had come and gone, except for him. Even the coffee vendor had left. The lights of the hospital rooms across the street stood out. Tom watched as nurses checked in on their patients, as family members and friends paid visits. Nighttime set in. Tom looked at his watch. Twelve hours had passed since he first took a seat in his chair. Sean was busy showing him a website that someone at work had told him about. It was called Caring Bridge, a way for parents to keep family and friends informed of their child's health and recovery. Tom looked at the screen in an attempt to show interest, but was quickly distracted by the movement he caught out of the corner of his eye. He looked up to see three familiar faces walking through the waiting room. It took a moment for him to register that these were the same faces he had seen fourteen hours earlier when he'd signed off on Emma's surgery. These people were Emma's surgeons.

A liaison nurse was pointing them in Tom's direction. They were all the way down the hall. Two of them still had their O.R. caps on. One was a woman in her late thirties. She was petite with medium length brown hair and glasses. Her name was Dr. Terry Buchmiller. Tom had written all their names on a piece of paper he'd shoved in his pocket earlier that morning. The man to her right was Dr. Russell Jennings. It was hard for Tom to forget him or his facial hair, for that matter. This was the man who'd broken all the news to them in the recovery room. On the other side was Dr. Borer, the urologist. His face was serious, in general. *But what does that mean right now?* Tom wondered. All of their faces looked sobering. He'd seen a surgeon a few hours ago walk up to a family with his thumbs up and a huge smile on his face. *Why weren't any of these people giving him the thumbs up?* he wondered. Tom's heart climbed back into his throat. Jean and Sean exchanged a solemn glance. Neither of them had the courage to make eye contact with Tom. They waited for these three surgeons to reach them, wondering if everything was about to change, again.

Fifteen minutes later, the door to Kerry's hospital room opened. Tom held it as Jean, Sean and Dr. Buchmiller filed into the room. Kerry looked at Tom with terrible panic. "She's okay," Tom smiled, "It's over."

Kerry, Tom, Donna, Joe, Jean, Diane, Adam and Sean gathered around as Dr. Buchmiller explained that it was her idea to come to Kerry's room. "After all the time I've just spent with your daughter, it only seemed right to deliver the final update in person," she said while smiling at Kerry. Dr. Buchmiller sat down in a chair and gave the crowd a play by play of Emma's entire surgery. She weathered Donna's interruptions like a champ, answering all of her questions without fail. She repeated things when Joe didn't understand her. She spoke in detail about Emma's complications and the long road she had ahead of her.

One of the things Dr. Buchmiller mentioned was that it would be at least three months before Emma would be able to undergo her next operation—to connect her esophagus. Until then, Dr. Buchmiller explained, she would have to remain in the NICU.

The exhausted surgeon smiled at little Adam's coos and laughed when Diane confessed how she'd snuck him in there. She told Kerry and Tom that she thought Emma *was* going to be all right. She congratulated them on getting their baby to where she needed to be in order to have a chance at life. Dr. Buchmiller was kind, intelligent and encouraging. She was an angel, and she and her surgical team had just saved Emma's life. The whole room filled with hope and joy. Tom and Kerry never imagined they could feel so grateful. "I'm going to need to hug you now," Kerry informed Dr. Buchmiller as she got up to leave. "Thank you. Thank you. Thank you so much," she cried.

Chapter 7

SAYING GOODBYE

STORE AFTER STORE lined the route as Tom and the marathoners made their way through Framingham. Mile 6 was in sight and most runners still had a lot of adrenaline fueling their pace. This was the same excitement that had taken them out of the gates. Cowbells rang from two rambunctious fans on the sidewalk. They were ecstatic that a guy dressed in a pink tutu had high-fived them on his way past. Another guy, in a giant blonde afro, ran up to Mr. Ballerina and smacked his ass as he ran past him. Clearly these clowns knew each other. At least, Tom hoped they did. *I could wear the tutu if I had to*, Tom thought, *but that wig would be way too hot and itchy.* Who was he kidding? There was no way he'd ever wear a tutu. *I **would** grow a huge beard*, Tom thought, *then on race day shave it off into a nice handlebar mustache.* He smiled and shook his head in agreement with himself. It was something he would do on his second or third marathon. *Kerry will HATE it*, he thought. *It's perfect.* But it wouldn't have been right for today's race. *That's not something you do on your first marathon*, he thought. Not to mention, today wasn't about Tom getting a laugh. Today was a religious experience. His run had a purpose. Today was for Emma and there was nothing funny about that.

Tom thought about Thomas and Ryan, wondering if they would be proud of him for finishing. His own father, also named Tom, had run marathons, too. Tom remembered that day in the fourth grade when his class project was based on his father's marathon achievements. Standing in front of twenty-two awestruck students—his future wife included—little Tom held up an 8x10 picture of his dad crossing the finish line.

He bragged about his "Tough-As-Nails Pop" and how he'd run through all five boroughs of New York City, twice. Tom marveled the crowd as he graphically described the mounds of eggs and pancakes his dad would consume to keep his strength up. He passed around his dad's two medals and let each child hold them. But nobody was allowed to try them on. Even Timmy, Tom's twin brother, had to hand them back over when he was finished admiring them. Tom was the only one who could wear them. He wore them on the bus and all day at school. He wore them to football practice, then home. He kept them on until his dad got home from work and patted him on the head.

Tom wondered if someday Thomas or Ryan might wear *his* medal. The wind blew and sweat dripped from his hat. A familiar face came into focus. It was the picture of the little redheaded girl on the back of his new friend's shirt. Quickening his stride, Tom caught up to Needham Joe and tapped him on the shoulder. "It's Gracie, right?" Tom asked. Joe smirked. "Actually it's Joe. Gracie's my daughter," he said.

"Is she here today?" Tom asked.

"She's here," Joe said.

"Twenty miles and counting," Tom announced. "The wind's picking up a little, huh?"

"I don't mind it," Joe admitted, "feels good to me. So, the last time I saw you, Emma was born. What did I miss?" Tom didn't feel right bending Joe's ear for such a long time. He'd spent an entire mile talking about Emma. Not to mention he wanted to save his breath, at least a little bit. So he turned the tables and redirected their conversation: "Tell me about Gracie, first," Tom said. "She obviously gets her good looks from her mom?"

Joe talked about his daughter who was born with a congenital heart defect. He recalled the horror of finding out from the doctors, just how serious her condition was. Tom listened as he spoke about his wife and two older daughters: how they had weathered all five of Gracie's open-heart surgeries together. He described her little chest and the huge scar she had going down the center of it. His wife, Joe was convinced, was the reason Gracie had curls. She would lay in the hospital bed with her, twirling Gracie's hair around her finger for hours while they watched *The Little Mermaid*. His other daughters would get jealous that she got to skip school to be in the hospital. Joe talked about her dance recitals and how she blew everyone away every time she took the floor. He bragged about her self-esteem, how she threw her heart into everything she did. Joe laughed about the trouble she'd get into, and how she got away with everything—even with her sisters—because she was such a gift to all of them. Joe went on and on about her sense of humor. He explained that she was the first one he'd look at when he told a joke because he could always count on Gracie to crack up, no matter how bad the punch line was. Tom listened to every word. Gracie sounded like a daddy's girl. This was everything he'd always wanted in a daughter. This was exactly how he had pictured life with Emma, aside from the curly red hair.

"That's enough about me," Joe said looking at his watch, "I've been yappin' for almost eight minutes and thirty-five seconds." Tom looked up. They were approaching Mile 7. He'd been so invested in what Joe was saying that he hadn't noticed an entire mile was in their rear view mirror. The crowd was thinning out a bit more. He and Joe had managed to successfully stay in sync, moving like two Froggers through the maze of runners. He noticed that some folks were turning up their engines, or else it just seemed that way now that things weren't as dense. Tom had meant to pay attention as they ran past the Framingham Train Station somewhere near the 6.5 mile mark, but he'd forgotten. He'd read in one of his books how sometimes runners get stopped as a freight train passes. History told that many leaders of the pack had suggested they were robbed of their victory because they got cut off from their opponents at the Framingham tracks. Tom was surprised that he hadn't been stopped in his tracks. It was the kind of thing he had come to expect nowadays.

"Oh man," Tom said, "I haven't looked at my note for two miles." He unfolded the damp piece of paper and scanned to where he'd left off.

"Last I heard, she was born ten weeks early," Joe announced. Tom nodded. He silently caught up on what he'd missed. Then Joe shook his head and looked down as Tom read aloud what was written next:

Mile 7: Saying Goodbye....

KERRY AND TOM stood outside of the NICU for a good forty-five minutes before they were finally allowed to go in. They washed and dried their hands, then doused them with a glob of Purell. This had become the new tradition, upon entry. Emma's nurse was tall with dark hair. She introduced herself as Nancy and didn't seem at all flustered at the state of her tiny patient. Unfortunately, that wasn't the case for Kerry and Tom. Looking at their daughter, it was impossible not to panic. Emma's skin was so tight, it looked like it could tear open at any second. Her entire body was bloated and red. Two tubes came out of her mouth. One was taped down, quite efficiently, to her face. Her eyes were glazed shut. Gauze was everywhere. A tube exited the right side of her chest and was draining red liquid. Another tube came out from her groin and was draining yellow liquid. A fifth tube came out from her stomach. IVs and lines ran up her legs and arms. There was some kind of wiry contraption taped down to her chest. A big red bubble protruded from the other side of her stomach. A clear plastic bag was taped around it. Kerry looked closer—the bubble was rigid. It was Emma's intestine. She assumed this was the colostomy. Machines were working all around her.

This baby did not look like *their* Emma. She didn't even *resemble* the child they'd seen fourteen hours prior. Tom was speechless. He didn't know where to begin. Kerry watched as the nurse pricked Emma's heel and collected the dripping blood. "What are you doing that for?" she asked. "Blood gases," Nancy answered. "We check her blood to see if she's got the right oxygen/carbon dioxide exchange going on. Depending on what we find, we can tweak the settings on her vent." Kerry nodded her head. She looked at the vent, then back at Emma, remembering Dr. Buchmiller's words: *"She's going to have a long road ahead of her."* That seemed like the understatement of the century.

Emma was too fragile to handle. There was no reaching in, no kissing and no touching. All Tom and Kerry could do was stare at her, and it was the most gut-wrenching thing either of them had ever seen. "She must be in pain. Oh, my God, she must be in so much pain. A little baby shouldn't have to suffer like this!" Kerry cried. She covered her mouth with her hands. "You're giving her something for the pain, right?" Tom asked. The blood vessels on his head were ready to burst. Nancy nodded her head and assured them that Emma couldn't feel anything. "How do you know that?" Kerry fired back. "We can tell by her heart rate," Nancy said, pointing to the top number on the monitor. "If babies are in distress, their heart rates tend to elevate. Right now hers is at an acceptable level for what she's been through."

Punching an imaginary wall, Tom kept his eyes locked on Emma's heart rate. Every time it went up, he squirmed. Every time it went down, he exhaled. He felt his own heart start to pound faster and faster. Kerry felt him squeezing her shoulders, and she turned around to bury her face into his chest. Her tears soaked through his shirt. This was not what they had imagined. This was not the baby whose strength they were celebrating just an hour ago. What they saw in that isolette looked doomed. Their daughter had been reduced to a jumble of tubes and wires connected to myriad machines. Her tiny body was unrecognizable. The only thing that slightly resembled Emma was the tuft of black hair on her swollen head. Kerry turned back for one last glance. "She's not going to remember any of this," Nancy said. "Maybe not," Kerry sniffed, "but I sure will."

The next morning, Kerry's family gathered in her hospital room. They took turns being escorted by Tom into the NICU to visit "Mighty Emma". Tom's father had dubbed Emma that name the night before, and it stuck. While Tom took Joe and Donna for a visit, Jean and Diane hung back with their sister. A nurse walked in the room holding a little plastic cup and glanced over at Adam, asleep in the stroller. "Is he yours?" she asked, looking at Kerry. "Because you know, we only allow siblings to visit."

"He's mine," Kerry responded. It was hard for her to get past the nurse's uncanny resemblance to Dame Judi Dench. Knowing the next question was coming; Kerry quickly did some calculations in her weary head and came up with a number.

"How old is he?" the nurse persisted, handing Kerry her medication.

"He's fourteen months," Kerry snapped back. She swallowed two pills, then handed the empty cup back to the nurse. *Dame Judi's not going to break me*, she thought. Diane and Jean fidgeted in their chairs and held their mouths tightly clenched. Any eye contact would have set them off.

"Wow, he's really small for fourteen months," the nurse continued. Kerry lifted her chin and looked at her square on. "If you think he's small," she snarled, "you should see my three-pound daughter. She's recovering from a twelve-hour surgery over in Children's NICU right now." Kerry held her stare. Her eyes dared the nurse to make one more comment about Adam. Looking down, the nurse walked backwards towards the door. "I hope she's doing okay," she muttered, "Let me know if I can get you anything."

Diane and Jean were looking up now. They didn't want to miss the performance their sister was putting on. It was most impressive. When the door clicked shut, they all burst out laughing. "I'm serious, nobody should mess with me right now...not even the Queen of England! I am NOT in the mood," Kerry growled. Jean shook her head and looked at Diane. "Don't piss her off—she will RIP your head off," she warned.

Even though she took pleasure in making the nurse uncomfortable, it was strange for Kerry to be talking about a daughter to anyone. Having had two baby boys, *daughter* was not in her vocabulary. Yet, ever since she was a little girl, Kerry had imagined having one. She pictured a dark-haired little beauty with pouty lips and big eyes. She'd envisioned every stage of her childhood: a delicate baby girl being baptized; a rowdy toddler in a purple tutu; a tough five-year-old scoring her first goal in soccer; a brainy eight-year-old reading all of Judy Blume's best sellers; a brave ten-year-old getting her ears pierced for the first time; a love-struck sixteen-year-old going to her prom.

Kerry had pictured these scenes in her head for as long as she could remember. She recalled the "deal" she'd made with God: To give up reading trashy magazines if he ever sent her a daughter. This, Kerry believed, was the responsible thing to do, having read that tabloid smut is a detriment to young girls' self esteem. These were all the things Kerry had thought about when she dreamed of having a daughter. Not once, had she ever pictured the little girl that lay in her isolette. *Who could have ever dreamed **this** up?* she wondered.

Adam woke up crying. Diane took him in her arms and opened her shirt. He latched on immediately and quieted down. Kerry looked at them, longingly. Jean saw this and popped up. "I'm going to get some coffee," she said. "Can I get either of you anything?" Diane shook her head *no*. "Can you get me an *US Weekly* and a *Star* magazine please?" Kerry asked. Jean agreed. She opened the door to find Kerry's nurse carrying two new IV bags on her way in. Jean politely held the door, then shot a wide-eyed look to both her sisters and let out a snort as it slowly shut. Dame Judi Nurse took a moment to process what she was seeing, then delivered her puzzled gaze to Kerry. "My sisters and I are very close. What's that you've got there? More liquid for my veins?" Kerry finished. The nurse nodded her head and hooked up the IV bags without so much as a peep.

At 1 p.m., everyone had had a chance to visit Emma and was preparing for their long trip back to Wyckoff, New Jersey. Diane, Jean, Joe and Donna all lived in Kerry's hometown, so they planned to caravan on the way back. "Just promise me you're not going to do fifty-five the whole way, Dad," Jean moaned. "I'm gonna have to break away if you're too slow." Tom laughed. Joe agreed to keep up, then kissed Kerry on the head. He was crying. The older he got, the weepier he'd become. Coupled with having to leave his daughter and granddaughter in this condition, her father was certifiably tearful.

Donna was emotional too, but that was no surprise. She held Kerry's face. "I'm unpacking in New Jersey, then I'm turning right around and coming up to Rhode Island," she said. Kerry's blotches started to surface. Her eyes watered. She agreed with her mom's plan. Donna continued: "I don't know what you're going to do...but you'll figure it out...and I'll just be at home with the boys to help...have faith in God, Kerry...stay close to him! We'll be praying for that little miracle...for Mighty Emma...and we'll be praying for you...stay close to God, Kerry...." Donna sniffled, "...I don't know *why* you and Tom are going through this." Kerry rolled her eyes. That seemed to be the question of the hour. She sadly kissed Adam and Diane goodbye breathing in as much "baby" as she could. Jean leaned in for a kiss and Kerry whispered: "I don't know what I'm going to do without you here." Jean did her best to swallow her emotions as she squeezed her sister one last time. "You're going to be okay," she said. "You can do this."

Although they were somewhat relieved when the door shut, being alone with their fears wasn't easy. Tom pulled out his computer and opened it. He'd written an email the night Emma was born, which he wanted to show to Kerry. "I sent this to everyone. What do you think?" he asked, handing her the laptop. Kerry read:

Hi Everyone—

We are proud and thrilled to announce that our little girl, Emma Ann Sheeran, was born today at 1:40 p.m. She weighed in at 3 lbs 8 oz and is 30 weeks old! She is the most beautiful thing I have ever seen and is our miracle baby.

Kerry is recovering nicely and hanging in there. To say the least, it has been a rough couple of days. We are so blessed to have this little girl.

Emma is in the Neonatal Intensive Care Unit (NICU) at Children's Hospital in Boston. There are some complications with her health, which the doctors are evaluating right now.

She has some intestinal and esophageal problems that are being addressed at this time. She will be going into major surgery tomorrow morning (Monday 1/28) and will have a long road to recovery. She is a tough little girl and came out kicking with a couple of loud yells. I am confident that she will pull through.

Please continue to keep her in your thoughts and prayers. And thank you all for your messages, thoughts, etc. Kerry and I really appreciate it. I will pass along any updates when I can. Attached are a few pics.

Love Always,

Tom & Kerry

Kerry handed the computer back to Tom. "It's good," she said. "She's not thirty-weeks-old, she was born at thirty weeks gestation...but whatever." Kerry looked out the window. The sky was grey. A woman walking down the sidewalk almost lost her shopping bag to the wind. It was hard to remember which day of the week it was. Tom busily typed out his next update, running things by Kerry as he wrote. But something felt off and she couldn't seem to shake it. The opening line of Tom's announcement didn't jive:

> 'We are proud and thrilled to announce that our little girl, Emma Ann Sheeran, was born today at 1:40 p.m.'

Proud? Thrilled? Does Tom really feel that way? she wondered. Those words couldn't have been further from the truth, as far as she was concerned. They sounded celebratory. They sounded happy. Kerry wasn't feelings either of those. *Should I be?* she wondered. *Am I some kind of a heartless wretch that I can't even take a moment to celebrate the fact that we just had a daughter?* She pictured the announcement in her own words:

Hi everyone-

We are terrified and distraught to announce that today our tiny 10-week premature baby with a mountain of medical problems was ripped from Kerry's uterus.

Oh, and it's a girl!

Luckily, Tom was doing the typing. "Actually, I didn't know you were going to send something out so soon," Kerry said. "I would've liked to have seen it before."

"What's wrong, you don't like what I wrote?" he asked.

"No, it's not that. I just wasn't ready to tell the world yet," she replied.

"What do you mean, Ker? Tell the world what?" Tom asked.

"Everything!" Kerry's voice began to shake. "I wasn't ready to tell everyone her name...her weight. I wasn't ready to tell everyone about her esophagus and her intestines. I wasn't ready! And now everyone knows her name...and everyone knows she's here...and I just wasn't ready for everyone to know all of that yet, okay?" Kerry snapped. Tom was stunned. This didn't make any sense to him. He closed his computer and sat down beside her on the bed. Reaching for her hand, he tried to make eye contact. But hers were locked on the window, so he looked outside with her. The wind was blowing a little girl's hat off her head. She was giggling, holding her mother's hand. Her mother caught the hat as it flew off, then scooped the girl up in her arms and carried her across the street. Tom and Kerry kept their eyes on the mother and daughter, until they turned the corner and were no longer in sight. "I'm sorry," Tom said. "I didn't know.

The rest of the day had its ups and downs. Emma's stability waivered with questionable heart rates and blood gases that weren't quite up to par. The doctors explained that she was on high alert for any infections she might develop as a result of the surgery. Even her IVs and central line were a possible source of infection, so the odds didn't really seem in Emma's favor. One of the nurses had given Tom and Kerry a binder with lots of information about infants in the NICU and what's to be expected. It was helpful and honest, which they appreciated. It reinforced one point in particular: the NICU experience is like a roller coaster ride. One day a patient could be doing great, the next he or she might be going to hell in a handbag. It didn't say that exactly, but it may as well have. This was simply reality. Just as the blond doctor at Brigham & Women's had explained, there is a lot of potential for problems when a baby comes out too early. And Emma's potential was quadrupled. While it wasn't easy to ingest this knowledge, it was knowledge nonetheless. Tom and Kerry had been completely blindsided by everything else. At least at this point, they weren't going to be stupid enough to think it would be smooth sailing from then on.

Kerry's milk came in the following morning. Big time. She filled four five-ounce bottles at five o'clock, and then again three hours later. It was hard for her nurse to keep up with the supplies. Kerry was given special labels with hers and Emma's names on them. It felt good to fill the bottles. She anxiously waited for Tom to arrive so that she could visit Emma and hand over the milk to the NICU nurse. Kerry had been picturing that moment for the last hour. Her nurse walked in with some more supplies: "Looks like everything's in working order," she said. "You're doing very well in general." Kerry nodded her head with hesitance. "They're probably going to discharge you tomorrow," her nurse added. *No!* Kerry thought. This sounded insane. *They wouldn't dare kick a recovering mother out of a room when her daughter is hanging on by a thread across the "bridge"*, she thought. "They can't discharge me, I can't go home," Kerry explained. Her face flushed. The nurse carefully placed the stickers on the four bottles without looking up. "I know this is hard, but insurance is not going to let you stay regardless of what's happening with your daughter," she explained. Kerry shook her head in disagreement. "Then I'll tell them my incision is hurting me. I'll tell them I'm in pain," she said. The nurse was now shaking *her* head. "I just need another couple of days," Kerry pleaded. "Just a little more time."

The NICU was more solemn then it had been the day before. At least, it was in Bay 6. Kerry sat in a rocking chair next to the isolette. Emma looked a little less swollen, and was filling her catheter bag with urine. It appeared to be an unusually large amount of pee from such a small human, but Emma's nurse explained that it was because she'd been given a lot of fluids during her long surgery. "What goes in must come out," the nurse said. Emma was being given drugs to help her get rid of the fluid. The only problem was, the doctors had to make sure her already-troubled kidneys weren't working *too* hard to eliminate everything. There was a fine line that had to be walked. Kerry had learned that this was the case with many treatments. For instance, tiny babies with premature lungs need oxygen to help them breathe. But too much oxygen can lead to vision problems, and in some cases cause blindness. Stevie Wonder, Kerry remembered, was given too much oxygen as a baby.

These same babies need food to thrive and grow. Yet some of their guts are too delicate to handle the digestion process and they wind up tearing holes through their intestines. This kind of problem, Kerry had read, can lead to lifelong gastro-intestinal troubles, or ultimately death. *It's like all these babies are balancing on a tightrope*, Kerry thought. She was amazed at how every single function of Emma's body had an important purpose. Every breath she took, every beat of her heart, every drip of urine, every drop of blood was being accounted for. It was thorough, precise, and completely overwhelming. The doctors and nurses were playing a constant game of defense, trying to stay ahead of the nasty curveballs their little patients might throw.

Tom walked in with three coffees from Starbucks. He handed the tall one to Kerry and the medium one to Emma's nurse. "This is for you, Deb," Tom said. Deb had worked a shift with Emma the day before, so Tom had gotten to know her a bit. Deb had also gotten to know Tom a little. Unfortunately his neurosis had been heightened, resulting from his recent addiction to Starbucks. Ever since he'd been shut down on revisiting smoking, caffeine had become his drug of choice. And much to Kerry's dismay, Tom had picked the most expensive coffee in town. "You know, they have free coffee in the family area around the corner," Deb said. Kerry's eyes lit up, but Tom refused to engage. "I need the good stuff," he explained. Tom looked at Kerry: "Drastic times call for drastic measures," he said. His squinty eyes suggested that Kerry refrain from dishing him any shit. If five-dollar coffee was going to somehow help, then five-dollar coffee it was.

As Kerry saw it, the problem wasn't just the amount of money he was spending. What concerned her even more was how completely wired Tom had become. This wasn't good. Tom was a worrier by nature. Some might say he was capable of working himself into quite a tizzy. Coupled with the circumstances unfolding before him, the result was one big bag of nerves. Interestingly enough, in the last twenty-four hours Kerry's nerves had settled a little. Yet Tom's had headed in the opposite direction and the nurses were taking the brunt of it. His questions spewed non-stop. Deb was so busy trying to answer him, she could hardly concentrate on what she was doing. And God forbid she stepped away for a second to tend to another patient, Tom would be calling after her to address one of the many alarms that were sounding on Emma's machines. It was intense, slightly embarrassing and difficult for Kerry to watch. But Tom had bought her a five-dollar coffee, so it only seemed fair that Deb put up with her husband.

Deb was in her mid-forties. She had short black hair and glasses, and wore a plaid checkered vest. Her demeanor was calm and serious. A gold cross hung around her neck. She'd been a nurse for twenty-plus years and had started her medical career in the Air Force. Her husband was also in the Air Force. They had three boys and lived in a suburb outside of Boston. Deb was a tough cookie. She'd seen her fair share of complicated patients over the course of her career. Emma Sheeran was now on that list. Although Emma's type didn't scare her, it definitely kept Deb on her toes. When a patient is being followed by multiple department heads for multiple reasons, it can become intimidating for some NICU nurses. Even the most seasoned will say that twists and turns can show up at any time. And with kids like Emma, the potential is tenfold. So while Deb remained calm on the outside, her brain was on high alert. She was responsible for Emma and she took her responsibility very seriously. It was difficult and stressful. And an uber-caffeinated father like Tom Sheeran wasn't helping.

Kerry looked around for the first time since Emma's arrival. Three other babies shared Bay 6 and all of them were in isolettes. She couldn't see the actual babies, but did notice that the one to her right was covered in pink blankets, so she assumed their neighbor was a girl. The baby's parents sat silently, barely even making eye contact with each other. As far as Kerry could tell, their baby seemed fairly stable; none of her alarms were going off. The mother looked to be in her twenties. Her bleached blond hair was disheveled. She had it pulled back into a messy ponytail. The father looked young too. His baseball hat was pulled down so low, it was impossible to see his eyes. Although, even if she could have seen them, Kerry wouldn't have looked into them. She was hardly capable of acknowledging her own presence in the NICU, never mind someone else's. The mother had a piece of string she was wrapping around her finger, incessantly. The father caught a glimpse of his wife's purple finger and gently swatted her other hand away. A minute later she was back to wrapping. He reached for the string again but she wouldn't give it up. This went on for an hour or so, until the two of them quietly got up and walked towards the exit.

Another couple walked past Tom and Kerry and stopped at the crib diagonally across from Emma. Tom smiled and said hello, but Kerry didn't look. She was finishing a lullaby in Emma's ear and wasn't about to be interrupted. When her song ended, she closed the plastic portal and sat down in her rocking chair. Seconds later, Emma's oxygen saturation began to drop. One of the alarms sounded and Deb rushed over. She carefully turned up two of the settings on the breathing vent and waited for Emma to recover. Then, Deb reached in and gently tapped her on top of her head. Another nurse came to the bedside and offered to help. Tom stood up. His heart was racing. His eyes were bulging. Kerry jumped up too. "What's happening?" Tom asked. Deb continued to tap Emma's head. "Come on, Emma," Deb said. She looked over at Tom and Kerry. "She dropping her sats...she need to remember to breathe," Deb explained. Kerry looked at Emma, who was losing her ruddy complexion. "I don't get it!" Kerry said, "I thought the machine was breathing for her!" Deb was unusually calm. She turned the vent up a little higher. "Just give her a second," she said. Eventually the numbers started to rise: 58... 64... 65... 70... 78... 84... 86... 87... 88—at which point the alarm was silenced and all those around collectively exhaled. "She's okay," Deb announced. "We've been weaning her vent settings all morning and it probably just caught up to her." She explained that this was the normal course for post-op preemies and to expect more of the same. "Clearly we need to give Emma some rest," Deb said. "We'll let the vent do most of the work for now."

When everything seemed to have calmed down, Tom got up to use the bathroom. Kerry sat alone in a fog, rocking. A nurse approached her and tapped her on the shoulder. "Do you mind if I switch chairs with you?" she asked, "I have a mother who wants to *kangaroo* her baby." Kerry had no idea what the nurse was talking about, but stood up anyway and gave her the chair. She accepted an office chair that swiveled from side to side as a replacement. Swiveling towards Deb, she asked: "What's kangarooing?" Deb explained that it was a skin-to-skin ritual that newborns and parents thrived on in the NICU. Parents would basically open their shirts and lay their undressed baby on their chest for a good old-fashion snuggle. Apparently, research had shown that this kind of contact is *so* soothing, it can positively affect these tiny humans' heart rate, respiratory rate and all over health and development.

Kerry pictured herself sitting in a rocking chair with Emma's tuft of black hair poking out of her shirt. She felt the warmth of her daughter's little body and the beat of her heart. She pictured her tiny mouth smiling, and all the nurses standing around in awe at how relaxed and happy this made Emma.

How lucky, Kerry thought. I *can't even hold my baby's hand.* The mother now sitting in her chair probably had no idea how good she had it.

Kerry swiveled to her right. She glanced at the couple sitting diagonally from them. The man was tall, thin and balding. He was reading a newspaper as his wife fixed the baby's lavender blankets. The woman was also tall, with dark brown hair and glasses. She appeared friendly, smiling sweetly at the nurse who was caring for their baby. She looked familiar, and it took Kerry a good minute to realize that this was the lady she'd seen handing the nurse her breast milk a couple days earlier. Things seemed fairly calm in this family's world. Hardly any alarms were sounding. Kerry compared their baby's numbers on the monitor to Emma's. Her heart rate was lower and steadier; her oxygen was higher; her respiratory rate, slower. *They probably don't realize how blessed they are to have a stable baby,* she thought. This had become a trend the more her eyes began to wander. Emma's alarms sounded again. This time it was her heart rate monitor. The screen read "tachycardia", which meant a super-fast heart rate. It was the fourth time in ten minutes that this had happened. The hairs on the back of Kerry's neck stood up as she remembered what Emma's other nurse had said about fast heart rates. *She's in pain,* Kerry thought. She stood up and peered at her helpless, swollen, bandaged baby. *How am I supposed to just sit here and watch my daughter suffer?* she wondered. *She's been sliced open from top to bottom and that was just to save her life. Now we have to sit here and watch her fight for it? WHY?* Her helplessness was unbearable. If God had a lesson in all of this, Emma's mother sure as hell wanted to know what it was.

The rest of the day continued on with more of the same. Little by little, Deb was able to wean Emma's vent settings. By nighttime, she was switched over to a regular ventilator, instead of the maximum support "Hi-Fi" one she'd been on since the surgery. This was progress, as far as Kerry and Tom understood. The doctors had explained that the sooner they could get Emma off the ventilator altogether, the better. But weaning her vent settings meant weaning her sedation as well. The caveat went as follows: A completely sedated Emma feels nothing; a semi-sedated Emma feels traces; an un-sedated Emma is awake and aware. Sure pain medications help, but there was no way to avoid the fact that along with extensive surgery comes pain.

Tom walked Kerry back to her hospital room for their final night's stay. He'd been sleeping on a chair that unfolded into a bed next to hers. "I'm not going to miss this chair," Tom said as he wrestled to unfold it. Kerry's heart sank. *What will we do? How can we possibly go home without Emma?* East Greenwich, Rhode Island was an hour and fifteen minutes away, without traffic. They'd looked into options like the Ronald McDonald house but most seemed more appropriate for smaller families with further distances to travel. Tom was convinced they needed to rent an apartment in the Longwood area, within walking distance of the hospital. He'd already made an appointment for the following morning to look at a two-bedroom. But that didn't make any sense to Kerry. She pictured Tom commuting to Rhode Island to work, and she and the boys crammed into a little apartment in the middle of an unfamiliar city. Thomas would have to be pulled out of school and Ryan would have nothing to do all day. She wouldn't even be able to visit Emma because she'd be taking care of the boys, who were too young to be running amuck in a hospital. In her opinion, it wouldn't work. She empathized with his desire to take residence down the street from Emma, but it just wasn't a feasible solution for their entire family. Kerry knew she had to figure something else out, but in that moment was too busy trying to decide whether or not she was going to tear some of her staples open in order to finagle another night in the hospital.

Tom insisted on running to Starbucks in the morning, which rubbed on Kerry's anxious nerves. "I just want to get out the door before they come around with discharge papers and all that crap!" she quipped. "Okay," Tom agreed, "just meet me in the NICU. Do you want me to get you a coffee?" Kerry thought for a second. There was no reason Tom should spend another five dollars on a coffee for her. It was ridiculous. "Well, if you're going anyway, you may as well get me a Venti Caramel Macchiato, no sugar," she said. There was also no reason Tom should be the only one drinking the good stuff. Just as they opened the door to leave, her nurse came in and put a halt to her escape. Tom caught a glimpse of the nasty look Kerry was giving him as he ducked out the door. "I'll meet you in the NICU," he said bolting for his life. The nurse turned to Kerry. Her round freckled-face was riddled with pity. "Check-out's at 11 a.m.," she said.

Walking up to the NICU entrance, Kerry paused at the front desk and looked around. She signed her name on the chart, but nobody was there to buzz her in. Two heavy bags were slung over each shoulder. One had the clothes and toiletries she'd arrived with, the other was packed with her pumping supplies and all the hospital grade maxi pads she could fit. The longer Kerry waited for the receptionist, the heavier her bags became. Chatter was coming from inside the family "break room". She peeked through the glass and saw at least ten people sitting around drinking coffee. The room was small, so it was a noticeably large group. *So much for the peanut butter and crackers I planned on grabbing*, she thought. There was no getting through this crowd.

A tall beautiful black woman pushed a mop through the hallway. Her head was wrapped in a vibrant scarf, which stood out amongst her plain blue scrubs. The woman flashed a bright, big smile at Kerry. "Good morning, it's a beautiful day," she said in a Haitian accent. Kerry did her best to force a smile back at her. It took everything she had to refrain from snarling. *Please*, Kerry thought. *This isn't the time or place to be cheerful. And as far as beautiful days are concerned, today doesn't quite measure up*. Kerry turned around in a circle, hungry and more annoyed then before. The receptionist was nowhere in sight. *Clearly, nobody in this place gives a crap that I'm waiting to see my sick baby*, she thought. *Nobody cares that I have to drive home in two hours*. Kerry's nails tapped on the desk, louder and faster. Not a soul anywhere. She pulled on the NICU door, but it was locked. An angry exhale blew from between her teeth. Suddenly the sound of a toilet flushing rang in her ears, and Kerry turned to see the bathroom door open. The receptionist quickly made her way to the desk, looked at the chart, then picked up the phone. "Emma Sheeran's mom is here to see her," she said, nodding to Kerry as she buzzed her in. Scrubbing her hands, then dousing them with Purell, Kerry carried both her bags *and* the chip on her shoulder into Bay 6.

Two new people were sitting at the isolette across from Emma's. They were women who appeared to be in their forties. Both were plump with dirty blonde hair. One of them made a joke to the nurse about being from New Jersey. It was clear that they had just arrived, since the same woman kept referring to their time at the "*B.I.*", which Kerry assumed was Beth Israel Hospital. The baby they were with was tiny. Kerry looked a little longer then usual, since the women had their backs to her. "Welcome, Matthew" was written on a card taped to his isolette. His birthday and weight were written, too, but the weight was in kilograms and Kerry wasn't familiar enough with metric conversions to know what it translated to in pounds. Whatever it was, it didn't look like much. One of the women leaned her head on the other one's shoulder. *How nice*,

Kerry thought. *She has her sister with her.* It had been two days since Diane and Jean left Boston. Kerry longed for their support.

Tom grabbed Kerry's bags and piled them on a shelf behind Emma's isolette, then handed her a cup of coffee. She took a sip. It was hot and delicious. She opened the top and took another sip, then licked the foam from her top lip. Tom pointed to Emma's urine bag, which was bulging. Peering through the plastic box at her daughter, she saw that Emma was red and sedated, but half the size she had been three days earlier. Her nose looked like a button, her legs like a plucked chicken. She almost resembled the visions Kerry had of her from their two brief pre-op visits. Turning to Deb, who was working for the third day in a row, Kerry asked: "How is she today?" Deb explained that Emma was quite stable throughout the night and that Dr. Borer was happy with the rate at which she was eliminating all of her excess fluid. "She's down almost half a pound since her surgery," Deb explained, "That's going to help bring her blood pressure down." Kerry shook her head in agreement. "I'm so glad it's going down," she said.

When Deb stepped away, Kerry looked at Tom. "Did you know she had high blood pressure?" she asked. Tom was in his own world, but hadn't known about Emma's blood pressure either. Ever since he'd arrived that morning, he'd been reading the New York Post, while casually watching the couple to their right. The mother wore the same clothes as the day before. The same ponytail hung from her head. She sat with her hand on top of her baby's belly. The father wore the same hat pulled down over his eyes. He stood on the opposite side of the isolette with a woman who looked to be in her late fifties. Tom and Kerry glanced at the older woman, who was crying and apologizing to the young father. It seemed she was the grandmother.

The young father eventually escorted the grandmother out of the NICU, only to return with an older man who looked to be the grandfather. He wore a blue Patriots jacket; his face was painfully distraught. Not a word was spoken as he reached in and lovingly stroked the baby's head. Kerry looked at the stable numbers on the baby's monitor. She noticed that no alarms were sounding. Glancing back, she saw the young mother's hand let go for a second to wipe her tears, then reach right back in to hold on to her baby. "This has been happening for the last forty-five minutes," Tom whispered. "They keep bringing people in to see her. He's like the ninth or tenth person." Kerry closed her eyes and pictured the family "break-room," packed with visitors. When she opened them, she saw the grandfather in the Patriots jacket wiping tears away. He reached for the young father and pulled him close. They hugged for a minute. Then the grandfather whispered something into the young father's ear. He walked over to the mother and did the same. Even her unoccupied arm seemed too weak to return the affection. The grandfather touched the baby's head once more, before being escorted back out by the young father. Kerry and Tom exchanged a puzzled gaze after the two men walked past them towards the exit.

A minute later, the young father returned to his baby's bedside. A nurse had followed him in. She grabbed on to the blue and pink drapes and drew them around the baby's isolette. The two women across from Emma's station looked up at the sound of the curtain rings sliding around the track. So did the tall couple diagonal to them. At this point, the only things visible were the nurse's and the young couple's feet. It was a relief to Tom, having felt like an unwilling voyeur for the last hour. Kerry too. Not only wasn't she interested in inviting anyone into her world; she also didn't want to be pulled into someone else's. So the curtains were closed now, and this was a good thing. "She probably has to have surgery," Kerry whispered to Tom. He shrugged his shoulders. "I'm trying not to pay attention," he whispered. Kerry shook her head in agreement, but it was hard not to notice the wallowing sobs coming from within the curtains. Kerry grabbed a section of the *Post* and buried her face in it. Tom did the same, but it was difficult to ignore the sounds of silence coming from all the machines being turned off. It was impossible not to see the computer monitor with the falling numbers and the muted alarms. "Let's go," Tom said grabbing Kerry's arm. "Let's take a walk."

When they returned thirty minutes later, Emma lay sleeping peacefully with a tiny pink bow stuck in her hair. But the bed-space next to hers was empty. Not even an isolette remained. The monitors were powered off and the curtains were once again pulled open. Kerry looked at Tom. His sad eyes confirmed what she was thinking. "Oh, my God," she said softly. Hugging her tight, he kissed the top of her head. Soon after, Deb arrived with some of Emma's medications and began administering them. Kerry wiped her tears and took a deep breath. "Did you do that?" she asked, pointing to the bow. Deb nodded, "She looks so pretty now that all the fluid is washing out, I just couldn't resist." Tom and Kerry stared at their beautiful little daughter. Her mouth looked distorted and uncomfortable. It was pulled in two different directions, from two different tubes. Tom pointed to one of them. It was taped to her chin, and attached to a larger tube, which connected to a plastic container on the floor. The container was full of whitish-clear foamy liquid. "What's that tube for?" he asked.

"It's called a replogle," Deb said. "It's connected to suction."

"What is it sucking?" Tom asked.

"Her secretions," Deb answered.

"The secretions in her mouth?" Tom continued.

"All of her secretions," Deb explained. Tom looked confused. Kerry grew impatient. She knew exactly what Deb was saying. Tom dug his eyebrows and opened his mouth—only to be silenced by his loving wife. "She can't swallow her own spit," Kerry quipped, looking to Deb for concurrence. "Emma can't even swallow her own spit, so this tube is sucking it all out of her mouth for her." Kerry's cheeks were red. She blew some more steam out of her ears. How dare Tom make her say these things out loud? Tom looked at Deb. "So without that tube, she'd be foaming at the mouth?" he asked. Kerry shuttered. It sounded like he was describing a rabid dog. "Without that tube, she'd be inhaling her secretions and she wouldn't be able to breathe," Deb explained. Tom looked at Kerry and shook his head back and forth. Emma wriggled a little, then settled into her sedation once more. "She's doing okay," Deb smiled. "In another couple of days she might even be off the vent." Kerry formed the tracings of a smile. "At least that would be one less tube in her mouth," Kerry said.

At 1 p.m., Tom tapped Kerry on the shoulder. "It's time to go," he said, "Our appointment's at 1:30." He gave her a sad but urgent look. Kerry froze. Her chest tightened. *How can we leave our daughter in a hospital so far away?* she wondered. *How can we leave Emma at all?* Everything seemed wrong. The voice in her head spoke:

"You'll figure this out. You have two other children who also need you."

Kerry's chest heated up. The warmth rose into her face and her mouth began to quiver. At this point, tears were inevitable. *Of course Thomas and Ryan need me,* she thought, *but not like this.* Kerry felt the stares of everyone within her vicinity, but remained unaffected. *I guess I should just get used to this,* she thought. Her episodes of falling apart in public were becoming a daily occurrence. And with zero privacy in the NICU, it just wasn't something she had the energy to concern herself with. So Kerry let it go, blotchy face and all. It was her ugliest cry yet, and no one bothered trying to stop her. "Okay," Tom coddled. "I know," he said, fighting back his own tears. Deb stepped closer and opened up her arms. She wrapped them around Kerry and held her for a good two minutes. This was no ordinary hug. It felt compassionate and protective. It felt honest and strong. Everything Kerry needed and wanted for Emma was infused into this embrace. Deb held on until Kerry caught her breath. She waited for Kerry to let go. "I promise I'll take good care of her," Deb said. "Call me whenever you want. We answer the phone all day and night." Tom and Kerry both kissed their hands, then reached in and touched Emma's leg. "Goodbye, baby," they said. "We love you."

Waiting for the valet was even worse. They stood outside the hospital entrance and watched all of the new mothers being wheeled to their cars with their babies in their arms. Their proud smiles were piercing. Their balloons were appalling. One woman had twins and held both car seats on her lap as the hospital staff made a fuss over her. The husband and attendants tried convincing her to surrender at least one seat, but the mother refused to let go of either. Tom did his best to ignore it. *Wow,* Kerry thought, *talk about rubbing salt into the wound. She gets to walk out of here with two healthy babies and I have to leave my little girl in intensive care?* Tears trickled down her face as she carefully climbed into their Honda Pilot. She glanced behind her and saw the empty car seat she'd made Tom install *"Just in case."* Her hands fumbled through her purse for her sunglasses. *Anything,* Kerry thought, *just to cover my eyes.*

Tom looked at his wife, then pictured a sunny day in the future:

> *He and Kerry were standing outside of the hospital. They were waiting for their car. He was holding Emma in her car seat. She was a healthy baby. No tubes, no wires. Kerry was taking pictures with their camera. She was pulling at the seat, waiting for her chance to pose with their daughter. Emma was gurgling and cooing. Everyone who walked past stole a glimpse of her, and then went on about how beautiful she was. The boys were with them. Ryan was stealing Emma's pacifier out of her mouth. Thomas was standing guard, ready to tell anyone who tried to touch his baby sister to "scram". Kerry was smiling. The sun warmed their bodies. When their car arrived, people made comments about how Tom and Kerry had their hands full as they watched them buckle each child into their seat. Tom stuffed three pink balloons into the back, then he slammed the trunk and got into the drivers seat. The hospital's entrance was in his rear-view mirror. He saw his own reflection. It was looking back at him with the biggest grin he'd ever seem. Tom's car was packed full of everything he'd ever wanted. And they were driving home.*

Chapter 8

THE UNDERDOGS

TOM AND JOE simultaneously crossed the 8th mile-marker, then checked their digital watches in unison. "Heartburn Hill is coming up, I think," Tom announced. Joe laughed. "No offense, brother, but I think your story's starting to give me heartburn," Joe admitted. Tom snickered. "Sorry, dude. Sometimes I forget just how heavy the subject matter is for other people. It's just become so normal for me." "Too normal," Joe agreed. "You're churning up a lot of memories. I've packed so many things in the "Do Not Go There" file in my brain. It seems to work better for me that way. If there's one thing Gracie's taught me, it's to look ahead and keep running." Tom smiled in agreement. "And with that, my brother, I must forge onward. I feel the wind at my back," Joe said with a wink. Once again, Tom watched as Joe weaved his checkered shirt through the crowd. He followed him for a minute or two, until the little redheaded girl's face faded into a blur of all the other men and women heading towards Boston.

Looking around, Tom noticed the scenery had become woodsier. Once in a while he'd pass a lonely house or a business of some sort, but for the most part the street was lined with partially green trees. Two men ran past Tom on the right. "My nips are killing me, dude!" one guy said to the other. "I think I just lost one of 'em in Framingham." Tom laughed to himself. This was one lesson he had learned early on. Tom remembered the horror on Kerry's face, one Sunday morning, when he walked into their kitchen with two bloody circles running down the front of his white shirt. Sympathy was nowhere in sight, given she was annoyed that he'd been gone nearly two hours. His wife's disgusted look, however, stung less than the warm water and soap that washed over his bare chest in the shower. It were as if someone had scoured him with sand paper, then poured lemon juice all over his flesh. After that day, Tom became quite familiar with *Body Glide* and all of its heavenly glory. Prior to any long run, he rubbed it on his nipples, in between his legs, on his butt cheeks—basically anywhere and everywhere. It didn't take long to realize: chafe really sucks. Anything that could prevent it was well worth its weight in gold.

Tom watched a train rumble by on his left. He remembered reading about the Framingham train tracks and how years ago, spectators could board a train to Boston and watch the entire race from their window. It seemed cruel to know that Boston was still far enough away that it required a train ride. And not just a ten-minute trip. The folks on that train probably wouldn't arrive in Boston for at least forty-five minutes. Sure they had to make stops, but still it was considerable mileage. Eighteen miles to be exact.

An older man in his seventies noticed Tom staring at the train. "Ya think we can beat it?" he asked. Tom laughed. "I'm thinking about it," he replied. The man was wearing shorts and a red, white and blue tank, which wasn't much considering the temperature. At first, Tom assumed he was just a patriotic guy. But as the man got a few steps ahead of him, Tom could actually read what was written on his back: *50 States Marathon Club*. This impressed Tom. He needed to know more, so he did his best to catch up to his superior. "How many states have you completed?" Tom asked. The man was surprised to see him again, having just left Tom in the dust.

"Fourteen," he answered.

"Wow," Tom said. "Fourteen? How many years has it taken you?"

"Fourteen so far this year," he corrected Tom. "This is my seventh time running the fifty states."

"What?" Tom asked. It was unimaginable. The guy didn't have the greatest physique. He was a little round in the middle, and wasn't displaying any award-winning guns. Not to mention, he was old! And it was only April, which meant he would have had to average more then three marathons a month. "Really?" Tom persisted.

"Really," the man answered. Tom had no choice but to believe him. And since he'd just been put to shame, he figured it was only right to tell the truth himself:

"This is my first marathon," Tom confessed.

"You never forget your first time," the old man said with a smirk. It was obvious this wasn't the first time he'd made the joke. Tom watched as he sped ahead. His unimpressive body somehow kept a strong, solid pace. He waved to the spectators with the charisma of a Hollywood star. The crowd's energy seemed to fuel his power. Tom longed for this old timer's confidence and strength. He wondered if he'd have it when he crossed the finish line in Copley Square.

Towards the end of the 7th mile, the road began to rise uphill. *This is Heartburn Hill*, Tom reminded himself. Not to be confused with the ever-famous Heartbreak Hill, which was still eleven miles down the road. Realizing he hadn't read his next passage from Kerry's note, he promised himself he'd do so at the top of the hill. It was incentive—part of the mind game that long-distance running had become. Since he'd never run with a personal trainer, Tom had no choice but to constantly challenge himself. *Who else is going to push me?* Tom often wondered. *Who else is going to set my standards?* It was one of his favorite things about being a runner. He'd set goals for himself, then achieve them. Then he'd set bigger goals and achieve those. Of course it was fun to hear peoples' reactions when he'd tell them he'd just run eighteen miles. But nothing mattered as much as how great it made Tom feel about himself. Tom was a positive, upbeat guy for the most part, but he never felt the pride that most athletes feel until he'd started running. Perhaps this was because he was a really good runner. It were as if he had unlocked a hidden talent he never knew existed. *If only Kerry understood*, Tom thought, *she might even become a runner herself someday*.

His calves relaxed and the hill pointed downward. Tom unfolded his letter and scanned to:

Mile 8: Bradycardia spells. Codes. This is just the beginning....

KERRY SAT AT the computer, unable to type. She'd just read sixty-seven emails from family, friends and acquaintances. All of them spilled with concern for "Mighty Emma." Prayer chains had been formed. Food chains had been assembled. Love and well wishes arrived from across the country. A handful of people appeared to understand how desperate Emma's situation was. Others simply congratulated Kerry and Tom on the birth of their daughter. It had taken her hours to read through each and every letter.

Some mentioned they were sending food. Others wanted to send preemie clothes and music for Emma to listen to. One of Tom's aunts had gotten an entire order of Marist missionary nuns to pray for Emma. Another family friend sent a rosary that had been blessed by Pope John Paul. Kerry's old roommate, who was living in China, insisted it was a good thing that Emma was born early, as she arrived just before Chinese New Year and had made it into the Year of the Golden Pig—which meant she would prosper and thrive. Countless people offered to "drop everything" and come help if need be. Everyone sent prayers and good thoughts. Not only was the outpouring of love over whelming for Kerry, but also the optimistic outlook some of these people seemed to have.

How can they say she's going to be fine? Kerry wondered. *These people have no idea what kind of shape Emma's in. How can they possibly suggest that she's absolutely going to pull through? What if she doesn't? What do I do with all the cute little preemie clothes they send me? Send them back? I can just picture it now: I'll be planning her funeral and having to box up a room full of toys, clothes and gifts that she never even got to see. It will make it one hundred times worse.* Kerry's stomach turned. *And what if people start sending me things embroidered with Emma's name?* It was definite; Kerry did not want ANYTHING given to her with Emma's name on it. *This is why I didn't want Tom to send that email from the hospital,* she thought. *This is exactly why.* The whole world had heard about Mighty Emma, now. Kerry realized this. And since there was no turning back, she did her best to be cordial and composed an email suggesting that in lieu of gifts—friends and family might offer up as many prayers as they could manage for Emma. This, of course, was based on something the voice in her head had suggested:

> *"I know you're not convinced that prayers can help,*
> *but if there's any chance they do…*
> *shouldn't you make sure Emma gets as many as she can?"*

It seemed reasonable enough, so Kerry hit *SEND* and turned off the computer.

In the living room, it was Super Bowl Sunday. Thomas wore one of Tom's Giants T-shirts, which hung down past his toes. Donna had driven up from New Jersey a day earlier, and was feeding Ryan his lunch as he sat in the high chair. "You're such a good eater, Ry-Ry," she cooed with each bite. Thomas refused to eat his turkey roll-ups, which Kerry had chosen to ignore. Unfortunately, ignoring things wasn't in Donna's forte. Every second that went by, without him taking so much as a nibble, became an aggravation to her. "Come on now, Thomas! Pick up your food and take a bite," she insisted. His stubbornness swelled with each one of his grandmother's demands. He pushed his plate to the center of the table, then sat back in his chair and waited for a reaction. Of course he got one: "Thomas Sheeran, if you don't eat your lunch, there will be no dessert for you," Donna growled. Thomas thought about it for a second, then delivered his response as concisely as he could: "NO, Grams!"

This was nothing new. Thomas and Donna had been butting heads at mealtime since the terrible twos had reared its ugly head. Most times, Kerry cringed through these types of battles. But today, she could have cared less. Maybe it was the posttraumatic stress she was suffering from. Perhaps it was the pill she had taken. Whatever it was—it felt good not to care for once. Kerry had never taken anti-anxiety drugs before. In fact, she was so unfamiliar with this type of medication, she kept referring to it by the wrong name:

> "*My doctor sent me home on Lithium,*" she had explained to her friend Jen earlier that day.

> "*Lithium?*" Jen had asked. "*Isn't that, like, a battery?*"

> "*Valium, maybe? I don't know what it is,*" Kerry had admitted, "*but I like it.*"

Tom wasn't taking anything, unfortunately for his wife and the NICU nurses. He called them every hour or so for an update on Emma. Being so far away felt terrible. He was still annoyed that Kerry had put the kibosh on his "Boston apartment" idea. At least if they'd gone through with it, he could walk over to the NICU anytime he wanted and see for himself how Emma was. Instead, he was now helpless and distant. The only thing that could connect him to his baby girl was a phone line. So he developed a routine in which he would pace around the house for as long as possible, then dial the 617 phone number, which he'd already committed to memory. Every once in a while he'd say to Kerry: "*You gonna call them for an update?*" Yet her answer was consistently the same. "*You just called them forty-five minutes ago. Let them do their job!*"

The truth was, Kerry didn't want so many updates. It made her nervous each time Tom picked up the phone. No news was good news. Plus, any time Kerry asked questions to the doctors and nurses, their answers always stressed her out more. Medical folks, she had learned, can never say things like: *"Everything will be just fine"*. It isn't in their vocabulary. Instead, they are programmed to speak very indirectly about the future. *"We'll see,"* Kerry noticed was one of their favorites, as was *"Every patient's different."* Some provided her with too many possibilities. Others didn't provide enough. It had become a game of trying to read what the medical folks were saying, and Kerry didn't have the guts to play it at the moment. Emma had been weaned off the vent that morning, and their fingers were crossed all day that she'd be able to hold her own. *"We'll see,"* the nurse had said at 10 a.m. *"If Emma tolerates it, we can keep her on the CPAP. If not, we'll have to re-intubate."* Unfortunately Kerry had asked about the risks of re-intubation, which ran the gamut from tracheal puncture to damaged vocal chords. CPAP, constant positive airway pressure, was a much better option. Kerry hadn't seen it yet, but was told it was a mask that pumped air and oxygen up Emma's nose. CPAP was much less invasive and a step in the right direction as far as her recovery was concerned. No, Kerry really didn't want to call and find out that Emma had had to be re-intubated, because all the Valium in the world wasn't going to remedy a step backwards.

The late-lunch battle forged on, until Kerry took Thomas' plate to the sink and formally dismissed him. Donna was disgusted by her surrender. "No dessert," she announced. On the surface it appeared Donna was speaking to Thomas, but Kerry knew those words were meant for her. Walking through the kitchen on one of his pacing loops, Tom smiled as his little boy jumped into his arms. "When can we get our baby?" Thomas asked with a cheeky grin. Tom pulled his son in tight and rocked him from side to side. He looked to his wife for an answer, so she responded: "We don't know yet, honey. Emma has to grow bigger and stronger. It's going to take a while." Kerry shrugged her shoulders at Tom. Maybe she'd said the right thing, she wasn't sure.

Later that night, Kerry held Ryan in her arms as she sang him his lullaby. Her breasts were so filled with milk, she contemplated trying to nurse him. It seemed like a perfectly acceptable idea, considering her ample supply and non-existent demand. Emma wasn't able to tolerate milk yet. There was too much of a risk considering reflux and her fresh surgical sites. For now she was only being given something called TPN

(Total Parental Nutrition) intravenously. So Emma was out, for now, but Ryan wasn't. And he LOVED to nurse. Ryan was devastated when Kerry had stopped breastfeeding him six months earlier. This, ironically, was the only thing keeping her from opening her shirt as she held him close in her arms. Certainly Ryan would grow reattached to her after his first drink. Unable to bear the thought of having to cut him off a second time, Kerry kissed his head and stood up. *He's such a sweet, happy baby,* she thought. She glanced at Thomas, who was snuggling his Diego blanket, fast asleep. A tear dripped down her face and into Ryan's hair. Kerry kissed the spot where it landed. "Nite-nite, Ry," she said. "Mommy has to go pump." Carefully laying him in his crib, she turned off the lamp. Another tear trickled down her cheek. *Not nursing Ryan is the right decision,* she thought. Neither he nor Thomas needed any additional disappointment in their lives. She'd already given them their fair share that past week.

Donna and Tom were screaming at the television when Kerry walked into the kitchen. She quietly placed her four bottles of milk in the fridge. "Children sleeping!" she scolded, although neither was listening to her. Super Bowl XLII was well underway. The first quarter had just ended and the Giants were up by three points. Kerry had missed an exciting first quarter in which no touchdowns were scored—only a field goal by the Giants, after a record-setting nine minute and fifty-nine second opening drive. But the Patriots now had the ball and things looked to be in their favor. Three seconds into the second quarter, things *were*. The Pats scored with a one-yard touchdown run. "Damn you, Maroney!" Tom yelled. Usually this kind of profanity would have elicited a response from Donna, but she was equally disgusted with New England's running back. "I knew our first quarter lead was too good to be true," Donna cried. The fact was, the Giants were beyond what most folks consider an "underdog" to be.

Far from perfect during their regular season, The Giants had lost six of their sixteen games. Their preposterous hope was to become the first NFC wild card team to ever win a super bowl. Kerry and Tom were juniors at Ramapo High School in 1991 the last time the Giants had won the Super Bowl, and seventeen years was a long time to wait for another championship. Especially for a fan like Tom. Of course the cards were truly stacked against them on this particular Sunday, considering New England had come into this game with an undefeated record. One more win and the Patriots could call it a perfect season.

Five weeks earlier, they'd beaten the Giants 38-35 in the final game of the regular season and *that* taste was still in everyone's mouths. No, the odds were not in New York's favor.

"Who needs a beer?" Tom asked.

"I'll take one," Donna said.

"I'm good," Kerry said. "I just popped a pill." Donna shook her head at the devilish smile her daughter was giving her. "What?" Kerry asked. "Do you want one?" Donna bit her tongue and laughed. She wasn't about to ruin the first smile she'd seen from Kerry in days.

"You know, you can't drive if you're taking those," Donna informed her.

"I can't drive anyway, because of my C-section—so it doesn't even matter!" Kerry said happily. This was a whole other issue she'd had to work out: driving. Dr. Wilkins-Haug had told her not to drive for six weeks, which meant she'd at least wait two. But in the meantime, she *had* to see Emma. Luckily, her friend Renee had stepped in and offered to help. "*I'll freaking drive your ass wherever you want, sweet cheeks,*" Renee had promised the last time they spoke. "*I'm heading in that direction anyway for work, so it's no problem, toots.*" Kerry knew that it wasn't exactly "*on the way*" for Renee to drop her in the city, but she was desperate, so she chose to believe her. "*I'll pick your ass up, too. I'm usually heading home around 5 o'clock,*" she had said. Renee had promised her a ride to see Emma whenever she needed one. This brought Kerry a huge sense of relief. It meant she didn't have to mess with anyone else's schedule or terms. Nothing was worse then being even more helpless and vulnerable then she already was. Nothing. "*I'll be ready and waiting at 5:45 a.m.,*" Kerry had promised.

At halftime, the score remained 7-3 Patriots. "Can you please call?" Tom asked looking at Kerry. "I've called the last seven times."

"You just called them an hour ago," Kerry whined.

"Ker, can you call? Please?" He took a sip of his Stella Artois. "I can't sit here, watch this game and even remotely enjoy it, unless you call them right now. So please, just call."

"Fine," she said. The pill she'd taken had put her in the mood not to argue, so she dialed the phone number and asked to speak to Emma's nurse:

"This is Kate," the nurse said.

"Hi. This is Kerry, Emma's Mom. How is she?" Kerry asked.

"Is your husband making you call now?" Kate laughed. Kerry liked Kate already. "Emma's doing alright, holding her own on CPAP. She has had a couple of spells in the last thirty minutes, but that's probably because I was messing with her. She's all settled for bed, now. I've got her very comfortable," Kate said.

"Bradycardia spells?" Kerry asked.

"Yeah, just a couple of dips, but she came back wicked fast both times without any major problems," Kate explained. She sounded young. Kerry wondered if she were fresh out of nursing school.

"What do you mean messing with her?" Kerry asked.

"Oh, just weighing her and taking her temperature and stuff. I gave her a little sponge bath and cleaned her up. She was still all dirty from her surgery," Kate explained.

"Oh, okay." Kerry responded. "Thank you, Kate."

"No problem. She's such a little muffin. I held her for like fifteen minutes," Kate said. Kerry froze. Suddenly she wasn't so sure about her feelings for this nurse.

"Thanks, Kate," she repeated. "Good night." Her voice cracked a little. She stared at the phone after she hung it up, and did her best to keep the tears from escaping her eyes. Her universe was upside down. Suddenly the voice in Kerry's head snapped:

"Get over it.
You should feel blessed that someone is taking such good care of her."

Kerry shook her head side to side. She hated the foreign feeling that ran through her veins and was creeping up her throat. A scene flashed in her head:

Kerry was holding Emma in the sink, carefully washing her with a white washcloth. The water was warm and bubbly. She gently scrubbed her soft black hair, then pulled it into a sudsy point with her fingers. Emma smiled at her. Her body was perfect. There was no colostomy, no g-tube. Kerry ran the washcloth over her smooth belly. It gleamed. She kissed her daughter's head, then rinsed her clean and wrapped her in a fluffy white towel. Rocking her in her arms, Kerry beamed at her daughter's flawless perfection. It was the first bath she'd ever had and Emma loved it.

Grabbing a towel, Kerry wiped her tears off the phone. She quickly collected herself before reporting back to Tom. "Everything okay?" he asked.

"Yep, she's alright," Kerry quickly answered. "She's all settled in for the night."

"Good," Tom said. He exhaled and sunk back into the coach. The game had become seriously intense. Although the Giants had dominated in runs and possession-time against the Patriots, they remained behind 7-3 at the half. Tom and Donna were excited. They took joy over how *on fire* defensive man Michael Strahan was. "He's all over Brady," Tom squealed. Eli Manning, the Giants' quarterback, was flexing his muscles as well, proving to the world that he was a contender. By the end of the third quarter, the score remained the same. Kerry wasn't sure if the Giants had it in them to score a touchdown. She worried about the ramifications on Tom, should they disappoint him yet again. He was already in a vulnerable state. *Throw the poor guy a bone, will you, God?* Kerry thought. She quickly corrected herself. *God doesn't answer prayers about little girls; he certainly isn't going to divinely intervene in the super bowl. Hail Mary?* she wondered. *Nah, too cliché for a football game. Never mind,* she finished.

The fourth quarter had Kerry, Donna, Tom, and the rest of America on the edge of their seats. With eleven minutes and five seconds remaining, Manning threaded a five-yard pass to David Tyree who caught his first touchdown of the season. The Giants were up 10-7, but not for long. The Patriots came back on a seven-yard pass to Randy Moss on third-and-goal. It was awful. Tom nearly blew the roof off with his guttural bellows. Kerry braced herself. She'd seen that look on Tom before. In 2004, to be exact—the same day the Red Sox beat the Yankees in the ALC championship after being down three games straight. *That* devastation lingered for days. It was further fueled, of course, when the Sox went on to win their first World Series in eighty-six years, the same night Thomas was born. Tom still hadn't recovered from that monstrosity. "Don't get yourself so worked up," Kerry said. "The Pats have had an ideal season. Did you really think the Giants could pull this off?" Tom turned towards Kerry, gripping the arm of the couch. Lasers beamed from his pupils directly into Kerry's eyes.

Donna slugged back the final sip of the one beer she'd been nursing the entire game. Tom reached for a cold chicken wing, but threw it back on the tray. *How can I possibly eat,* he wondered, *when the Giants are down 10-14 with less then a minute left!?* Manning had successfully driven the ball down the field while avoiding a rush by New England. He'd just nailed a thirty-three-yard pass and the ball was at the Patriot's twenty-four-yard line. "It's now or never!" Tom cried. The veins in his neck bulged. His teeth were sweating. Kerry looked around—she was the only one still sitting on the couch. Tom and Donna paced around the living room, looking as if they were ready to vomit. Then, with thirty-five seconds left, Manning threw the most beautiful pass any of them had ever seen. It sailed twenty-five yards into the arms of the Giant's wide receiver, Plaxico Burress.

TOUCHDOWN!

It was over. The Giants won. New England had nothing left. *Everyone* went crazy—the folks at Arizona stadium *and* the father, mother and grandmother at a little grey house in East Greenwich, Rhode Island. The unlikely super-bowl-party trio danced in a circular embrace around the living room, screaming at the tops of their lungs. "They did it!" Tom cried. "I can't believe it!" Donna squealed. The Giants had ruined the Patriot's perfect record: Final score Giants 17, Patriots 14. They defeated the undefeatable. New York's underdog had pulled it off. Kerry wondered if her underdog might be so lucky. "That was incredible!" she screamed.

Apparently *perfection* wasn't all it was cracked up to be.

The next day, Kerry arrived in the NICU at 7:30 a.m. carrying a cooler filled with breast milk. She handed it to Maria, the spunky little grey-haired nurse standing at Emma's bedside, who opened it and gasped: "Whoa, Bessie! That's a lot of milk! We're gonna have to get a separate freezer just for you!" Kerry smiled. *Bring it on,* she thought. *I'm powerless to do anything else here, at least I can make her some milk.* She peered inside the isolette. Emma was hardly visible. Her tiny face was covered with the CPAP contraption. She wore a white hat with special Velcro around it, to keep the massive nosepiece in place. Two plastic prongs went up her nose, forcing her nostrils upwards.

"She looks like Hannibal Lector, doesn't' she?" Maria asked. Kerry raised her eyebrows and shook her head in displeasure. "Does it hurt her?" she asked. Maria explained that while it might not be the most comfortable piece of equipment, she'd be hurting a whole lot more if she weren't able to breath. "ABCs baby, it's all about the ABCs," Maria said. She waited a second for Kerry to shoot her a puzzled look, then went on to explain: "Airway, Breathing, Circulation. That's what it's all about. We have to keep her <u>A</u> airway propped open, so that she can <u>B</u> breathe and <u>C</u> circulate oxygen throughout her body. Didn't you ever learn that in first aid?" Kerry nodded her head *yes*, and took a small step away from Maria, while still maintaining eye-contact.

Maria unscrewed one of Emma's ports and administered some medicine through the syringe. "What are you giving her?" Kerry asked. Maria finished what she was doing, then checked her watch and typed something into the computer. "I'm sorry, Mommy, you asked me what I just gave her? Caffeine," Maria said. Kerry was afraid to pursue this any further, yet needed to know how caffeine had now made it onto Emma's laundry list of medications. *Is she truly her father's daughter?* she wondered. Aware she had successfully confused Kerry yet again, Maria offered up an explanation: "Sometimes these babies need a little Starbucks, a little jolt to get their hearts pumping. We just give 'em a little kick when they need it." She winked at Kerry, who smiled back at her. "I learn something new everyday," Kerry said.

Before sitting down, something taped to Emma's isolette caught her eye. It was a light blue note card etched with a hand written note:

> *"I stopped by to see Emma today and said a prayer. She is beautiful.*
> *-Sr. Carlotta"*

When she looked up, Maria had walked away, leaving her to wonder about Sr. Carlotta. Glancing around, she saw only one other note card taped to a baby's isolette in Bay 6. *Hmmm,* she wondered, *maybe only the Catholic babies get notes?* It didn't seem fair. *Then again, God seems to be working in some very mysterious ways these days, so perhaps it's true.* One of Emma's alarms sounded and Kerry jumped. She looked up at the screen to see that Emma's numbers were dropping. "Maria?" Kerry called. "Maria?" Maria walked back over and opened Emma's isolette. "Come on, chicatita, give me a nice deep breath," she said. Kerry's eyes were glued to the screen. The numbers kept falling. "Come on, baby—don't be a naughty girl in front of Mommy," Maria continued. She was tapping Emma's chest and gently shaking her. Kerry felt her own chest heat up. She was confused. *Is this a bad spell? Or does Maria's playful banter mean it's nothing to worry about?* Emma's heart rate was now in the forties, her respiratory rate was in the thirties, her oxygen hung in the sixties.

Maria reached in with both hands and turned Emma on her side. Kerry looked at Maria, helplessly. "Tell your baby to take a nice deep breath, Mommy," Maria said. The alarms were louder and more intense then ever. Stress-induced hives popped up all over Kerry's face and chest. She reached in and held Emma's leg. "Breathe, Emma. Come on Emma, take a breath!" Kerry insisted. "Breathe, Emma. Come on, peewee. Come on, baby." Her fingers squeezed her daughter with each demand. Suddenly, the alarms became silent. Kerry looked at the screen. All the numbers were going up. She looked at Emma. Her skin was regaining its vibrancy, like something out of a cartoon. Maria carefully wrapped her in a blanket and shut the top of the isolette. She shook her head. "Show off," Maria declared. "She just did that to get your attention, Mommy." Kerry scrunched up her face:

"I...I don't get it. Was that a bad one? It seemed like a bad one."

"Nah," Maria replied. "That wasn't too bad. Trust me, you'll know if it's a bad one." Kerry looked to the ceiling and exhaled. That was as far as she was willing to take their conversation. Maria made another note in the computer, then walked around the corner and quietly spoke to one of the neonatologists. Kerry's hands made their way out of Emma's bed and up to her own neck and chest as she began to scratch her hives uncontrollably. She scratched and scratched until an hour passed. Until she was certain her daughter was stable. Until she realized there was blood underneath her fingernails.

Music played in the next bay over. Kerry had become somewhat entranced in the song, perhaps because it was set to *repeat*. It only took her forty-five minutes or so to figure that out. The song was one she'd heard on the radio: *"Bubbly"*, by Colbie Caillat. The verses had dug themselves into her head.

I've been awake for a while now
You've got me feelin like a child now

Cause every time I see your bubbly face
I get the tingles in a silly place

It starts in my toes
And I crinkle my nose
Where ever it goes I always know
That you make me smile
Please stay for a while now
Just take your time
Where ever you go

At first, she enjoyed the distraction. The music wasn't blaring, just softly playing somewhere amidst all the bells and alarms. But after ninety minutes passed, and Colbie was still singing the same song, Kerry couldn't help but to grow slightly irritated. She checked her watch. It was 11:45 a.m., so she reached for her pumping supplies and blew Emma a kiss. "I'll be back after lunch, honey. Be a good girl while I'm gone, please," Kerry whispered.

She turned to walk out and noticed the two sisters were sitting at tiny Matthew's bedside. They both glanced at her, so Kerry quickly looked down and turned in the opposite direction. *How long have they been there?* she wondered. The NICU's general lack of privacy had become commonplace, and Kerry began to wonder things she had no business wondering: *Where's the father? Why haven't I seen him yet?* Of course there was always the possibility he'd been there when she wasn't. And since she had made the conscious choice to commute back and forth from Rhode Island, as opposed to holding vigil twenty-four/seven in the NICU, Kerry had no business being curious about anyone else's whereabouts. After all, nobody really knew what her situation was either. For all she knew, all the doctors, nurses and parents could be wondering how a mother could leave her daughter in the intensive care unit of a hospital an hour and fifteen minutes from her house. No, Kerry had no business wondering where this boy's father was, because he could very well be wondering the same thing about her.

After pumping, Kerry wandered downstairs into the cafeteria. Much to her pleasure, the hospital issued vouchers for all of her meals. This allowed Kerry to eat for free, based on the simple fact that she was a breast-feeding mother. It felt strange to identify herself that way, considering Emma hadn't had a drop of her milk, but she wasn't going to argue.

Kerry's breasts had developed a very intimate relationship with her pump. They were seeing each other about four times a day and had grown accustomed to one another's signals. With the boys, all she had to do was hear them cry and her milk would come rushing in. Not so with Emma. It only took the flick of a switch to get things flowing—and *boy*, did it flow. Each tug from the pump generated a powerful spray of milk. And Kerry wasn't going to admit this to anyone, but every now and then it sounded like her pump was talking to her. Sometimes in the morning she'd hear: *"MAKE MILK, MAKE MILK, MAKE MILK, MAKE MILK."* Once in a while—usually in the hospital pumping room—it would assert: *"LET'S GO, LET'S GO, LET'S GO, LET'S GO."* The only time it said the same thing, consistently, was when she'd set her alarm to pump at 3 a.m. While everyone else in the house lay fast asleep, Kerry would be curled up in her bathroom—captivated by the beautiful song her pump would always sing: *"EM-MA, EM-MA, EM-MA, EM-MA."*

"Hi, I'm Cheryl."

Kerry's daydream was interrupted in front of the deli section of the cafeteria. "You're Emma's mom, right? Matthew and Emma have the same birthday," Cheryl said. Kerry jumped when she realized the voice she was hearing matched the face of one of the "sisters". Cheryl's expression was kind and genuine. Her smile melted the ice she'd just broken. Kerry gave in and returned a smile.

"I'm Kerry," she said. "I noticed that, too…about their birthdays."

"January 27th, a day we'll never forget," Cheryl said. Her sister was standing next to her, not speaking, yet nodding her head with every word.

"Hard to believe it was only a week ago," Kerry noted, while scratching her neck. "Are you Matthew's mom?"

"Well, Liz gave birth to Matthew, but we're both his moms," Cheryl explained. Luckily the light bulb over Kerry's head wasn't beaming in her new friends' faces.

"Is Matthew your only child?" Kerry asked. The couple exchanged an indefinite glance, then returned their eyes to her.

"We have a daughter, Isabel, she's fifteen months. How about you?" Cheryl asked.

"I have two boys—one's three and the other's nineteen months." Kerry said. "We live in Rhode Island," she added. Kerry looked ahead, she was the next person in line to order her sandwich. The woman behind the counter didn't seem at all interested in waiting for her to finish up her conversation, so she reached her hands out to Cheryl and Liz and squeezed theirs. "Thank you for saying hello," she said, "It was nice to finally meet you both." Liz and Cheryl reciprocated the sentiment and vowed to make eye contact the next time they were sitting within three feet of Kerry, as long as she promised to do the same. Kerry laughed and waved goodbye. As she ordered her chicken salad wrap from the crabby lady behind the counter in the cold cafeteria, she felt warm.

The rest of the day was fairly uneventful. Kerry buried her face in trashy magazines all afternoon, allowing for less conversation with Maria. Emma behaved, for the most part. She was more awake then she'd been the past week and was clearly agitated by the CPAP. It was hard to watch her little body wriggle around. Her scrawny arms swatted at her face, attempting to free herself of the nosepiece. Kerry had to fight off every motherly urge to comfort her baby. She wanted to rip the damn contraption off of her, but she couldn't. The only solace she could offer was in song and touch, so any time Emma whimpered, Kerry cupped her head and sang. By 2:30 p.m. she had composed a lullaby:

> *Peewee Sheeran, she's my peewee girl*
> *Littlest peewee in the whole wide world*
> *Sweetest peewee in the whole wide world*
> *Most delicate peewee, my peewee girl.*
>
> *Mighty-Emma, she's my mighty girl*
> *Mightiest baby in the whole wide world*
> *Strongest baby in the whole wide world*
> *Toughest baby, my baby girl.*
>
> *Sissy sassafras, my sassy girl*
> *Sassiest baby in the whole wide world*
> *My sissy sassy, you're my sassy girl*
> *You're my sissy sassafras, my sassy girl.*

Close your eyes, Emma, and go to sleep
Hug me tight and have sweet dreams of me
Hugging you tight, and kissing you goodnight
You're my baby Emma—now go to sleep.

It wasn't the best lullaby ever written, but Emma seemed to like it. Even better, the more Kerry sang it, the less she heard the Colbie Caillat song. By 3 p.m., Kerry had sung herself to sleep. When she awoke thirty minutes later, Tom was standing next to her in a blue Giants baseball hat, placing a picture of Eli Manning on top of Emma's isolette. Three hot cups of Starbucks coffee sat on the nurse's stand, letting off steam. Maria stood with her arms folded, glaring in disgust and refusing Tom's request to borrow medical tape. "I don't care how much coffee you bring me," Maria warned, "there's no way I'm helping you hang that picture of a rat on this poor child's isolette." The whole scene confused Kerry, but she assumed one of the coffees was for her, so she reached over and indulged.

Tom disappeared for a minute, then returned with ten to fifteen pieces of scotch tape stuck to his hand. Maria shot him a dirty look, but he held his tongue. There was no reason to explain how he'd bribed the receptionist with Lifesaver mints in exchange for some adhesive. After all, he'd taken the time to carefully cut the Super Bowl MVP's glorious image out of the New York Post that morning, he damn well was gonna hang it. Tom had explained his intentions to both the boys, who were equally excited to decorate their sister's crib with some valentine hearts. No, he wasn't about to let a little nurse with hot pink sneakers and major attitude get in their way. A smile snuck across his face as he created his masterpiece: Eli holding the Vince Lombardi trophy, surrounded by Ryan and Thomas' hearts. "You're going to scare her with that dirty rat looking in on her," Maria warned. "Plus, while you were getting your precious tape, she told me she's a Tom Brady fan."

Two older male doctors walked past Emma's station and caught a glimpse of the shrine. Their nauseated expressions formed in unison and shot directly into Tom and Kerry's faces. The same happened three minutes later, when a nurse offered to verify Emma's medication for Maria. There was no playfulness in her gasp—the nurse was visibly sickened. "I'm not sure this was a good idea, honey," Kerry said. "Don't we want everyone on our side here?" Tom assured his wife that it was absolutely necessary. "If mature adults working in a children's hospital can't separate their disappointment from Emma's care, then we're in the wrong place!" he explained. Kerry shook her head in agreement, although the sour puss on Maria's face had her believing otherwise.

A short, stocky nurse pushed a rocking chair past them with all her might. They watched as she delivered it to a mother in Bay 2. Kerry had seen this mother in the break room a couple of times. She looked exhausted. The nurse helped the mother get settled in the chair, tucking pillows all around her. The mother was wearing a men's flannel shirt and stretch pants. Her hair was long and brown. "CAITLIN" was written in pink on a sign that hung from the baby's crib. Kerry watched as the nurse lifted the baby from the crib and carefully placed her in the mother's arms. The mother fed Caitlin with a tiny bottle. Kerry turned towards Maria. "When can I hold Emma?" she asked. Tom looked at her like she was dreaming, but Kerry held her eyes on Maria.

"How long ago was her surgery?" Maria asked, clicking though the charts on her computer.

"Over a week ago," Kerry quickly answered. "How long does a mother usually have to wait?"

"That totally depends on the patient," Maria said. "But given she's had a pretty decent day, I don't see why you couldn't try. Let me double check with the doctor." Kerry's displeasure with Maria was slowly starting to disappear. She and Tom smiled and looked on anxiously as Emma's nurse scurried towards the doctors' station. The excitement Kerry was feeling prompted her to tell Tom all about her encounter with Liz and Cheryl in the cafeteria, and how she'd solved the "Mystery of the Missing Father." Her smile grew brighter as she recalled their vow *"to acknowledge one another"*, then beamed when Maria came around the corner pushing a rocking chair. "You're lucky, Mommy," Maria said. "This is the last one on the whole floor."

Tom watched with a twinge of envy as Kerry took her seat. His jealousy didn't stop him from eagerly reaching in and helping Maria corral all the tubes and wires attached to Emma. When they realized it was too much for two people to handle, they called for the assistance of another nurse. "You're lucky she's cute," the second nurse explained to Kerry, "cause I'm ready to knock that ugly hat off your husband's head." The threat went in one ear and out the other, for this was the moment Kerry had longed for, ever since she'd heard Emma's faint cry in the delivery room. The moment she wasn't sure she'd ever be granted. This was something she'd pictured every hour of every day for the past seven days and here it was, about to happen.

Exposing her torn-up red chest, Kerry opened her shirt. Then Maria cautiously lowered her three-pound daughter and all ten pounds of her accompaniments onto her heart. After carefully fastening two buttons on her shirt, Kerry wrapped her arms around Emma. Tom covered them with a warm blanket. Everything else in the room—all the noises and lights and distractions faded away. All that was left was a mother holding her child. Maria pulled the privacy curtains and paradise rose up all around them. The touch of Emma's skin was solace to her mother's damaged nerves. The rhythm of Kerry's heart cradled Emma into a peaceful slumber. Tom kissed both their heads. As Kerry slowly rocked back and forth, the voice spoke to her:

"Nobody should have to wait to feel this. It's the most beautiful feeling in the world. Nobody should ever have to wait."

Kerry had to agree.

An hour later, Tom woefully reminded his wife that Renee was due to pick her up within the half hour. The team reassembled to separate the mother/daughter pair. Maria made sure each of Emma's IVs had enough slack before quietly closing the top of her isolette. Kerry finally scratched her nose, which had been itching for the last forty-five minutes. She wiped the tears that had already dried on her cheeks. Reaching down for her magazines, she began packing her bag. Tom handed her a water bottle, then tapped her affectionately on the rear. As Kerry stuffed it into the side pocket, a familiar sound began to ring in her ears. Everyone's eyes darted to the monitor and were met with falling numbers, again. Only this time they were falling lower then before, and staying low.

Maria reached in, as she did earlier, and tapped Emma on the head. She repositioned her to her other side, yet there was no change. "Come on, Emma. Come back!" Maria demanded. But she wasn't coming back. Emma's numbers continued to fall as she turned greyish-blue. "Why isn't she coming back?" Tom screamed. Kerry stood frozen, convinced that this was going to end exactly as it had that morning—with Maria blowing it off. She pictured Maria making fun of Tom for being such a worrywart and blaming the whole thing on the Eli Manning picture. This would all fix itself. They just had to wait another couple of seconds and Emma's airway would open up. She'd start breathing again and her little heart would catch up and make sure all the oxygen was circulating throughout her bloodstream. It was as simple as ABC. "COME ON EMMA!" Tom screamed.

The alarms blared at maximum as two other nurses appeared at Emma's bedside. It had been close to two minutes at this point and Kerry's denial was dwindling. "PLEASE GOD!" Kerry begged. Her hands were on her head, tugging at her hair. "OH, MY GOD, PLEASE!" she screamed. Maria ran over and pressed the little yellow button behind Emma's bed, which read *CODE*. Tom saw this, and lost the last drop of color remaining on his face. A team of doctors and respiratory therapists scampered to the scene, asking Tom and Kerry to step back while they worked on Emma.

"Bag her!" a balding doctor in his early thirties yelled out. The CPAP contraption was pulled off and a respiratory therapist covered Emma's tiny face with an oxygen bag. Everyone watched as the young man squeezed the bag ferociously, delivering as much air as he could into Emma's lungs. The breathing machines were now obsolete; all that was left was a man and their baby. Kerry and Tom were paralyzed. They wanted to grab Emma and blow breaths into her lungs. They wanted to hold her and pat her on the back and demand that she breathe. But instead, they stood seven feet away, unable to move, watching as their flesh and blood fought for her life. "PLEASE GOD!" Kerry screamed.

"We got her!" the balding doctor announced. All eyes were on the monitor, which showed three sets of climbing numbers. Once Emma's oxygen reached the nineties, her pink complexion returned, though much paler then it had been before her spell. Kerry and Tom stood like statues, unable to speak. When she was stabilized, the respiratory therapist took the bag off Emma's face and replaced it with the CPAP. Her little chest rose and fell in an effort to catch up on all the breathing it had missed. The man turned up all the settings on her machine, and instructed Maria to keep them as such for a while. One by one, all the people who had run to Emma's aid dwindled away. Soon only Tom, Kerry and Maria were left. Maria hugged Kerry, then reached for Tom as well. "*That* was a bad one," she said.

Refusing to leave when Renee arrived, it took two neonatologists and three nurses to convince Kerry that Emma was again stable. "If worst comes to worst, we'll re-intubate," one of the doctors explained. And although that didn't sound like music to her ears, at least it was a plan. Tom carefully reminded Kerry of her importance to the boys, and how this was one of those times in parenting where they needed to divide and conquer. He agreed to spend the night at the hospital. This was a no-brainer for Tom. The hospital provided ICU parents with bedrooms at no cost—the only price one had to pay was to have a child hanging onto his or her life. Before Kerry left, she sang Emma her lullaby and wept through every verse. A man pushed an ultrasound machine around the corner and stopped at Emma's station, but Maria shooed him away. "We have to reschedule her brain scan for tomorrow," she said. "Emma is not up for being messed with right now." The man kindly agreed and turned the machine around. Tom took his post at her bedside and kissed his wife goodbye. On the lonely elevator ride down, Kerry's head swam: *What was that? Just reminding me how quickly you can take her away? I don't understand you at all. You're torturing me. I thought you loved me.*

"How's the little peanut doing today?" Renee asked as Kerry climbed into the car.

"Don't ask," Kerry replied.

"Oh, man. I'm sorry, Ker. I don't know how you're even able to take any of this. I'd be a mess," Renee said.

"I am a mess," she said. "She almost...." Kerry stopped herself. "Emma had a really hard afternoon."

"What are they saying? When will she be able to come home?" Renee asked.

"Come home?" Kerry laughed. It was suddenly obvious Renee had no idea about Emma's current state. "Coming home isn't even in our foresight. She has to make it through the night. And when morning comes, she has to make it through tomorrow. And maybe, if she does okay, they can try feeding her soon." It was as if Kerry were admitting it to herself. She went on to explain all the pitfalls of Emma's terribly complicated body mixed with prematurity. Kerry talked for sixty minutes straight about Emma's bladder, kidneys and bowels. She baffled Renee with tales of bradycardia spells, and brain scans. She painted a picture of just how messed up Emma's esophagus was. "She has to survive the next couple months before they can even do the surgery to connect her. And that's just the beginning!" Kerry explained. Renee was both stunned and confused by everything she was hearing.

"Did your doctor put you on any drugs? Cause I'd need some major drugs if I were you," Renee admitted.

"Nothing major!" Kerry laughed. "That's the craziest part... I still have two other babies to take care of. Kinda have to be lucid for that."

When Kerry arrived home, Donna was changing Ryan's diaper and getting the boys ready for bed. She looked spent, so Kerry happily took over. Thomas cried and pulled on her leg as she zippered Ryan's jammies. "I wanna treat!" he whined. He carried on as she brushed Ryan's teeth. "He hasn't been like this all day. This only started the minute you walked in the door," Donna said. "I WANNA TREAT!" Thomas screamed. Donna explained with annoyance that Thomas had refused to finish his dinner, therefore forfeiting dessert. He pulled on Kerry's shirt and bared his giant baby blues: "Mommy, pwease? I wanna treat," Thomas whimpered. Kerry looked to her mother for a smidge of mercy, but there was none to be found. Donna's lips were pursed and Kerry knew what that meant. "Say goodnight to Grams," Kerry said. Ryan merrily obliged, but Thomas refused to acknowledge she was even in the room. Grabbing his arm, Kerry waved it back and forth. "Goodnight, Grams," she said in her best three-year-old voice.

Disappearing downstairs, Donna retreated into the den to catch up on her emails. When she thought it was safe, Kerry scurried down and snuck into the kitchen. She grabbed an Oreo from the cabinet, then bolted back to the boys' room. "Don't let Ryan see you eating this," she said, handing the cookie to Thomas. His face lit up and Thomas hugged his mom, just as she'd hoped he would. Watching him lick all the cream from the middle, Kerry answered his questions about *where* she'd been and *why* he couldn't go with her. She dusted all the crumbs on to the floor and agreed to not make him brush his teeth again. Then she kissed him twenty to thirty times as she sang him his lullaby. She did the same to Ryan. "I'm so happy I got home before you went to sleep," Kerry said as she turned off their light. "I love you guys so much."

Before heading downstairs, she noticed the light was on in the nursery. It was hard to resist sitting in the glider, so she rocked back and forth for a few minutes with her eyes locked on the empty crib.

Back downstairs, Donna heated up their dinner in the kitchen. "One of your friends dropped this off. Kim, I think? Short blond hair? Should I make a plate for Tom?" Donna asked. Kerry looked in the pan. There was enough lemony chicken and rice to feed an army. "No, he's staying at the hospital tonight," she said. Kerry went on to describe the day's events, despite her exhaustion and failing ability to converse. Donna's incessant questions didn't help: "How long was she out? Why did they bag her? Is there permanent damage?" When Kerry couldn't take it anymore, she pushed her plate to the center of the table and collapsed into a heap. "I don't know, Mom! I don't know why any of this is happening. If God wanted to take Emma, I don't know why he didn't just take her before she was even born! It's like she's being dragged through the mud, knocked down every time she tries to get up," she cried. Kerry's hives popped out more and more with each word. "If he's just going to take her, then what is the point of all of this?"

Donna stood up and walked around the table. She was blotchy and teary as well. "I keep asking the same question," she said, wiping her daughter's cheek with her balled-up napkin. "And the only thing I can come up with," she continued, "is: so that you can know her."

"What do you mean?" Kerry asked.

"I mean, maybe God's giving you this time with her, so that you can hold her and kiss her and name her. So that, *if* she dies—you can say that you knew her. Some people don't even get that chance," Donna said. Kerry tore the balled-up napkin in half, and gave a square to Donna. The two of them were dripping with tears and boogers, and blowing their wet noses in unison. "It's the only thing that makes any sense to me," Donna said. Kerry pondered it for a couple minutes. It sounded nice. Much nicer then what she had been thinking. But Kerry wasn't going to fall for that. Changing her perspective wasn't going to change how she felt about *Him.* Maybe," Kerry said, "maybe that's it."

Kerry was feeding Ryan his last bite of oatmeal when Tom called at 8:30 a.m. the next morning. He was happy to share that Emma's night was "uneventful", minus the three minor spells she had between 1-3 a.m. He was preparing to leave the hospital and head to his office. Work had piled up during the last ten days, and if he were going to seal the deal in

Singapore, he was going to have to lock himself in his office for the next twelve hours. Tom's fingers combed through the fuzzy beard that had grown in thick on his face. "Who is her nurse today?" Kerry asked. Tom told her that a young Asian woman was taking care of Emma. He stroked his beard. "Do you think, honey, that maybe, tonight...we could...you know...." Tom began.

"What's her name?" Kerry interrupted.

"Her name's Jessica, I think. I've never seen her before. Anyway, babe...can we have sex tonight? Please?" Tom asked. Kerry's anxiety heated up. The thought of Emma being in the hands of someone whom she had never met made her sick. "Please, babe, can't you work from the hospital? Just until noon?" she begged.

"I've got a conference call at eleven-thirty, and I *have* to do it from the office," Tom explained.

"But what if it happens again?" Kerry asked. The scene of Emma's code played out in her mind, as it had been doing all night long. Kerry closed her weary eyes, then squeezed them tight, but it didn't help. It still played back—repeatedly. It pained her to know that she wasn't going to be able to see Emma until the next morning. "I don't wanna leave her, Ker, but I don't really have a choice," Tom said.

He didn't want to have this argument just then. If Tom could've lived by Emma's side twenty-four hours a day, he would've. But the rest of the world wasn't standing still, even if Kerry was. It felt like his life was twice as complicated at the moment. Seventy-five percent of the people he worked with didn't even know Emma existed. And frankly, Tom wasn't sure they'd even care if they did. He could only assume that when a billion dollar corporation wants to build a multi-million dollar command center, they're more concerned with budgets and deadlines then they are with little babies in the hospital. Not to say Tom was working with cruel people, because he wasn't. It just wasn't the center of *their* world. Tom knew this and chose not to share Emma's struggles with most of his clients. He needed to keep business separate from personal. Not only was it professional, it helped him keep from completely falling apart. If Merrill Lynch wanted revised drawing and a new proposal in their hands by 9 a.m. Wednesday morning, Tom was going to have his work cut out for him all day, and he knew it. "If it makes you feel any better, I can drive back up here late tonight," Tom offered.

Kerry took a few seconds to think, before concluding that wasn't a good plan. Tom sounded exhausted. And if she were going arrive first thing Wednesday morning, there was no point for him to risk falling asleep at the wheel, just to be there eight hours ahead of her. "No," Kerry said, "don't do that. I guess we're going to have to get used to this, at least until I can drive."

She had finished feeding Ryan, and was now emptying the dishwasher. Thomas ran up behind her as she was putting a stack of plates on the top shelf and accidentally knocked into her side. All the plates came crashing down. Half shattered on the counter, the rest scattered across the floor like confetti. "Thomas!" Kerry yelled. Tom heard the ruckus in the background. "What was that?" he asked. Thomas began to hysterically cry as Kerry ordered him out of the room.

"Ker, what happened?" Tom asked.

"Nothing," she snapped, "everything's fine." Ryan, startled from all the noise, was crying too.

"So, Ker...about tonight...." Tom said.

"NO! I couldn't even if I wanted to...and I don't!" Kerry screamed. She hung up the phone, not knowing which direction to head in first. The room was a disaster area. "Oh my gosh!" Donna screamed from the stairway. "What happened? Is someone hurt?"

"Just a huge mess, that's all," Kerry said. She stood, dumbfounded, staring at her kitchen atrocity. Tying her long blue robe, Donna raced to the broom closet and pulled out all the dustpans and brushes she could find. Ryan's whimpers were turning into shrills, and Thomas' shrills were now ear-piercing. Kerry thought about Jessica, the nurse who was taking care of her baby. She wondered if she knew just how delicate Emma was, or how she liked to be sung to. Kerry wondered if Jessica would know that she needed to tap Emma on the head when she had a spell...or to press the code button if she wasn't recovering...or to turn her on her side if she wasn't breathing well. Kerry thought about the brain scan and wondered how soon Jessica would call her if something were wrong with Emma. She wondered if she could trust a woman she'd never met to keep her baby alive while she was cleaning up broken dishes in Rhode Island. Slumping down on the floor in a heap, she pressed the phone to her forehead and began to cry. Donna caught wind of her sniffling amongst the chaos and bent down to check on her. "Did you get hurt?" Donna asked.

"It's all too much," Kerry cried.

"It's a huge mess, but it's okay. They're just plates. We can clean this up," Donna said.

"Not the plates, Mom," Kerry said.

"Did something happen with Emma over night?" Donna asked. Her morning-eyes were riddled with panic. Both boys were still wailing.

"No, she had an okay night. It's just...Tom's going to his office...a nurse I've never met is taking care of her...she's having a brain scan today and I'm not even going to be there if something's wrong," Kerry explained. Her voice was getting higher and more agitated. "And I'm supposed to take the boys to story time at the library and wait for someone to tell me if my daughter's brain is bleeding...or if she stopped breathing...or if someday she might be able to swallow food...or pee and poop...wait and see if she's going to have any quality of life whatsoever? I'm just supposed to go about my day and wait for somebody to tell me this! HOW AM I SUPPOSED TO DO THIS?" Kerry cried.

"You just DO IT!" Donna answered. "And, you ARE doing it," she insisted.

"Not very well," Kerry said. Her eyes scanned the kitchen. Thomas stood in the corner, mewling. Ryan, too, had worked himself down to a whimper. Chards of red and white ceramic plates covered a twelve-foot radius.

"You're functioning," Donna said. "You're waking up and caring for your boys and you've got Emma in the best place for her right now." Donna tucked Kerry's hair behind her ears, and tipped her chin up so that they were looking eye to eye. "You're not curled up in a ball, somewhere," Donna continued. "You're functioning. That's all you can expect from yourself right now." Kerry kept her eyes locked on her mom's to make sure she was speaking the truth. *If all I have to do is just function, then it seems possible* she thought. In fact, the lower Kerry set expectations for herself, the better it made her feel. Suddenly the old adage "one day at a time" made total sense. If Bonnie Franklin could do it, then so could Kerry. And to her knowledge, neither of Bonnie's daughters was born prematurely with esophageal and intestinal atresia. Already, Kerry felt stronger. She remembered what she'd read in the NICU binder: *"Expect it to be a roller-coaster ride for your child. Some days are good. Some are not."* Yesterday was not a good day. That didn't mean that today wasn't going to be. And since it was written in the parent's handbook, she assumed that most likely this had been the case for some other babies who'd faced struggles, before Emma. Perhaps other parents had felt exactly as she was feeling.

"Okay," Kerry said.

"Okay," Donna agreed.

Her mother swept up the plates while Kerry scooped up both boys. For now, all she could do was stop them from crying. *One minute at a time is more like it,* Kerry thought. Although, that didn't sound as good when she sang it in her head.

Chapter 9

ALL PART OF HIS PLAN?

THE KILLERS BLARED in Tom's ears. It was hard to resist screaming along with the soulful chorus of *"All These Things That I've Done"*, but Tom jammed-out differently when he was running. Instead of vocalizing *every* word, he would lip-synch the first half of a verse, then softly mumble the second half out loud. It was a little strange, but rather then worry about who might be pointing and laughing, Tom chose to believe that most normal people carried on this way, especially during a run. In his mind, the rest of the world was moving to the same beat that played in his ears. He'd decided to put his earphones in at Mile 9. It seemed like a fair enough reward. Kerry's letter was holding his interest and all, but a little musical entertainment went a long way. Thinking back, Tom remembered sitting in front of his computer for two days straight, carefully downloading music onto his iPod. He had created five different categories:

1: Fartlek
2: Forrest Gump
3: Deep
4: Long
5: Mixed

Fartlek, which translates to "speed play" in Swedish, were some of Tom's best training runs. Basically, a fartlek run meant running at an unstructured pace. Light jogging, regular running, and sprinting. The idea is to exercise both one's aerobic and anaerobic systems. Tom's goal during these types of runs was to get his heart working anywhere from sixty to eighty percent of it's maximum rate. His Children's Hospital trainers had suggested these runs to the marathon team early on, and

Tom had stuck close to their advice. So when it came to choosing this genre of music, Tom's choices were equally unstructured. Alicia Keyes might kick of the first couple of miles with a light jog, but as soon as the Black Eyed Peas came on, he would explode into a full on sprint. It was easy this way, turning his playlist into his own personal trainer. The key was to stay true to the process. He knew which songs he'd chosen, precisely, to switch his gears. There was no talking himself into thinking "Boom Boom Pow" meant: *slow it down, Tom.*

Forrest Gump was a medley reserved for the days when Tom felt so pumped, he could almost go on forever. It paid tribute to a certain Steven Spielberg flick he'd seen about eighty times. *Run, Tom, Run!* trickled through his head every time this glorious state over came him. Know as "Runner's High", this endorphin rush is chemically produced by the hypothalamus and pituitary glands in humans. In simple terms, it's a great sensation that makes athletes feel as though they could run forever. Given the aforementioned term, Tom felt it only apropos to fill this genre with several songs from The Grateful Dead, The Doors, Pink Floyd and Led Zeppelin. The Forrest Gump category not only made reference to a guy who overcame all odds and ran clear across the country, it's euphoric attributes also reminded Tom of his countless, party-packed, sinful college nights.

Deep was a collection of songs that evoked special sentiments from Tom. When he was feeling sad, stressed or just plain low, running was a form of therapy for him. Sometimes a good cry was all he needed to help him claw his way to the surface of whatever was weighing him down. These kinds of runs were usually done either very early in the morning or after the sun went down. When Tom was in a mood like this, he wasn't interested in socializing with anyone, aside from the occasional deer or turkey. Sometimes he had to dig deep to rid himself of whatever was bothering him. And the songs he chose to listen to helped him accomplish this. Lots of Springsteen, Paul Simon and U2 made up this category. If The Boss were crooning "Living Proof" at 5 a.m. on a Thursday morning, guaranteed there wasn't a dry eye on the streets of East Greenwich, Rhode Island.

Long referred to the category of songs he set aside for the one day a week when Tom achieved his most mileage: his long runs. Over the course of nine months of intensive training, he had slowly built up to twenty-two miles in one shot. Adding a mile or two with each week, he reserved two to three and a half hours (usually on a Saturday or Sunday) to accomplish this goal. Given how long and far he was running, he wanted his music to engage him like a novel. Country music was always good for telling a story. Coldplay's lyrics were unmatchable, most of their albums were included in this genre. The Police and Duran Duran instantly brought him back to his childhood, transporting Tom directly into his parents' basement where he and his siblings would jam out to albums on their Emerson record player. It was amazing how lost he could get in his own head because of one single song. That was the whole idea.

Mixed spoke for itself. It included all of the above, and then some. Lots of songs from that particular point in time filled this spot. John Mayer's "Say" was in there, as was Leona Lewis' "Bleeding Love." Rhianna belted hits like "Disturbia" and "Take a Bow," while Mary J Blige insisted she was "Just Fine." When Tom wasn't in the mood to define himself in any way he put on Mixed. Sometimes it was nice not to think about anything at all. Sometimes Tom felt the need to just throw on his sneakers and go out for a run. Once in a while, it was okay to run without rules. Without goals. Sometimes he might want to change his mind and quit halfway through, or maybe tack on an extra five miles, or head for the trails if he were feeling up to it. Queen's "Bohemian Rhapsody" would very often be echoing Tom's thoughts when he just had to get out…just had to get right out of wherever he happened to be at the moment. Mixed displayed an element of freedom for Tom—the reason he fell in love with running in the first place: because it was something he could do anytime, anywhere for however long he wished. And given all the shackles that were constantly pulling him back, Tom found comfort knowing he could break free whenever he had to, as long as he had his sneakers with him.

At the end of Mile 9, Tom had a pleasant view of Fiske Pond on his right, followed by a quaint traipse through the Natick Historical District. Each Victorian he passed reminded him of Kerry's wish to someday own a house with a *"huge wrap-around porch"*. So far it hadn't worked out that way, given their current residence in a 1960s Colonial, but she never complained. The center of town was home to some decent crowds of spectators. On his right, a big green gazebo spilled with kids, adults, music and fun. This was not the place for Tom to slow it down, or even walk, temporarily. Fans would have had him back at his original pace in a hot second, should he have even tried. The kids, alone, were thundery in their enthusiasm. Tom partook in as many high-fives as he could handle, before the sheer impact had him fighting just to stay on track.

Miles 10 and 11 continued through the busy town center. Tom had read that the Marathon's race director coordinates a "Plan B" with several towns throughout the route, in case of any emergencies. Natick was one of these towns. Should something bad happen—a terrorist's bomb; a gas leak; an earthquake—officials could re-route the runners. A lot of planning went into the safety of both the runners and the spectators. Police and firefighters were staggered strategically throughout the route so that they could react, should such an occasion arise. After passing a medical tent, Tom pondered the amount of planning it must have taken to pull off such a huge race. Community after community coming together in good spirit to allow him and all the other participants to take over their streets for the day. It gave him such a powerful feeling to be a part of something so big. Tom couldn't wait to share this feeling with his father. He wondered if Kerry would understand when he told her about it.

Towards the end of Mile 11, the crowds had thinned out a bit. Yet a wave of excitement seemed to be coming towards Tom and he couldn't, for the life of him, figure out what all the hubbub was about. That is, until he found himself running next to the most famous father/son pair to ever hit the marathon circuit: Team Hoyt. Tom was well aware just how special it was to be running next to this inspirational twosome.

Dick was a sixty-seven-year-old retired lieutenant colonel (of thirty-seven years) from the Air National Guard. He was nearing his one thousandth race, which included 10ks, marathons, dualthlons and triathlons. Dick was an Ironman six times over. In 1992, he even went so far as to bike and run across the United States. Dick Hoyt was an impressive athlete, to say the least.

His son, Rick, a graduate of Boston University, was equally impressive, being that he joined his father on every single one of these races. Born in 1962, he developed cerebral palsy and was diagnosed as a spastic quadriplegic, a result of oxygen deprivation to his brain at the time of birth. His mother, Judy, and Dick were encouraged to institutionalize him, given what doctors seemed to think was a poor quality of life. Luckily for Rick, his parents had other plans. Through perseverance and dedication, they fought to give him all that life had to offer. They recognized that regardless of his inability to walk or speak, Rick had a voice. Interactive computers gave him the ability to communicate— which is why his father was able to hear him in 1977, when he asked if they could run a five-mile benefit together. When Dick pushed Rick in his wheelchair across that first finish line, Team Hoyt was born.

As Tom ran past this dynamic duo, a lump swelled in his throat. In his marathon research, he'd read countless testimonials from parents, fellow handicapped people, even presidents of the United States paying tribute to Team Hoyt's strength, courage and ability to inspire. Dick's arms were chiseled with muscles that had pushed his son up thousands of hills and broken through hundreds of barriers. His face showed unpretentious determination, without a trace of the attitude Tom might have expected to see due to the attention he and his son received. Rick, too, appearing humbled by the cheers, outstretched his arm in an effort to return some love to the adoring fans. Tom hovered next to them for a couple of minutes. He soaked in as much inspiration as he could before passing them completely. When Mile 11 was behind him, he was hungry for more. So he unwrapped Kerry's note and read the next line:

Mile 12: Tests, questions, spells—they never end. Her inability to gain weight has us worrying....

BAY 6 BUZZED with excitement. Little Baby Matthew had officially become a member of the "Kilo Club". NICUs love to keep things metric, but in layman's terms, it meant that his weight had reached the equivalent of a whopping two pounds, three point two seven four ounces. One small step for man, one giant step for baby-kind when it came to preemies in the hospital. Not only did it demonstrate that progress had been made, it gave Matthew a certain level of strength he'd been lacking. When Kerry walked in, she was stopped in her tracks by the congratulatory certificate displayed on Matthew's isolette. Bottles in hand, her face was thin and make-up free. Her hair was in two braids with a blue bandana tied around her head. It was a common look for Kerry, as of late, especially effective in masking grey hair. She blew her sleeping baby a kiss, then walked over to Matthew's mothers and lit up with excitement.

"Kilo Club?" she asked.

"Yes, can you believe it?" Cheryl said.

"It's the only club nobody ever really wants to be a member of," Liz laughed. Kerry gave them both hugs. She peeked in on Matthew, who was none the wiser regarding his recent achievement. Waving a quick "hello" to Tom and Erin—parents to baby Rose, diagonal to Emma—she put her milk on the nurse's stand, then took a seat next to Emma's isolette. Another blue note card was taped to the front, amongst all the green tinsel and shamrock decorations. She pulled the note off and read:

"I visited Emma this morning and said a prayer.
The nurses have her dressed up so adorable. Her Irish ancestors would be proud.
-Sr. Carlotta"

Kerry grinned as she re-examined her daughter's apparel. She hadn't noticed the kelly green onesie covering Emma's frail body. A white beret sat on top of her head. The CPAP had been replaced by high-flow nasal cannula, which was much more comfortable for her little nose and frankly, more attractive. Emma was six weeks old at this point, yet hadn't even gained a full pound from her birth weight. All of her X-rays showed that her esophagus hadn't grown either. Granted, X-rays couldn't be counted as completely accurate, but Dr. Buchmiller was not impressed with what she had seen. *"We won't know just how much of a chance we have of connecting her until we do a fluoroscopy,"* Dr. Buchmiller had said to Tom and Kerry a few days earlier. They'd learned that a fluoroscopy is a special real-time method of imaging which uses a fluoroscope to pick up a patient's internal structures. Dr. Buchmiller had explained that during this test, a special dye would be injected into Emma's g-tube, with the hopes that her stomach would reflux some of it into the bottom part of her esophagus (the part that originally routed into her trachea at birth). Next, they would inject the dye into the top portion of her esophagus. This would allow them to see exactly where both parts ended, and if there were any chance the two could be connected. *"We can't even think about planning her next surgery until she gets bigger and stronger, and we have a clearer idea about those two ends,"* Dr. Buchmiller had said.

Kerry tucked Sr. Carlotta's card into her purse and looked around for Emma's nurse. The computer flashed its typical screen-saver: *Boston Children's Employee of the Month*. Randall Jenkins, an endoscopy technician in the Gastroenterology Procedure Unit, was the current award winner, credited with "spreading good will...and making coworkers smile." His bald head and kind face was still fresh, considering Kerry had been staring at a completely different person's grill for the entire month of February. Colbie Caillat sang "Bubbly" in the background. Kerry rolled her eyes at Liz and Cheryl.

"I know, seriously?" Cheryl whispered.

"It's like what they do in prison camps to torture the inmates," Liz snapped.

"I heard this song on my way home last night and almost punched my radio!" Kerry whispered. "Seriously?"

"I heard that the mom plays it because she thinks it soothes the baby, " Cheryl whispered.

"I'd be happy to bring in a mix I made for Cheryl a few years back: Paul Simon, Sarah McLachlan…I mean, how much more soothing can you get then Sarah McLachlan?" Liz whispered. The music was coming from Bay 8, an area none of them had ever stepped foot it, even though it was only thirty feet away. Since their children were stationed in Bay 6, there was never any reason to continue down the line in the NICU. This mother had probably walked past Cheryl, Liz and Kerry a million times, but they couldn't know for certain who she was. And they hadn't a clue whether her baby was a boy or a girl, or what his or her health issues were. But they did know, that if a mother thought something was helpful to her baby, nobody better mess with it.

"How's Caitlin doing today?" Kerry asked.

"Same," Cheryl said. "I saw Shawna on my way in." Shawna was Caitlin's mom. Her checkered flannels were as recognizable as her sad face. Tim, her husband, wore an equally distraught look. Caitlin was stationed in Bay 2 on the end closest to the entrance, so passing by them was unavoidable. Back in February, it seemed Caitlin might have a chance at heading home, but an infection was holding her back. This seemed fixable to Kerry, because according to the NICU binder, infections were to be expected during long hospital stays. As she understood it, a baby could get an infection from bacteria that had worked its way into an IV or a central line. This is why, she'd learned, the nurses were so diligent about cleaning the lines and ports before they accessed them.

But Caitlin's infections weren't confined to the area around her tubes and lines, they were devouring her liver. Each time any of them passed by Caitlin's crib, it was clear things had gotten worse. She was receiving breathing support now, which she hadn't needed a month ago. Kerry had stopped running into Shawna in the pumping room. Shawna hadn't the time or energy to keep up with it. Her two other kids brought on a whole other level of responsibility, which Kerry could relate to, of course. One day, while getting coffee in the break room, Kerry had overheard Shawna on the phone. Shawna was lecturing her eight-year-old son on the poor grade he'd received in religion class. It stuck with Kerry that this poor, exhausted mother still had to react to her second-grader's grades. Caitlin had gotten sicker, and life at home was piling up. And despite Tim and Shawna's attempt to smile anytime they said *hello*, it had become more then obvious they were hanging on by a thread.

Emma's alarms sounded. Kerry opened her isolette immediately and tapped her on the head. "Come on Emma, take a breath, peewee," Kerry said. Her oxygen was dipping, but it wasn't going lower then eighty, so Kerry's level of concern was not at it's highest. She turned Emma on her side and continued to encourage her breathing. Within seconds, Deb arrived at her bedside and jumped in. "Let's give her a little extra help," Deb said as she turned up the oxygen. She reached for a syringe and filled it with water, then quickly flushed her replogle with five ccs. It took a few seconds, but Emma recovered. Her oxygen climbed back into the nineties and her respiratory rate followed suit. Deb shut the top to Emma's isolette and turned towards Kerry.

"I was thinking all about Emma on my ride home from work last night," Deb said.

"Oh?" Kerry replied.

"I've been trying to figure out what's causing all of these spells," Deb said. Kerry was intrigued. For the past seven weeks Emma had been having bradycardia spells non-stop. Some of them were the dreaded "code" type—where everything plummeted all at once. Yet others seemed to slowly creep up on her. Her oxygen might start to dip, one percent at a time, while her respiratory rate went in the opposite direction—like her lungs were still trying to give it their best.

"It seems more mechanical then it does cerebral," Deb explained. "Like a plug is forming in that tube of hers and causing her to aspirate her phlegm," she said. "Her phlegm the replogle should be sucking out." Kerry tried to comprehend everything Deb was saying.

"How can Emma breathe, when all this gunk keeps building up and spilling into her airway?" Deb asked. Her reasoning was based on the fact that Emma's secretions were thick and that anytime she flushed Emma's replogle, it loosened up whatever was blocking the little holes at the end of it. Deb could see the gunk moving out of the tube. She could hear the suction more clearly. But most of all, Emma's best moments (Deb had noticed) were directly after her replogle had been flushed. Another one of Emma's core nurses walked over and joined in the discussion. "I was talking to Nancy," Deb added, "and she agrees: the problem is the replogle." Nancy put her hands on her hips and shook her head. "It needs to remain patent in order to do its job. We told the doctors they should put in an order for her replogle to be flushed every hour," Nancy said. Kerry was astonished. This was huge. She'd been watching her baby struggle to breathe since day one. She'd nearly resigned to the idea that any one of these days *could* be Emma's last. All it took was one bad spell, one time when she wasn't strong enough to fight back. Kerry was used to feeling the pity that everyone in the NICU had for her and Tom. She was used to feeling scared. Emma was a stressful patient; her alarms were notorious to the entire medical staff and all the surrounding parents. And now, two seasoned NICU nurses had told Kerry that there might be a way to fix this. It seemed too good to be true. "My hope," Deb said, "is that less spells equals Emma's ability to thrive."

Emma had been getting feedings through her g-tube for the past month. Kerry's breast milk was being fortified with formula and oil, and given to her in tiny doses so as not to overwhelm her underdeveloped system. At first, her body completely refused to digest it. It would sit in her little stomach for hours, until a disappointed nurse finally had to take it back out and mark the "residuals" on her chart. Even when Emma's digestive system finally kicked in, the amount she was able to tolerate was so small, it seemed impossible she'd ever even gain one ounce. "If her body isn't working so hard just to breathe, then maybe it can focus on other things...like gaining weight...making poop and pee...it might even give her heart a break," Deb added.

Emma's heart, they had discovered, had two tiny holes called VSDs. It stood for Ventricular Septal Defect, also known as heart murmurs stemming from the wall that divides the left and right ventricles of the heart. This was common in preemies, but for a preemie in Emma's condition, it just added another layer of concern. Cardiologists had been periodically monitoring the holes to see if they were getting bigger or smaller. Doctors had said that often times, after a year or so they will close on their own. But Tom and Kerry had been warned that sometimes they don't, and surgery is required. This news, of course, didn't help Kerry's relationship with the Man Upstairs. Every time it crossed her mind, she had the same thought: *Anything Else? ANYTHING FREAKING ELSE?*

"It's time for her cares, if you want to get started," Deb said. Kerry washed and Purelled her hands, then opened the drawer under Emma's bed and selected many supplies. She quietly opened the isolette, then laid everything down on her tiny mattress. Gently, she unsnapped Emma's onesie and opened her diaper. Kerry washed her hands again, then opened a green and white package containing a size six French urinary catheter. Without touching it, she placed it on a sterile drape, which Deb had laid out for her. She then opened up a pair of purple sterile latex gloves and gingerly slid her fingers inside without touching the outsides of the gloves with her bare hands. With her left hand, she opened a small packet containing surgilube and squirted some on the sterile drape. Then with the same hand, she carefully cleaned all around Emma's lower half with a soapy towelette, front to back, followed by a similar cleanse using antiseptic. When everything was set, she removed the catheter from its package (with her right hand), dipped it in in surgilube and slowly inserted it into Emma's urethra. Within seconds, urine streamed out of the catheter and into a catch container. When the stream stopped, she slowly removed the catheter and placed it on the drape. Then she put the blue plastic top on the catch container and screwed it on tight.

After throwing out all the wrappings, Kerry washed her hands again. Next she removed all the tape and gauze around Emma's g-tube site. She examined Emma's skin. It looked red and irritated, so she pointed this out to Deb. Then she carefully cleaned the area with soap and warm water. She dried it completely with a piece of gauze, then applied a small amount of antibiotic ointment to a Q-tip and dabbed it on the red spot. She placed a new piece of gauze around the site, then used special tape to hold it in place.

Again, Kerry washed her hands, then turned her focus towards Emma's colostomy. The bag had lifted off her skin a bit, and looked beaten up— so Kerry decided it was time for a change. Before removing it, she took out more supplies, including a tiny new colostomy bag, then traced and cut a circle the size of Emma's stoma (the extracted portion of her large intestine) on the adhesive part of it. She took the old bag off and cleaned around the stoma with warm soap and water. Next, Kerry dried the area completely, then opened a little packet of stoma adhesive barrier and applied it to the area. She painted a thin layer of stoma paste around the stoma, and carefully secured the new bag in place. The hole Kerry had cut fit perfectly around Emma's stoma. *I love when that happens*, Kerry thought. She pressed down to make sure the bag was stuck to Emma's abdomen. Then she placed four cotton balls inside the bag and closed it with a tab. *I can't wait*, Kerry thought, *until there's actually enough poop for these cotton balls to soak up.*

Finally, Kerry took Emma's temperature. This was the last and easiest step. Happily, she reported a normal temp to Deb, who made a note of it in her chart. Kerry kissed Emma's beautiful cheek, and caught what she thought was a smile on her little lips. Emma's eyes were closed, as they had been the entire time. She hadn't noticed everything her mother had just done. Kerry sat in her chair and picked up the latest copy of *People* magazine.

A pregnant nurse bustled past Bay 6. She looked to be in her thirties, with a short brown ponytail. Kerry gazed at the nurse's swollen belly, which was wrapped in her arms, as if it were a package to be carried. She glanced at Cheryl and Liz, who were also gazing.

"We're still supposed to be pregnant right now," Kerry said.

"I would only be thirty-three weeks if I were," Liz said.

"I'd be thirty-seven," Kerry sighed. "I feel like it won't hurt as much once I'm past my due date. Every time I see a pregnant woman, I'm reminded that *I* should still look like that."

"That doesn't really happen to me with pregnant women," Liz admitted, "as much as it does with twins."

"Yeah, I can't look at twins. Not yet," Cheryl concurred. Kerry shook her head in agreement, then bowed it. It was completely understandable, given what they'd been through. The reason Matthew was born fourteen weeks early was a complicated one, and it involved his identical twin brother, James.

When Cheryl and Liz had learned their inseminated egg had split, they felt as though they'd won the lottery. Given that Liz was over forty and already had carried a perfect baby girl to term, it seemed almost impossible that they should be so lucky with fertility—twice. And the random occurrence of identical twins was just unimaginable.

The babies both shared one placenta, which is common with identicals. Early on in the pregnancy, Liz's obstetrician had mentioned that approximately fifteen percent of twins who share a placenta go on to develop something called Twin to Twin Transfusion Syndrome (TTTS). She had explained that sometimes the shared placenta contains abnormal blood vessels, which connect both babies' umbilical cords. Blood can circulate unequally, or in the wrong direction, from one twin to another, causing the babies to receive too little or too much. The baby that receives too little blood is known as the "donor". This twin's development and growth is compromised. Their urinary output is often so low, it can lead to renal failure and/or oligohydramnios (a low level of amniotic fluid). The baby that receives too much blood is known as the "recipient". This twin's heart suffers from all the strain put on it. The increased blood volume becomes too much to handle, and often times this twin will develop heart failure. Additionally, their urinary output is increased, which can result in polyhydramnios (a high level of amniotic fluid.) The obstetrician had explained that TTTS cannot be prevented, and that it's not hereditary or genetic. She had also warned them it could happen at anytime during the pregnancy.

These were potentials Cheryl and Liz took very seriously, yet were pretty convinced they had dodged as they walked into their twenty-week appointment. At first, their twin boys barely showed signs of the syndrome. But within three short weeks, Liz was coming in for "taps" to James' amniotic sac. By twenty-six weeks, Matthew's urinary output had become incredibly low, and James' little heart had become overwhelmed with all it was being asked to handle. The doctor delivered them via emergency C-section at Beth Israel Hospital, around the corner from Boston Children's. James only survived long enough for his mothers to witness the precious, few beats of his heart. Matthew clung on to his brother's spirit and lived, despite his failing kidneys and a bowel perforation. He was transferred to Children's Hospital a week later—where he took his rightful place in Bay 6, across from Emma Sheeran.

The Haitian woman with the colorful head-wrap pushed her mop in and out of each bed space, smiling at every person who stepped out of her way. Her face was smooth, but her hands were dry and rough. She hummed softly as she slowly cleaned under each crib, unable to resist peeking in on the little patients inside. When she was finished, she stopped and rested the mop's handle against her head. "It's a beautiful day," she said with a radiant smile. Kerry, Cheryl and Liz returned pleasant grins. "His light shines on all of us," she added. Then she turned around and wet her mop, before continuing on.

"My mom thinks I should go to confession with her before she goes back to New Jersey," Kerry said.

"Confession?" Cheryl laughed. She swiveled her chair towards Kerry.

"What'd you do now, Kerry?" Liz asked.

"She knows how pissed I am at God, and being that Easter is right around the corner—she thinks it's time for me to face up to all the feelings I'm having," Kerry explained.

"Did she say that to you?" Cheryl asked.

"No, I would never tell my mom all the thoughts I've been having. She would crumble if she really knew. She just sees that I'm not interested in going to church and that I fall silent every time she mentions His name," Kerry explained.

"*His* name?" Liz asked.

"Oh, I'm not even sure if I believe God exists right now. I certainly couldn't argue whether or not a gender had been assigned to the Almighty," Kerry said. All three of them laughed. Liz stuck a piece of paper in her book and closed it. She continued with her thoughts:

"Two weeks after James died and Matthew was holding on for dear life, we all got hit with the stomach flu. Isabel, Cheryl and myself, all sick as dogs. Fevers, chills—the works. Violently ill for, like, three days. Do you know what I mean? We don't even get a pass on the stomach flu?" Liz quipped.

"Seriously," Kerry agreed. "Poor Sr. Carlotta came by the other day…sweetest lady that ever lived…and we're talking about everything that's happened, and Emma etc., and she asks me: *"What have you learned about yourself during this entire experience?"*

"What'd you say?" Cheryl asked.

"I said, I never knew that my body broke out in hives when I was under extreme amounts of stress," Kerry answered. "That's all I could think to say."

"Aww, Sister Carlotta. So sweet, though. Leaves us notes on Matthew's isolette when we're not around. She does it for all the babies in here," Cheryl said.

"How about when people say, *Everything happens for a reason,* and they think that's actually going to make you feel better. Like, oh yes, of course. There must be a great reason that James was chosen to take one for the team. I'm sure we'll figure it out someday!" Liz snapped.

"Or how about: *It's all part of God's plan.* Like I should be happy that his plan involves having my daughter struggle to live and breathe on a daily basis. That's awesome. Great plan. When I look around this hospital and see all the kids...paralyzed and confined to wheelchairs, suffering with incurable diseases, fighting since the first day of their lives just to live on this earth...I have a really hard time swallowing that God planned this out for all of them, and that there's some awesome reason behind it. I'm sorry... It doesn't make any sense to me. None," Kerry said.

"People should really just shut up if they can't think of anything better to say," Cheryl said.

"Seriously," Kerry said.

"Seriously," Liz concurred.

Two men pushing an ultrasound machine right next to Emma's bedside interrupted their conversation. The man with red hair explained that he and the gentleman with dark hair and glasses were from Neurology, and that Emma was due for her next brain scan. Kerry backed away and allowed them some space to set up and work. The man with the dark hair opened up Emma's isolette and removed her little white beret. The man with red hair applied surgilube to the "wand" and rolled it across Emma's head. Almost immediately, impressions of her brain appeared on the screen. Kerry had read about "IVHs" (intraventricular hemorrhage) the last time Emma was scanned, and had learned that the reason it's common in premature infants is largely because their brain tissue is so delicate, due to the fact that technically it's still supposed to be growing and strengthening in utero. This, in addition to an immature circulatory system, results in blood not always getting to everywhere it needs to in the brain. Blood vessels become weak and start to break down, and bleeding ensues.

The men whispered and pointed to different parts of Emma's brain. Their backs were to Kerry, so she couldn't read their lips. But she thought she had heard the words "*grade four*" spoken by the man with dark hair. The problem was, she knew that brain hemorrhages in preemies were categorized into four different grades. Grades one and two are the most common and usually resolve without any terrible complications. Grades three and four, however are extremely serious, many times resulting in permanent brain trauma. Cerebral Palsy, among others, is a common injury in this grade of bleeds. Kerry knew this, as she watched the men continue to point and whisper and discuss. The dark-haired man seemed so focused on one section: he pointed and whispered, pointed and whispered. Minutes passed. Kerry's heart convulsed. Her eyes darted over to Cheryl and Liz, who were both biting their lips. Finally, she couldn't take it another second.

"What's wrong? Is something wrong?" Kerry shouted. The men were startled, unsure, momentarily if Kerry were even speaking to them.

"I'm sorry?" the man with the red hair asked.

"You keep pointing and whispering about my daughter's brain, and…just tell me, is she having a bleed? I thought I heard you mention grade four. That's the worst kind. Is she hemorrhaging?" Kerry squalled.

"She's fine, there's no sign of any bleeding." The man with red hair said. He pointed to the man with dark hair and continued: "Robert asked me what a grade four would look like on this kind of an ultrasound. I was just showing him the area of the brain it is most likely to appear in"

"Oh," Kerry replied.

"Robert's a student. You have to remember, this is a teaching hospital," the man with the red hair finished.

"Thank you." That was all Kerry could think to say. She took a deep breath, then slowly exhaled. Some color returned to her face. The men quickly finished up, then nodded their heads at her and rolled the ultrasound machine into the next bay.

Cheryl and Liz buried their noses as deep as they could inside their books. Kerry sat down in her chair. She took a swig from her water bottle, then screwed the cap back on and reached for her *People* magazine. She flipped it open to the article on Halle Berry and her newborn baby girl, then slammed it shut. "I thought of one more," Kerry said. "*God only gives you as much as you can handle.*"

"Ohhhhh!" Cheryl yelped, covering her ears with her hands.

"I *hate* that one," Liz grumbled.

Chapter 10

SHIT HAPPENS

AN AMBULANCE BLARED its sirens and was coming in hot behind Kerry. Pulling over to the right as fast as she could, she glanced in her rear-view mirror and made the sign of the cross. Her breath was taken away, temporarily, but given how late she was—Kerry had no choice but to get back on the road, quickly, and start looking for a parking garage. Boston was insanely busy. Not only was it Marathon Monday, the Red Sox were playing the Orioles at Fenway. She expected to have to walk about three to four miles just to make it to Kenmore Square, and it was already 1:30 p.m. Kerry was cutting it close, but had faith that the *chip* in Tom's racing bib was accurately recording his whereabouts. If it were at all off, she was screwed. Tom's biggest mistake was telling her about this device, knowing that Kerry timed everything down to the last possible minute, always.

A song came on the radio and Kerry's eyes lit up. She reached down and turned up the volume. Cheap Trick was singing *"Surrender"* on her Seventies Sirius station, which was not only a coincidence, but also a rare treat for her ears. Kerry remembered the last time she'd heard this song, and the unexpected impact of one word in particular. In an instant, she was transported back to one of her many car rides up to Boston in early 2008....

Given how intense life was both at home and the hospital, Kerry's drives to and from Boston became filled with self-reflection. It was an hour and fifteen minutes each way of trying to figure out how she, Tom and their family were going to keep on keeping on. It was really the only alone time she ever indulged in. Whether she spent it crying, screaming, thinking, or just listening to the radio, Kerry enjoyed it. Sometimes she'd get lost in a song. Many times she felt like the music was speaking to her directly. But never so much so as the afternoon she'd heard this 1978 teen anthem.

Emma had been having a rough time, requiring multiple blood transfusions to keep up her strength. Her next surgery was nowhere in sight. Donna had gone back to New Jersey, and Thomas was having a hard time with the babysitter. Kerry hated how much he and Ryan missed her when she was gone. It was just another stab to her ravaged heart. Tom was under a ton of pressure at work, which was nothing new. Jane was a wreck, and never hesitated to tell both Kerry and Tom how worried she was about them. Her anxiety over the state of her granddaughter had become too much to handle. Of course, Jane wasn't alone—lots of family and friends struggled to contain their fears. This became difficult for Emma's parents. It was one thing to be living their existence. It was another, to be constantly reminded just how difficult each and every day was. The pressure to hold it all together was intense, and Kerry was still dealing with a lot of anger. Every night, when she sat in the glider in Emma's nursery, she mourned the loss of the dreams she had dreamt for her daughter.

Then one day in early April, while driving through Pawtucket on her way to Boston, this song played on the radio. *Surrender*, Kerry thought. *Huh.* Not in the sense of giving up, but rather in *accepting*. It seemed so simple. If only Kerry could surrender to the reality of what had happened, maybe she could move forward. The voice in her head chimed in:

"Stop wishing things were different, Kerry. They are not."

This wasn't the first time the voice had suggested this, just the first time Kerry actually heard it. But why was it clicking just then? *Does Tom already know this?* she wondered. *Does everybody?* The fact was, Emma was born on January 27, 2008 with severe complications and nothing Kerry could say, pray or do was ever going to change that. Suddenly, she knew this. That very moment, Kerry surrendered. It was life altering. Her view of Emma's situation was completely different. Her view of life changed.

As it turns out, Kerry realized, shit happens. And from what she could see on every floor of Boston Children's Hospital and everywhere around the world—it happened a lot. Shit can happen at any time, to anyone, anywhere. It doesn't discriminate. Occasionally it hits some people a lot harder then others, but usually without cause. What Kerry was happiest to realize, however, was that instead of standing there drenched in it, she had the power to react. Again, the voice spoke, proposing a valid, albeit slightly crude, question:

"How can you clean shit off of you, if you haven't even surrendered to the fact that you're covered in it?"

Suddenly, Kerry was clear. Yes, Emma had countless obstacles to face, but none of them would be as difficult as trying to change the past. *Shit happens, and it will continue to happen—and all I can do is accept it and deal with it,* Kerry concluded. It all seemed so glaringly obvious. She wondered why nobody had said this to her before. She wondered how God fit into all of this. A shift had taken place, as Kerry sat behind the wheel of her Honda Pilot. All because of one word in an old song.

A pack of twenty-something partiers crossed in front of Kerry's car as a parking attendant waved her into his garage. His white flag seemed oddly appropriate. It was clean and crisp. Hers was tattered and worn. She'd had to wave it quite a bit over the last year. *Surrender,* Kerry thought. *At least now, I know how to do that.*

* * *

THE WOMEN OF Wellesley College lined up along Rt. 135 and screamed at the tops of their lungs. Men were darting to the side of the road, periodically, and it wasn't until Tom passed a blond holding a sign over her head that read: *KISS ME!*—that he understood why. This part of the route was well known to runners, and well liked. It was electric. It's tradition, Tom had read, dated back to the early 1900s, when the Wellesley "girls" would stand on a stone wall in front of their college and cheer on the marathoners. Of course, back then all the runners were males. From what Tom had learned, it was quite a highlight even in 1907. Over a century since then, women now accounted for about forty-two percent of the runners, and they, too, anticipate the energy these particular fans give off just before the halfway mark. Tom was excited to be passing through this part of the race, feeling as good as he did. It meant his run was fifty percent complete. It also meant he was about to see his first set of supporters. *Perhaps,* he thought, *I will end up getting a kiss from someone in Wellesley after all.*

His older brother, Sean, had taken the day off to cheer on Tom. He'd even brought his daughter, Bella. The two of them had camped out in front of a bagel store in Wellesley Center. Their eyes grew weary, having scanned each and every Boston Children's checkered shirt that had passed by. Sean, too, had access to the chip information, and had a general idea of when to expect his brother. Nonetheless, it was easy to get distracted by all the hoopla at the midway mark. C&C Music Factory blared from two gigantic speakers across the street. Three men wearing clown wigs drew attention when they stopped running for a moment to break-dance for their happy spectators.

Lots of runners stopped to say hello to the friends and family members who held up signs and cheered from the sidewalk. Sean worried, momentarily, that Tom might run right past them. They had no signs, no cowbells...only their voices. Sean checked his watch. It was 2:15 p.m.—the exact time he had estimated Tom was due to pass. "There he is!" Bella screamed. "Uncle Tommy! Uncle Tommy!" She waved her arms frantically. Sean joined in, and eventually Tom spotted his fans and ran towards them. He picked up his niece and gave her a big, sweaty smooch on the cheek, which she quickly wiped off. He hugged his brother. Their faces were beaming. "You're halfway done, dude!" Sean exhorted. "Way to go, Tommy!" Sean was genuinely impressed with his little brother. Growing up, Tom had always been into sports but was never a *great* athlete. He got knocked around as a linebacker in football. He could count on one hand the number of goals he'd ever scored in soccer. Even baseball had delivered some challenges, especially when the coach picked Tom to fill the most undesirable position in little league: catcher. No, Sean's little brother had never caught the winning pass, scored the winning goal or hit the winning homerun. But it never really mattered, because Tom still loved to play. Sean knew this about his brother. And here Tom was, running the race of all races—and he was killing it. "I'm so proud of you, dude. So proud," Sean said, patting Tom on the back. "You're really doing this, aren't you?"

Tom gave Bella and Sean a quick overview of his marathon experience thus far, then hugged them one last time before taking off. He jogged backwards for a few seconds, waving goodbye, until he was startled by the tripping of his own feet. He apologized, profusely, to the woman he had bumped into, then forged onward through the town's busy center. The sidewalks were packed with well-wishers. On the right side of the road just up the hill, he was coming upon the Boston Children's hospitality tent. It was perfect timing, considering Tom had eaten his last packet of GU back at Mile 10 and was hoping to load up with some supplies. As he got closer, he saw a familiar bearded face. Joe sat in a folding chair with his sock and sneaker off, holding a big bag of ice on his right ankle. He looked up and saw Tom.

"Hey brother, fancy meeting you here," Joe said.

"What the hell, dude? What happened?" Tom asked.

"Ahhhh. I tweaked my ankle. It's FUBARed," Joe explained.

"How bad?" Tom asked.

"Wicked bad, bro. I'm a gimp." Joe said. Tom was upset. This wasn't fair. He'd tweaked his own ankle a million times during his training. This was the injury he most feared would get *him* today. Yet here it was, happening to his new buddy: a good guy, who was running in honor of his little girl. It wasn't acceptable. Tom tapped a volunteer on the shoulder and asked where the first aid kits were kept. Then he quickly grabbed what he needed and kneeled on the ground next to Joe's leg.

"I'm gonna wrap this up for you, and you're gonna finish this race," Tom said.

"Thanks, but I limped all the way to this tent from Wellesley College," he explained. "Those kids were screaming so loud, I lost sight of my footing and hit the curb. I'm screwed, I can hardly even walk," Joe said. Tom shook his head. He grabbed the bag of ice and dried off Joe's foot with a paper towel, then rested it on his thigh and straightened his heel out. "I've had to do this one hundred times, trust me it works," Tom promised. He wrapped around Joe's lower leg, then carefully moved down and around his ankle. Over the top of his foot, down and around. Over, down, and around. Over, down and around. Tom did this until he ran out of ace bandage. The only thing still exposed was Joe's heel. Tom ripped off a piece of tape with his teeth and wrapped it tightly around his lower leg. Then he handed Joe his sock and sneaker. "Let's see what you can do," he said with anticipation.

As they ran past a sign for Route 16 East and Cambridge/Boston, Joe punched Tom in the arm and laughed. "Amazing bro!" Joe squealed, having abandoned his limp for a fairly confident stride. "Told you I was an expert wrapper!" Tom said. "What were the odds, that I'd run out of

GU just in time to save your ass?" The wind was blowing at them, a bit. Not so much it slowed them down, but just enough to remind them it could if it wanted to. The sun hid behind the clouds, yet Tom's chill from his dried sweat still burned off. He hoped to gain back the ten minutes he'd lost Wellesley. This meant he'd have to turn it up a notch for the next few miles. *Perhaps*, Tom thought, *I'll get my chance to take off ahead of Joe.* The idea of this gave him a rise. There was just something about making people eat his dust every now and then. Especially after he'd been eating Joe's for some time. Runners know this. They think about it every time they come upon another runner on the same path. It's the exact moment when they commit to passing someone—the rush. On the outside, it's a nod of the head or a nonchalant *hello*. On the inside, however, it's pure victory. And once a runner has moved past someone, it's absolutely imperative they hold their place as leader. Slipping back from a spot at the front means handing over one's pride. It's just plain embarrassing. A runner should always contemplate such things before making this big move. Which is what Tom was doing at that very moment, before Joe interrupted him.

"So?" Joe asked.

"So what?" Tom said.

"What did I miss? Catch me up." Joe insisted, pointing to the note in Tom's hand.

"Nah, dude. Our story is long and tough, no need to drag you along with it!" Tom said.

"Do I look like I'm dragging? I'm invested. What's happening at Mile 14?" Joe asked.

Tom gave in and once again unfolded his inspiration. He read:

Mile 14: Trouble during her fluoroscopy. Not even the police can slow you down....

KERRY SAT IN a rocking chair next to Emma's bedside and wrote out a stack of thank-you notes. Peewee's isolette had been traded in for a genuine big-girl crib, and all six pounds seven ounces of her rested quite comfortably in it. A huge sign, written with red marker in Kerry's handwriting, was taped above the head of her crib and read: PLEASE FLUSH EMMA'S REPLOGLE EVERY HOUR TO AVOID SPELLS. Tom and Kerry had dubbed themselves the "Replogle Nazis", ever since Deb and Nancy's hypothesis on Emma's plug-induced spells had proven true. So true, in fact, that anytime a nurse would neglect to keep up with her timely flushing duties, Emma would inevitably fall victim to her own secretions and a plugged up tube. The days she spent with her "core" group of nurses were Emma's best. The ones she spent with nurses who were unfamiliar to her case were her worst. Hence, Tom and Kerry's need to intervene.

Gone were the days of nurses teaching them about the NICU. Now *they* were the educators when it came to Emma. They had discovered that while being stationed in one of the best hospitals in the country, they were still among human beings who were capable of making mistakes. Therefore, they became educated on what it meant to be a Patient Advocate. Emma's core nurses had encouraged them to become such. The NICU, as a whole, considered parents to be important members of their patients' "Care Team". Kerry and Tom spent almost every single day with Emma, which made them experts on what worked and what did not. Keeping the replogle patent worked. So there was no hesitation to remind a nurse who had gone past the hour mark to kindly give it a flush. Of course, no nurse likes to be told how to do his or her job. But this particular step in Emma's care warranted a prompt from her parents every now and then. The alternative was watching their daughter struggle to breathe, which made it a no-brainer.

They had also learned to constantly ask questions regarding the "next steps" for Emma. Waiting around wondering when her next tests were going to be run was *so* two-months-ago. Tom and Kerry were now helping to steer the ship. They took part in both neonatal and surgical rounds, requesting X-rays be done and conclusions be made regarding Emma's next surgery. Until they connected her esophagus, Emma wasn't going to leave the hospital. And given the amount she'd grown over the past month, the next logical step was to perform the fluoroscopy. Which is why they pushed to schedule it for April 3, 2008, two days before Kerry's original due date.

A new face flashed on the computer screen: Josh Bain, a technical support specialist in the Information Services Department. He was touted as being proactive in his approach to help coworkers with their computer issues. A new "Employee of the Month" meant that a new month had arrived. "It's April Fools Day?" Kerry asked Tom. "I didn't even realize March was over." The weather was raw and windy. It may as well have still been March.

Tom walked over to the sink and washed his hands, then returned to prepare for Emma's cares. Her colostomy bag practically erupted with poopy cotton balls and couldn't wait another minute to be cleaned. Every time Emma cried, another squirt of poop came out. Her body had filled out. Even her cheeks had some chub to them. The fluid on her kidneys had completely drained. Dr. Borer, Emma's urologist, was borderline giddy when her recent renal ultrasound showed that her smaller, compromised kidney had grown in leaps and bounds. And though Emma was still connected to gaggles of tubes and wires, she was a lot less fragile then before. They could pick her up and hold her if she cried. She squeezed their fingers tight and smiled at the sound of their voices. This encouraged them. It was progress. And yet, she was still considered one of the most complicated patients in the NICU. But that was okay, because being *complicated* was still better then being *critical*. There were others, at this point, who had replaced Emma at the top of *that* unenviable list.

Caitlin had taken a turn for the worse. Tom and Kerry had spoken to Shawna and Tim a week earlier, only to hear she was now in need of a liver transplant. Her infections weren't clearing up. Shawna had revealed that Caitlin was born with a benign tumor in her liver. Its initial harm was that it was taking blood from her liver and sending it to her heart and lungs in abundance. But even a twelve-hour surgery to try to correct the blood flow problems proved insufficient. *"She's as yellow as a dandelion,"* Shawna would say, a result of her baby's malfunctioning liver. On top of that, the central line to her heart became infected shortly after her operation. Caitlin's body essentially began to shut down as a result of it, sending her liver disease to a horrible new level. Her entire abdomen swelled with fluid from her blood vessels. Shawna and Tim were distraught to find out their daughter's only hope was a liver transplant. *"It's what we have to do if we want to keep her,"* Shawna had explained to Tom and Kerry. Her eyes had become even more tragic. Tim could barely lift his gaze from the floor.

Tom closed Emma's freshly cleaned bag, then asked permission from Kate, the night nurse, to hold her. "Finish her cares first, then we can weigh her and you can hold your little muffin as long as you want," she barked. Tom scowled and pointed to the Grande Mocha Latte sitting next to her computer. Kerry smiled.

They had become very close to Kate over the past few months. She worked pretty regular hours and was almost always assigned to Emma. Kate was a beautiful twenty-eight-year-old. She had a cute figure, long brown hair and was planning her wedding. Kerry had talked with her for hours on this subject. She'd offered up advice on handling in-law issues, picking dresses and avoiding "Bridezilla" moments. Kate was a straight shooter who never hesitated to remind them of their duties as Emma's advocates. They respected each other immensely. Kate worked four nights a week, 7 p.m. to 7 a.m. She spent many long nights with Emma while Tom and Kerry were home in Rhode Island, asleep in their bed. In addition to her expert nursing care, Kate had a special place in her heart for their baby. She was there when Emma cried and needed to be held, for an hour or more if need be. She enjoyed giving her "tubbys" any chance she got, because Emma always cooed at her while in the bath. She bought Emma clothes and a blanket, and called her "muffin" and "diva woman". She dressed Emma up, sometimes in Red Sox T-shirts, and took pictures with her phone, then sent them to Tom and Kerry. Kate was a Godsend, as far as they were concerned. All the love, affection and attention she was missing from her parents, Emma received from Kate and the core group of nurses who took care of her. The amount of gratitude Kerry and Tom felt was indescribable. All the free Starbucks in the world could never repay what they owed these women.

Across from them, a pretty woman with strawberry blond hair rocked a tiny baby boy with a blue cap in her arms. Jackie was Matthew's night nurse, whom they'd also grown very close to. She liked to laugh, and Kerry's sarcasm would often set her English cackle into an uproar. She got a kick out of Tom and Kerry's banter, and never hesitated to peek in at Emma every time she passed her crib. "*Oh, my God,*" she'd whine, "*she's so freaking cute!*" Jackie had to help out on more then one occasion with Emma during a bad spell, referring to them as "*Missy-Moo's temper tantrums.*" She was thirty years old, single and downright happy. She offered constant support and guidance, and snickered right along when Kerry poked fun at her "big gazongas". She cared deeply for Matthew, *especially* when Cheryl and Liz weren't around. Often times Kerry would catch her singing or giggling to him. She read him board books and shook rattles in his little hand. None of this was part of her job description, which is why it was all the more entrancing to witness. She was the kind of woman Kerry had always pictured a nurse to be, having seen so many of her own family members shine in the same profession.

Jackie was simply someone Kerry and Tom looked forward to seeing anytime they took their spot in Bay 6.

"Who's watching Thomas and Ryan tonight?" Jackie asked.

"My mom," Tom answered. "We've got nurses all over the tri-state area taking care of our kids."

"You're lucky," she said. "Nothing beats family, huh?" Tom shook his head. Kerry felt instantly guilty, given she'd had a strained conversation with Jane that afternoon.

Earlier that morning, Tom was checking his voicemail. As usual, there was a frantic message from his mother with regards to his health and well-being. *"I'm worried about you, Tommy. I don't know how you can even deal with everything with Emma, and pull the hours you're pulling at work. It's awful! You're going to have a nervous breakdown. It's terrible! It's too much for you to have to handle!"* These messages were very common. Even more so, now that Tom had been avoiding her phone calls. Kerry had seen the displeasure on his face every time he listened to them. She'd heard it in his voice when he spoke to his mom on the phone. Jane's expressed worry had obviously been upsetting Tom, but he didn't dare say anything to *her* about it. Which is why Kerry felt it was her job to let Jane know just how unconstructive it had been. *"Tom knows this is difficult, he knows it stinks,"* Kerry had explained, *"but reminding him just how bad it is day in and day out doesn't help."* The silence on the other end of the line was filled with Kerry's last-ditch effort to explain: *"I realize this is difficult for all of us. I'm telling you this because I know you love him tremendously. And he'd never want to say something to you about it—which is why I thought I should tell you."* That hadn't helped. Jane was completely taken aback by what Kerry had said. *"I AM worried about him, Kerry,"* she'd responded. The conversation ended abruptly, with a clear understanding that neither of them understood the other. Kerry's attempt at lessening angst in her husband's life had backfired. Even the voice in her head seemed disappointed:

"That was stupid. After all she's done for you?
Let it go. You oughta know better."

"Nothing beats family," Kerry agreed.

Two days later, Emma's nurse connected her replogle to the portable suction machine. The "travel" nurse stood bedside, preparing to bring her down for the fluoroscopy. Kerry was on edge, given she'd never met this particular nurse before. "Emma will spell if you don't flush her replogle," Kerry explained. The travel nurse introduced herself as Amy and shook her head to acknowledge what Kerry had just said. She made friendly chitchat about her daughters, and asked Kerry about her boys. Slowly, Amy started pushing Emma's crib.

"What will happen if she has a spell while they're doing the test?" Kerry interjected. Amy explained that she had portable suction and oxygen with her, and that she would handle it just as they would in the NICU. "As a matter of fact," Amy said with confidence, "all the rooms in X-ray have wall suction and oxygen, so she's doubly covered." Kerry smiled. They pushed Emma's crib out of Bay 6, down the hall and through the NICU doors. Her nerves were jumping, but since Tom had to be at a meeting in Connecticut that morning—it was up to Kerry to hold her shit together and get through this test with *their* baby. *Divide and conquer,* she reminded herself.

Her dear friend from high school, Michele, planned to stop by later that morning to visit Emma, so Kerry tried to think about that. It was a rare event that Kerry could show off her beautiful girl to anyone, and she looked forward to it. Not taking her eyes off Emma the entire elevator ride down, she kept her hand glued to the crib. When they arrived at radiology, the room was filled with five or six medical personnel. Their faces were new to Kerry. None of them had ever met Emma. Scattered butterflies, frogs and bunny rabbits covered the walls. The radiologists prepared for the exam, as the assistants stretched Emma out on the table. The voice in Kerry's head grew louder:

"Make sure you tell them about your baby."

"She has bradycardia spells when her replogle gets clogged," Kerry blurted out to the young woman securing the equipment above Emma. The woman glanced at Kerry, then at the travel nurse, then back at Kerry. Her eyes had dark circles beneath them, her face was wary. She gave a quick nod, then busily unattached Emma's portable lines and reattached them to the wall suction and oxygen. Emma wriggled around and smiled at the attending radiologist.

The medical team chatted about Emma's case, and reviewed the necessary steps they would have to take in order to achieve the desired images. Then they began the test. Kerry stood behind Emma's head and watched as they injected dye through her g-tube. The image of her torso appeared on the screen in front of them. After a minute or so, frustration was evident, when Emma's stomach refused to reflux the dye up the distal portion of her esophagus. Kerry did her best to telekinetically move the dye, knowing how helpful this would be for Emma's assessment. It didn't work, however, and the team was forced to move on to phase two.

The wary assistant asked Amy to help her remove Emma's replogle, but when they realized it was taped down fairly well, the two of them agreed it would be just as effective to turn off the suction, temporarily, while the radiologists injected the dye into Emma's esophageal pouch. The wary assistant did this, and shortly after, the team continued the test. Kerry watched the screen as the dye ventured a couple of inches down, then rested in the pouch of Emma's unconnected esophagus. For a moment, Kerry was lost, wondering how her daughter's little body had gone so wrong when it had formed. Her thoughts, however, were quickly interrupted by the startling sound of a beeping alarm. Everyone's eyes shifted to the portable monitors, which read declining numbers. Kerry jumped to her baby's side. Emma's eyes erupted with panic. Her body pulled to get a breath.

"Suction her!" Kerry screamed. Amy flipped the switch on the portable suction machine and assured Kerry she was going to be okay. A minute went by and Emma's numbers had tanked. "Suction her!" Kerry screamed again. Emma was now completely blue, her eyes bulging. "Suction her!" Kerry screamed.

Amy assured her they were doing everything they could and that it was only going to be a matter of time before Emma came back. Everyone in the room scrambled around, desperately trying to help. Amy's face grew vacant; her confidence completely drained out. The suction wasn't working. Emma was now grey, and had lost consciousness. Her infant arms stopped flailing. The wary assistant frantically pointed out to Amy that the suction was connected to the wall, not the portable unit she had been using.

She quickly turned the wall unit on, but it appeared to be too late. Emma didn't resemble the baby who was lying on the table just minutes before. A woman in a white coat announced she was "calling code", and with the press of a button sent a hospital wide alert. Another woman's voice repeated "Code Blue, Radiology, Room 2" multiple times over the public address system. The room was instantly flooded with doctors and nurses. Time passed—minutes, seconds, and Kerry felt herself leave her body. It was almost as if she were stuck to the walls with all the frogs and bunnies, watching Emma perish in front of her. She heard herself plead as the woman in the white coat started chest compressions. She saw the strangers who pulled her away as she howled "Please God!" repeatedly. She wondered how she was ever going to be able to tell Tom that their precious baby had died. She wondered what she would say to the boys.

A team of doctors and nurses from the NICU arrived just as Emma's heart began to beat again. Within seconds, her vitals started to slowly climb. Kerry was still being asked to stand back, but refused the strangers' grips on her arms. She flew to her baby's side and stuck to it as the team rushed Emma back into the NICU. They passed her friend Michele, who watched at reception as Emma's crib barreled through the entrance. Michele held a pink gift bag with a little stuffed elephant sticking out from the top. It was all Kerry could do to give her an alarming gaze while shaking her head *no*. Once Emma was back in Bay 6, her vitals remained incredibly weak. The attending neonatologist called for suction, and a nurse fed a thin tube up her nose and down her airway, then vacuumed up an incredible amount of dye and secretions. Immediately, Emma's condition improved. Kerry took a breath for the first time in ten minutes. "Thank you, God. Thank you, God," she called out. Deb rushed around the corner into Bay 6. Although she wasn't assigned to Emma that day, word had spread about what had happened. Deb wrapped her arms around Kerry and squeezed with all the strength she could offer. Kerry broke down, blotches and all. The entire NICU tried to look away from the obvious disturbance. Once Kerry regained her breath and ability to speak, she knew: it was time to call Tom.

Ninety minutes later, red and blue lights flashed in his rear-view mirror as Tom angrily gave in and pulled his truck over on the VFW Parkway in Boston. Taking his time, the officer sauntered over to Tom's already-opened drivers side window. His belly grazed over the black belt, which held up his blue uniform pants. Gray hairs peeked out from underneath his hat. Other cars slowed down to get a look at the action as they passed. Tom's brain felt like it was going to explode. "Officer?" he yelled, sticking his head as far out of the window as possible. "Officer?"

"License and registra...."

"Officer!" Tom interrupted, "Officer, you've got to let me go."

"License and registration, sir," the policeman said earnestly, opening his black leather folder.

"Officer," Tom clamored. He held his Children's Hospital identification badge very close to the policeman's face. "My daughter, sir." His hands shook. The muscles on his jaw flexed.

"Sir, do you know why I...." the policeman continued.

"I know, but Officer, please listen...." Tom begged.

"Ninety-three miles per hour on the VFW, Sir? Do you know what the...."

"MY DAUGHTER JUST CODED!" Tom yelled. "I'M GOING TO THE HOSPITAL, RIGHT NOW." His voice trembled. "Just let me go," he finished. He was looking directly into the policeman's stunned face, holding up his badge.

The policeman looked at the badge, then into Tom's tragic eyes, and took a step back. He looked behind him. Instantly, he held out his hand to stop the approaching cars on the street, then pointed at Tom and commanded: "GO!" Tom, now looking stunned himself, slammed on the gas without even shifting into drive. His engine roared an angry roar. "GO!" the policeman repeated. And with that—Tom found the right gear. Seconds later he was peeling down the VFW Parkway at a very cautious eighty-nine miles per hour.

Chapter 11

THE AWAKENING

"WHOA, BROTHER," JOE said. "That's what you call: a bad day." He dumped a cup of water over his head. Tom cautiously looked into his cup before doing the same. His face was still sticky with Gatorade from his last attempt to cool off, and he wasn't about to make *that* mistake again. Joe's ankle was holding up well. He and Tom were in perfect stride. "Back in the day, I had to race to the hospital a couple of times myself," Joe explained, "when Gracie was in trouble."

"Oh, really? Same kind of thing?" Tom asked.

"Not exactly," Joe said. "Nothing ever happened during a test, like that. But Gracie's valves were so messed up, it wasn't uncommon for her to basically have a heart attack every now and again. She might wake up feeling kind of crappy, but you wouldn't know if she were coming down with something or if it were heart-related. Either way, my wife would always take her to the cardiologist, and half the time she'd end up in an ambulance on her way to the emergency room."

"Geez," Tom commiserated.

"Yeah," Joe continued, "usually I'd be sitting at my desk at work when I got the call. I had more then my fair share of "lead foot" episodes going down 93...wicked fast, but I never got pulled over." The two of them crossed the 16-mile marker and smiled at the old man on the sidewalk who was intent on reminding all the runners they had only 10.2 more miles to go. "Speaking of going fast, I feel the wind at my back, bro," Joe announced. And just as quickly as he announced it, he was off, ready to undertake mile 17 a little bit faster then his friend from Rhode Island was. Tom was glad he hadn't let Joe in on his earlier plans to make him eat dust, so there really wasn't anything to be ashamed of in that moment. At least, that's what Tom told himself.

The road was flat for the time being, but Tom's legs remembered how they'd felt the last time they had tackled this mile through Newton. It was his least favorite part of the run, given the long, gradual climb uphill for more then half a mile. He wondered why Joe chose to turn on his engines here and if he might, in fact, regret it. *He could run out of gas at the 128 overpass,* Tom thought. *If I even catch a glimpse of Gracie's red curls on the back of his shirt, he's toast.* The idea alone put some spring into Tom's step and carried him past a happy crowd of drinkers, who stood in front of a handsome brick building labeled 'LOWER FALLS WINE' on his right.

The never-ending hill and lack of scenery on this particular road called for a distraction. So Tom did the only logical thing he could think of, and unfolded his letter.

Mile 17: Preparing for surgery...

"I MET YOUR mother-in-law!" Jackie said with a touch of sass. Kerry smiled and opened her ears. "I wasn't even Missy Moo's nurse and she had me running around all afternoon: *'She feels cold, can you get me another blanket?...Her leads aren't sticking, can you get her some new ones?...She wants to be on her side, can you move her?... Is this g-tube moving around too much?...When are they gonna feed her again?...Can you flush the replogle?...Flush her replogle!...Flush her replogle!'"* Jackie snapped. Kerry couldn't stop grinning as she lined up her four freshly pumped bottles of milk. "I mean, I thought you and Tom were bad, but geez! This whole department needed a nap after Jane left," Jackie added. Kerry was laughing at this point. So were Cheryl and Liz, who gave up pretending to read their books. "Sounds like she was acting like a responsible grandparent, if you ask me!" Kerry insisted.

Jane had been on hospital duty for the last couple of days. With Emma's surgery coming up on May 1st, Tom and Kerry wanted to spend as much time with the boys as possible before "moving" to Boston temporarily. Jane had volunteered to spend a couple of days at Emma's bedside, which had worked out nicely. Not only was she absolutely enamored with her granddaughter, but Jane's inability to hold her tongue coupled with her twenty-plus years experience as an ICU nurse made her the perfect candidate for the job. Tom and Kerry were sure that "Gaga" wasn't going to let anything happen to her granddaughter on her watch. Jane's love burned for Emma. It burned. And as long as this fire was directed at the NICU doctors and nurses, all was well in the world. Jane was an honorary Replogle Nazi, and she had taken her responsibilities very seriously. Kerry appreciated this, especially after what had happened during the fluoroscopy. Her mother-in-law was really the only other person, aside from Tom, she could trust to make sure Emma stayed safe. That was huge.

Unfortunately, the same couldn't be said for Donna. She had proved during her last visit that the NICU wasn't the place for her. Donna and Joe had driven up a couple weeks earlier with the intent of spending some quality time with Emma. Jean had bragged, following her recent visit, about the amazing cuddles she and Emma had shared. It had Donna yearning to do the same, especially since the entire time she was living in Rhode Island, her child-care responsibility for Thomas and Ryan had prevented her from ever being able to visit her granddaughter in Boston. The day Donna and Joe had picked to come, however, happened to fall on the heels of an eye exam for Emma. She never did well after an eye exam. Something about prying her eyelids open with pointy metal instruments and forcing her eyeballs to move—it didn't quite jive with Emma's mojo and inevitably caused her to spell...a lot. Which is what had happened when Donna and Joe walked into Bay 6 after a five-hour car ride. Their much-anticipated reunion did not play out as they had hoped. Each time Emma's heart rate dropped, Donna gasped uncontrollably. The alarms were a trigger, sending her body into mini-convulsions. Donna couldn't hide her intense fear, cowering and yelping with each dip. After the seventh or eight time "freaking out", Donna was escorted out of the NICU by the head nurse and Kerry. Joe, who was speechless the entire twenty-minute visit, scampered out behind them. It was all too much. *"How can you watch her struggle like that?"* Donna had cried. Kerry hugged her, but Donna kept asking in a desperate attempt to understand. *"It's unspeakable! How can you watch that?"*

Colbie Caillat crooned "Bubbly" in the background as Kerry sat down in a rocking chair and pulled out a stack of sixty-four thank you cards. The Haitian woman cleaned out the bed-space next to Emma, in preparation for a new patient. Kerry smiled at her and said hello. "God is good," the woman said with a twinkle in her eye. Her head-wrap was neon pink. Kerry nodded her head while awkwardly shuffling her cards.

Eight more, Kerry thought, *and I'll be all caught up.* The problem was, there were just too many people to thank. Kerry hadn't cooked a meal in almost four months. Friends, strangers and neighbors had all rotated their time and cooking efforts in order to feed the Sheeran family. Prayers came in from all over the world. One friend wrote that he had lit a candle for Emma in every one of the eighteen churches he'd visited on his recent trip to Europe. Kerry's sister, Janet, said that each night her family held hands around their dinner table and prayed for Emma. A group of women in Florida known as the "Water Babies" prayed for Emma after each aqua aerobics class. Knitters, some that didn't even know Tom and Kerry, had knitted beautiful hats, booties and sweaters for "Mighty Emma". Kerry and Tom's hometown church in New Jersey was praying for Emma *every* week at *every* mass.

Their friends, Colleen and Jim, had just driven up from New Jersey with their two children the previous weekend, so that Tom and Kerry could spend the night in Boston while *they* stayed home to watch the boys. Thomas and Ryan were being fed, clothed, driven around and loved by the countless friends and family members who had offered.

Tom's buddy Mike and his wife, Abbie, were putting Emma's parents up in their house almost once a week. They lived in Wakefield, which was a hop, skip and a jump to the hospital, and much more comfortable. Kerry's close friends, Jen and Annie, listened to her complain on a daily basis. They held her up, especially on Emma's worst days.

Tom and Kerry's siblings paid visits to their fragile niece whenever they could. Sr. Carlotta and a small group of chaplains prayed over Emma's crib weekly, asking God to guide the doctors and nurses in her care, pleading for his mercy. Laurie, a social worker in the hospital, had adopted Tom and Kerry as friends and was genuinely concerned with each peak and pitfall Emma encountered. The list was as endless as the support Tom and Kerry had received. Every time they turned around, someone else was going out of their way for them. It was generosity at its best.

Cheryl waited for Jackie to walk away, then whispered to Kerry from across the aisle: "I heard someone lost her baby today," she said. Kerry covered her mouth with both hands. "Who?" she asked.

"I'm not sure," Cheryl answered. "A woman in the break room just told me she was slightly traumatized because she'd been sitting across from a mother who has been rocking her dead baby for the last three hours." Kerry closed her eyes. Liz looked at the ground and shook her head.

"Awful. God awful," Kerry mourned.

"I think it's nice they're letting her spend as much time as she needs," Liz said.

"I'd probably do the same thing," Kerry said.

"Just plain terrible," Cheryl agreed.

The three women sat quietly, rocking back and forth in their collective chairs. Their eyes were dazed, their thoughts, heavy. Matthew slept soundly in Liz's left arm. Emma wriggled in anticipation of her 7 p.m. cares. Colbie Caillat sang her refrain in the distance:

> *It starts in my toes*
> *And I crinkle my nose*
> *Where ever it goes I always know*
> *That you make me smile*
> *Please stay for a while now*
> *Just take your time*
> *Where ever you go*

The song repeated for another hour or so. Then, suddenly it stopped. It was the last time any of them ever heard it played in the NICU.

The sorrowful mood led Kerry to focus her energies on Emma and her failing colostomy bag. The sides had lifted off so much that no amount of stoma paste was going to save it. Reluctantly, she peeled it off and started fresh. This gave Kerry a chance to clean her up, so she grabbed a washcloth and ran it under some warm water before wiping Emma's eight-pound, seven-ounce body clean. When her fingers passed over the area where Emma's leg met her pelvis, she noticed something hard. Kerry removed the washcloth and felt with her bare finger. Pressing in the same spot on the opposite side, she confirmed that this was no normal lump, nor was it in her imagination. She finished up Emma's sponge bath, and waited for Kate to wrap up whatever she was doing with her other patient.

"Kate, feel this. Is this a hernia?" Kerry asked.

"I don't think so," Kate answered, feeling around. "Hold on...that's weird...I don't know...it's something, but I don't know. I'll get one of the neonatologists to look at it." Within minutes, a doctor was assessing the little lump. Minutes after that, a surgeon pressed on Emma's groin, unable to locate it. "It's right there," Kerry pointed out, moving his hand down two centimeters. The surgeon pressed again, then shook his head. Kerry couldn't get over how much he looked like Phillip Seymour Hoffman.

"It's an inguinal hernia. She'll have to have surgery," he announced. Kerry's eyes popped wide-open. "She's having surgery on her esophagus this Thursday. Can they fix the hernia at the same time?" she asked.

"I don't see why not. Call our surgical coordinator and have her put it on the schedule," Phillip Seymour Hoffman's twin instructed.

"Isn't that the nurse's job?" Kerry asked.

"I thought you *were* the nurse," he responded. "You aren't?"

"I'm her mom," Kerry said, looking down at her clothes, then over to Kate.

"Nice work, Mom." Phillip Seymour Hoffman's twin said. Kate patted her shoulders and quickly phoned in the request. The voice in Kerry's head echoed their sentiments:

"Nice work, Mom."

Later that night, Cheryl, Liz and Kerry couldn't seem to bring themselves to go home. It was 8:15 p.m., their babies were tucked in tight, and there was nothing to do but say goodnight. And yet, they didn't. For whatever reason, they didn't want to leave either their children or each other.

They talked about Caitlin and how deathly ill she'd become. A few days before, Shawna had told them she was taken off the transplant list. Caitlin's condition had become *so* grim that even if a liver *were* awarded to her, she wouldn't have been capable of surviving the actual surgery. Respiratory had her at the highest settings on the hi-fi ventilator, and her doctors had moved her into an isolation room at the back of the NICU. Her fluid retention was such that her stomach ballooned out to three times its normal size. The color of her skin was so astounding, even the hospital's top surgeons were unnerved. Cheryl, Liz and Kerry could see hope draining out of every doctor, nurse, friend and relative that stood by Caitlin's crib. It had been terribly heartbreaking to watch. The only positive thing to occur was some recent success in draining her excess fluid. It had taken the pressure off Caitlin's lungs, enough to dial down the vent settings and allow her back on the transplant list. But everyone knew that time was of the essence, and time Caitlin did not have.

They talked about their relationships. Cheryl described her first date with Liz, how it was snowing when she picked her up, and how incredibly anxious her driving had made the pretty English teacher. Cheryl talked about falling in love with Liz and how difficult it was for her parents to accept. Liz talked about her pregnancies, how she fielded questions from her students about paternity. She described the funny looks she and Cheryl would get, sometimes, when they held hands at restaurants, movie theaters and on planes. Liz talked about having to face the staff at the high school she taught at, with only one son to show for. Cheryl, Liz and Kerry all pondered how Matthew would be affected, growing up knowing he was without his identical twin. To them, it was a hole that could never be filled. But they had to wonder if Matthew would feel the same, given he would never know otherwise. Liz and Cheryl debated when would be the best time to tell Matthew, and concluded that as soon as he could understand—he should know.

They talked about their faith and how God factored into everything they had been experiencing. Kerry told Cheryl and Liz about her "confession" back in March to the young priest with the strongest Rhode Island accent she'd ever heard. "It was so weird," she said, "like I was talking to my brother-in-law." She told them that the only thing she had to say was how painfully angry she had been with her maker. How her inability to understand God's *plan* had her second-guessing his existence. Kerry explained how "Father RI" kept his cool and seemed to understand everything she was saying. How he had explained that God didn't mind that she was angry with him, as long as she still believed.

How God was crying right along with her, every step of the way.

"I guess that's what I still don't understand," Kerry had said to him. *"If God planned all of this for Emma, then why bother crying when it plays out exactly as he wished it would?"* She told them that Father RI didn't really have an explanation for it, only the encouragement to *"have faith"* and to *"trust in God"*. "I left church feeling just as confused as when I arrived," Kerry explained. "The only difference was, I had the green light to continue being angry, so at least that was *something*," she smirked.

They talked about how differently some people react to a crisis. How near-strangers had come out of the woodwork with their arms open wide, while some life-long friends had retreated into the shadows, keeping as much distance as possible from them and their problems. They were in the middle of sharing stories about their mothers not letting them off the hook for certain things, crisis or no crisis, when Shawna and Tim ran past them in a frantic whoosh. Only it wasn't a bad-frantic, it was an excited one. All three of them stood up and watched as the couple reached Caitlin's crib. Shawna and Tim smiled, bright, beautiful smiles. They hugged the doctors and nurses who were circling around them.

"She got a liver!" Liz gasped.

"She must have!" Kerry agreed.

"Oh, my God," Cheryl cried, "I've never seen Tim smile!" Tears dripped from all three of their eyes. Jackie walked over to them and was stopped in her tracks by all of the emotion.

"What in bloody hell is going on with you guys?" Jackie asked.

"We think Caitlin just got a liver!" Kerry said. Jackie welled up immediately and grabbed Kerry. Liz and Cheryl stood up and joined in. The four of them cried and hugged and danced around Bay 6, until Cheryl spotted Shawna and Tim walking towards them.

"Is it what we think?" Kerry asked. Shawna beamed a smile that confirmed what they had suspected. She said she was in Walgreens when the doctor called, and she just dropped everything in the aisle and ran out screaming: *"MY DAUGHTER HAS A LIVER!"* Tim mentioned that they had been told Caitlin would receive a split liver from a young adult male who had fallen. The other half was going to a forty-year-old man.

Knowing that someone had to lose their life in order to give Caitlin hers was intense—a tragic circumstance in and of itself. They all felt that. But in that moment, a very sick little baby was being given a second chance at life, which was an extraordinary gift by any measure. Shawna and Tim hugged all of them tight, then returned to Caitlin's crib to anxiously review the details of her upcoming transplant surgery.

"I think that was the most beautiful moment of my entire life," Liz said, "No offense, Cheryl."

"None taken, honey," Cheryl said. "And I won't tell our children that you said that either."

"Please don't," Liz begged.

As Kerry drove home that night, her head was swirling with the events of the day. Things had started out so sad and ended so tremendously. It had been a while since she'd celebrated anything, and the feeling in her heart was indescribable. Driving south on 95, a course she'd now driven hundreds of times, Kerry's mind was focused on a popular topic: God. Only this time, she wasn't seeping with anger. *Wonder* had moved in, and was causing quite a stir in that head of hers. Kerry thought about the priest, the Haitian woman and Andrew the chaplain. She thought about Sr. Carlotta, her parents and the Irish nuns who taught at her grammar school back in New Jersey.

All of these people had something in common: they believed in God. But did they all believe that God worked in the same way? She wasn't so sure. *Who's to say*, Kerry thought, *that God even has a plan? What if everybody as far back as Abraham has gotten this wrong?* Kerry had grown so tired of this theory—it just didn't make sense to her. *What if God makes mistakes too?* she wondered. The human body was so beautifully complex, this was something she'd been well educated on over the last few months. *Only a divine genius could have come up with the concept*, she thought. *But what if, like in all paradigms, imperfections happen. And when they happen, God—the creator—is just as upset as the rest of us. What if there are glitches that even God didn't foresee when he designed the human blueprint? Whether they happen during development or later on in life. What if everything that happens in the world, good and bad,* **isn't** *planned? Is it possible that even God couldn't have thought of everything?*

Kerry felt clear, and was amazed that this was the first time any of this had crossed her mind. She pictured the Haitian woman speaking the words *"God is good"* to her. *What if the woman was using "good" as a noun, instead of an adjective?* Kerry wondered. If God was indeed everything that was good in the world, it was a hell of a lot easier to put a face to him. All Kerry's life when she had thought about God, she'd imagined the essence of the almighty man who stood on a cloud and watched over, judging from above. *What if instead,* Kerry thought, *God is the neighbor who drops off dinner, or the friend who listens to me cry on the phone, or the nurse that thinks about my daughter on her way home from work? What if God is the hug from my mother-in-law, the prayer from a stranger, or the person who remembers that Emma's replogle is connected to wall suction? What if God is my mom or dad, sister or brother, nurse or surgeon—showing up when I need them…offering advice and consent whenever they can? What if,* Kerry thought, *God is my conscience…guiding me through my life…reminding me when something is important, and when something is a waste of time?* All of this made complete sense. *What if,* Kerry thought, *the sign that hung above my third grade classroom's door was right? What if: GOD IS LOVE?*

The Killers were rocking *"Mr. Brightside"* from her radio, and Kerry couldn't help but laugh at the coincidence. After all, wasn't this all about changing her perspective? God had created her with a rational mind, it seemed she'd be doing him a disservice not to use such a convoluted gift. It boggled Kerry that up until then, she'd been letting other people tell her who God was, instead of figuring it out on her own. Finally she understood that God *would* always be there for her, she just had to look for him—or her. *Did everyone else already know this?* Kerry wondered. Suddenly, it was so obvious.

Tom was in bed reading when she finally got home. He knew something was up the moment Kerry walked into the room. Her energy was off. She seemed…happy. Kerry threw her purse on the dresser and flopped down on top of him, kissing the side of his neck.

"What's going on?" Tom asked. "How's Emma?"

"She's fine," Kerry answered, rubbing her hand along his arm. Confused, Tom watched as she gently glided her fingers up towards his shoulder then down to his hand, forcing the book from his grasp. "Oh, she does have to have another surgery," she added.

"What?" Tom said, sitting up straight.

"It's just a little hernia, no big deal," she explained. "They're going to fix it during her operation next week." Kerry resumed her gentle massage, this time along his bare chest. "The most amazing thing happened tonight, babe," she said.

"What?" Tom asked.

"Caitlin got a liver!" she beamed. "They're probably going to do the surgery next week."

"Oh, my God! That *is* amazing," he said. "Amazing news!" This time, he was careful not to move. As excited as he was, Tom was enjoying Kerry's attention even more.

"God is good!" Kerry said. She kissed his neck and pressed her body as close as she could to him.

"God *is* good!" Tom agreed. They were kissing now. Their breathing was heavy. He reached for her shirt and pulled it off with one tug. She took off his glasses and set them on the bedside table. It appeared Tom's dry streak had officially come to an end. They rolled towards each other, into a cloud of passion.

"Thank God!" Tom cried. "Thank God! Thank God!"

"You should!" Kerry laughed. "You really should!"

Chapter 12

CONNECTIONS

TOM SNICKERED TO himself as he turned onto Route 16 East. The level ground under his feet seemed like a mirage, especially knowing what he would soon have to face. A lean blonde woman he'd been trailing all through Newton moved to the right side of the road and slowed down to a walk. Her hands were on her hips, and she sucked in as much breath as her lungs would allow. Tom thought about doing the same. He hadn't given himself a break in a while. Plus, Heartbreak Hill would be coming up pretty soon. Tom knew his parents planned on being stationed somewhere near the hill, and he really wanted to look strong when he passed them. A break at this point seemed perfectly reasonable. Tom followed suit and moved to the right-hand side of the road, resting his hands on top of his head as he slowed his legs down.

No sooner was he walking, when a stout, middle-aged man with dark brown skin tapped him on the back. As he passed Tom, the man said nothing, yet simply waved his hand in a beckoning motion. *What was that?* Tom wondered. He watched as the man did the same thing to the blonde woman who was still catching her breath. Almost instantly, she removed her hands from her hips and worked her way into a jog. *Ahhh,* Tom thought, *he wants us to keep running.* Perhaps it *wasn't* such a great spot to take a break, after all.

Encouragement was not to be underrated, according to Tom. In the nine months he'd been training for this race, it was the one thing Kerry didn't really offer up. *She doesn't get it,* Tom would remind himself every time Kerry got upset. Everything always seemed to come back to *her.* *"This is such a difficult time! Why are you doing this to me right now?"* Kerry would often ask. She didn't think it was fair that Tom should be able to take off and train, hours on end, while she stayed home and held down the fort. *"Why can't you just go out and jog three to four miles a few times a week like normal people? Why does it have to be a marathon?"* she'd ask. Tom felt badly that it was so time consuming, and even offered to train during his lunch hours and early in the morning, but nothing seemed to satisfy Kerry. *"Your timing really sucks, Tom! It's the toughest year of our lives, and you're out running for half of it!"* she had said.

Kerry was right—Tom was gone a lot. Every weekend, she'd wake up with the kids while he was getting in his long runs. A few weekends throughout the year had been dedicated to running in the half-marathons Tom had signed up for: Maine, New Hampshire, and Newport. The training runs with the Boston Children's group were an all day affair, especially when travel time was factored into everything. The whole thing was a major time-suck. And as for herself? Well, Kerry practically had to move mountains just to make an appointment for a pap smear, so the idea that Tom could commit to something *so* major at such a challenging time in both their lives—without her consent—was completely unfair in her eyes. Not to mention, exhausting for both of them. To the rest of the world, Tom looked like a hero. But to Kerry, he had been disappointing. She needed his help and didn't feel Tom was there to give it to her. *"I HAVE to do this!"* Tom would tell her, but that was never reason enough for Kerry. *"I'd like to see how it would affect you if the tables were turned,"* she'd say. *"If you had to pick up all the slack from something I suddenly decided I HAD to do."*

The blonde woman remained ten steps ahead of Tom, but the stout man with dark skin had advanced out of sight. *Maybe,* Tom thought, *I should have told her. Maybe, if Kerry understood, she would be happy about this.*

By the time Tom reached the Newton Fire Station, he'd regained his pace. As he made the sharp turn onto Route 16, he couldn't help but notice the countless firefighters lining both the sidewalks and inside the windows of this landmark. Immediately he thought about his cousins, who were among the long list of first responders on 9/11. To be admired by men and women of such equal caliber was unbelievable. Tom saluted as he passed their cheering screams and applause, and took a moment to drink in *their* encouragement. Another hill was quickly approaching, and he was going to need it.

178

Before he began his ascent, Tom reached for another little boost and read:

MILE 18: Emma's surgery....

MARIA WAS TAKING Emma's temperature when the anesthesia team approached Tom and Kerry for their sign-off on her surgery. May 1, 2008 had finally arrived, the day they'd been anticipating since her last surgery three and a half months earlier. Because of the inconclusive fluoroscopy, the surgeons couldn't be sure what kind of success they were going to have when they tried to connect her esophagus. Dr. Buchmiller had explained that once they opened her up, there were three possibilities for Emma:

1. The gap between the bottom and top portions of her esophagus could be *so* long; the only way they'd be able to connect it would be to use foreign tissue (i.e. cow intestine) to bring both ends "together". It would involve another surgery, and a much longer hospital stay.

2. The gap could be *too* long, but not impossible to connect; hence the need for traction sutures. This was a new technique brought to Boston Children's by Dr. Jennings. He had studied it being done at Cincinnati's Children's Hospital, where they'd succeeded in stretching children's esophagi over the course of two to three weeks, before attempting to connect them. In this possibility, Emma would have traction sutures tied to both parts of her esophagus, then pulled across her body and brought to the surface of her skin in the shape of an "X". Every day after this procedure, her surgeons would pull on the sutures and tie them a little tighter, therefore stretching the tissue. Emma would have to be intubated and heavily sedated during this time, as any sudden movements could cause countless problems including tears in her esophagus. Once the stretching was complete, they would bring her back into the operating room and attempt to connect her. Regardless of their success, this kind of connection usually caused narrowing, and would most likely result in Emma having to have multiple "dilations" of her esophagus throughout her lifetime.

3. The gap could be nonexistent, with both ends just the right length, ready to be connected.

Not knowing which of these three fates Emma was about to meet added to Tom and Kerry's strain. They signed anesthesia's consent forms and let out a simultaneous sigh. "The gig's up," Kerry whispered to Tom. A few weeks prior, Nancy had suggested they put themselves into a state of denial in order to manage their pre-surgery stress. Denial had been a friend to them both, eliminating so many of the "what ifs" that had crept into their heads. But now that May 1st had arrived, they had no choice but to face up. It was going to be a long, difficult day for their baby girl, and a torturous one for her mom and dad.

"Who left these here?" Kerry asked pointing to a bag filled with *OK, In Touch, Star* and *In Style* magazines.

"Your pals across the way," Maria answered, glancing at Matthew's crib. Kerry smiled as she thumbed through the jackpot of trash. Not one *Time* or *Newsweek* to be found. Even *People* was missing from the lot. *Perfect,* Kerry thought. She was touched that they had known enough not to give her anything with substance. At the bottom of the bag was a card from Liz and Cheryl. Tom peeked over her shoulder and together they read the beautiful words of support, written by the two people who knew exactly what they were going through. Tears were running down both their faces by the time they finished.

"Oh, no! Don't start crying now! You have all day to do that!" Maria admonished.

"Alright!" Tom quipped, wiping his cheeks. "Change of subject, how did you get to work this morning?"

"Hmmmm," Maria said, looking at her feet, "let me think... Oh, yeah...I ran here today."

"How far is the hospital from your house?" Tom asked.

"About 10 miles, give or take a few inches," Maria laughed. It fascinated Tom that this little nurse in her fifties chose to walk, bike or run to work up to four times a week. Even during the nastiest winter weather, Maria would find ways to work her exercise regime into her morning commute. Her hot pink running sneakers always stood out against the sea of clogs and crocs worn by her coworkers. She'd just run the Boston Marathon a few weeks back, and even that didn't seem to slow her down.

"I'd love to be able to do that," Tom said.

"Why can't you?" Maria asked. Kerry snickered. She was wiping her own tears away and tried to play it off as a sniffle, but Tom's glare hinted to a failed attempt.

"Maybe I will. I could run to my office in Wickford; its about ten miles from home. In fact, maybe I'll run the Boston Marathon next year," he said, sticking out his chin.

"Okay, babe, that sounds great," Kerry smirked.

"I'm serious," Tom countered. "I'll start training next week, and by April 2009 I'll run the marathon."

"If you can run anywhere near as fast as you can drive, you'll be in good shape! Right, Mommy?" Maria joked.

"Watch it," Tom warned. "You're still on thin ice with me," he said, pointing to the half-ripped picture of Eli Manning now pathetically taped to the side of Emma's crib.

"What I meant to say," Maria corrected herself, "was best of luck. I know you can do it." Tom looked over to Kerry, who was reaching in to comfort Emma.

"Well?" he asked.

"Yes, honey. Best of luck," Kerry muttered.

Delivering Emma through the doors of the operating room wasn't any easier this time around, yet somehow Tom and Kerry achieved it with a touch less panic then in January. They knew that that without this surgery, their daughter would have little to no quality of life, therefore making their "goodbye" sadly necessary. At the same time, Emma had grown so much. They'd fallen so deeply in love with her—it was maddening to even consider their lives without her at this point. Tom, a veteran to the surgical waiting room, introduced Kerry to the liaison nurses and gave her a rough idea of what to expect with regards to their updates. They were told Emma's surgery could take anywhere from eight to twelve hours.

"I asked Dr. Buchmiller to give me some kind of a sign that everything went well, if it does, when she comes to talk to us after the surgery's over. Just a simple thumbs up or something," Tom said.

"Okay," Kerry responded. "Is that weird?"

"You wait and see how you feel during the twenty seconds it takes for her to walk down that hallway, then let me know if it's weird," Tom replied.

The hallway did look pretty long, as did the faces of all the parents walking down it. Surrounded with heavy emotion, it was an atmosphere Tom and Kerry had become all too accustomed to breathing in. Tom claimed a quiet area in the back corner where they sat down and held each other, faces pressed close, for a good twenty minutes. Together, they prayed for Emma's safety and for God to guide her surgeons' hands. When they were finished, Tom offered to run across the street for some Starbucks while Kerry fielded phone calls from family and friends.

By the time Tom returned, Kerry was ready to weave herself a cocoon of trashy magazines. Tom opened his laptop and threw himself into his Singapore work. They hadn't looked up once, when the liaison nurse came by with her first update. All was well, Emma had been successfully intubated and her arterial line was in place. The surgeons planned to fix her hernia before placing her chest tube—to get it out of the way, before they REALLY had to mess with her. The next time Tom and Kerry lifted their heads was to learn the hernia repair had been a success and the surgeons were ready to move on to the main event. It was hard to believe three coffees and four hours had passed by the time either of Emma's parents even spoke.

"What should we do when she gets home?" Kerry asked. "I think we should baptize her in the church."

"Yes, definitely," Tom agreed. "We should throw the biggest party anyone's ever been to."

"We should," Kerry said.

"I'm talking big white tents, a huge bouncy house, rented tables and chairs, catered—the whole nine yards," Tom said.

"Catered?" Kerry asked. She winced at the sound of the dollar signs flying out of Tom's mouth.

"Yes, Kerry, catered! We'll get *Venda Ravioli* up in Providence to make a bunch of sandwiches...maybe a huge pot of chowder...some salads. It will be awesome," Tom explained. He stuck out his chin and was glaring at her with his *"I'm serious"*, and *"Don't even try to suggest I grill one hundred and fifty hot dogs and hamburgers"* face.

"I'll tie balloons all around the deck, in different colors...and we'll invite everyone we know...everyone who's been praying for her since the day she was born. Hell, we'll invite the whole NICU! She can wear a cute little party dress with little flowers...all poufy. I'll ask Jen to get one of those beautiful cakes from the Cake Lady, and Annie can make a mix of all *Emma* songs...Brown Eyed Girl etc....she's good at that. We'll blast music and the kids can run around and eat ice cream. It'll be the biggest celebration EVER. I love it!" Kerry squealed.

She and Tom jotted down all their ideas in her organizer. They even picked out a few possible dates. The longer they talked about it, the more excited they became. Kerry was debating menu particulars with Tom, when the liaison nurse interrupted with her latest update. Everything was going well. They were six hours in at this point. The surgeons were working on releasing both parts of her esophagus, which were tangled in a sea of connected tissue and blood vessels. In other words, this part was going to take a while. There was still no word on what kind of a connection, if any, they were going to be able to achieve.

Kerry put down her organizer and looked outside the window, which was facing another hospital. People smoked cigarettes on the sidewalk just outside the entrance. A man paced back and forth, furiously inhaling smoke while gesturing into his cell phone. He seemed oblivious to all the people who were purposely stepping aside to get out of his way. His long, skinny arms waved around as he spoke. The Red Sox jersey he wore was swimming on him. When he ended his call, he lit another cigarette and continued pacing the sidewalk. He narrowly missed colliding with an older man pushing his wife in a wheelchair.

At the seven and a half hour mark, the update was pretty much the same.

The only change was that Tom and Kerry had been assigned a different liaison nurse. It was Sandy. Tom remembered her crazy blond hair and awkward smile. He also knew, it was only going to be a matter of seconds before Kerry started making fun of her. "What is *she* so darn happy about?" Kerry asked. "I mean…should she really be smiling like that?" Kerry crossed her eyes and spoke in a ditzy voice: "Hi, nice to see you again! Your child's at death's door! Hope you're enjoying your lunch! Be back with my next update in ninety minutes!" she joked. Tom covered his face, appearing horrified. "You're terrible," he said. "I suppose it'd be better if she scowled at everyone instead!"

No longer able to concentrate on work, Tom began researching running sneakers on his laptop. Three hundred and seventy-five dollars later, he'd purchased some, along with two books, two shirts and two pairs of shorts. Upon sharing his excitement with Kerry, not shockingly, he was met with disfavor. "You've taken the only sport in the world that's free and found a way to blow hundreds of dollars on it…before you even know if you *like* it!" Kerry said. Tired of always having to defend himself, Tom swallowed his disappointment in his wife's attitude. *It would be nice to see a little enthusiasm from her, for once. A little support*, he thought. Running was something he planned to follow through with.

> *He was already picturing himself crossing the finish line at the marathon, with all of his friends and family watching and cheering him on. They were holding up huge signs decorated with his name. A marching band was playing in the background. Some random man wearing a top hat was putting a huge silver medal around his neck.*

This was something Tom was going to do. He felt it in his heart. But this wasn't the time or place to try to convince Kerry of that. He closed his computer, sat up and took a swig of his coffee. "I guess you don't want to hear about my new subscription to *Runners* Magazine?" he laughed.

Seven minutes before their next update, they were surprised to see two familiar faces walking towards them. Dr. Buchmiller still wore her blue O.R. shower-cap, as did the male resident surgeon walking beside her. Her face looked exhausted, although it bore a happy expression. When she finally made eye contact with them, Dr. Buchmiller was quick to raise both arms in the air with her thumbs pointed towards the sky. Kerry and

Tom grabbed each other's hands and fought back their urges to cheer, so they could hear what their daughter's surgeon had to say.

"She's connected!" Dr. Buchmiller announced. Kerry closed her eyes and covered her face. Tom pumped both fists in the air. The resident took a step back as the three of them fell into a puddle of emotion. "I'm going to have to hug you, now. You know that, right?" Kerry warned Dr. Buchmiller. Practically lifting the surgeon's tiny frame into the air, Kerry infused her embrace with enough gratitude to fill the entire hospital. Tom, unable to help himself, wrapped his arms around both women. When Dr. Buchmiller took a moment to wipe tears and collect herself, Tom and Kerry turned to the resident and did the same. "Thank you!" they cried over and over, "Thank you so much!" When their initial jubilation died down, it was amazing to hear the details of the surgery. The surgeons explained that once they had released both ends, Emma's esophagus fit together almost perfectly. The connection was, in a word, simple. The proud parents looked at each other and shook their heads. In three and a half months, that was the first time anyone had ever used that word to describe their Emma.

After they said their goodbyes to the surgeons, Kerry sat down and pulled out her phone. She rubbed her aching cheeks, not used to so much intense smiling. With about ten phone calls to make, she had no time to waste before heading to the recovery room. As she finished dialing her parents' number, she caught a glimpse of the thin man in the Red Sox jersey running out from the hospital across the street. His head was buried in his hands. Kerry swore she could hear him wailing, despite the giant window and the worlds between them. The line rang. Falling to his knees, the man pounded the cement ground with his fists. People stared, but nobody approached his cloud of misery. The line rang again. The man looked so alone. *Help him!* Kerry thought. *Please, someone do something.* The line rang again, and Donna picked up:

"Hello?" she said frantically. "Kerry, is that you?" Kerry returned her focus to the telephone. "Hello!" Donna yelled.

"Mom, it's me," she said. "They fixed her, Mom." Kerry glanced out the window again; a woman was hugging the man on the sidewalk. "Emma's fixed," she cried.

Emma's recovery was, again, difficult, but successful. Within a week, Kerry was giving her sips of breast milk from a bottle. Her g-tube still remained, given how long it can take some patients to learn the art of eating and drinking, but the replogle was no longer a permanent fixture in Emma's mouth. A few days later on Mother's Day, Tom and Kerry brought the boys to Boston and all four of them escorted their little princess on a stroll around the hospital's "Prouty Garden". It was her very first trip outdoors. Thomas and Ryan skipped along the flowered pathways, oblivious to the enormity of the situation. Kerry and Tom beamed as they took turns holding her and snapping pictures of their family. Their whole family, together, in the warmth of the sun. Three days later, the Sheerans said goodbye to all their friends in the NICU. Much emotion flowed from the doctors, nurses, social workers and parents who crowded around Emma's crib in anticipation of her departure to "the floor." Tim and Shawna, fresh off the heels of Caitlin's successful transplant surgery, vowed to keep in touch with them: "You're forever on our Christmas list!" they promised. Cheryl and Liz agreed that they were now all connected for the rest of their lives. As Kerry hugged them, she caught a glimpse of Roberta Hoffman's picture flashing on the monitor, Children's May 2008 winner. "I just can't bare the thought of you guys staring at another Employee of the Month!" she cried. Liz laughed, "We had a long talk with Matthew and he understands that six is our absolute limit!" she assured them.

After two days in a standard hospital room, it was time for their daughter to be discharged. Tom and Kerry's heads spun through a two and a half hour instructional from Emma's nurse on everything they needed to know: How to perform CPR; How to operate the feeding pump; When to administer each of her seven medications, multiple times/daily; What to do if her g-tube pops out; How to determine if she has an intestinal blockage; How to determine if her esophagus develops a stricture; Where to order certain compound medications; Where to order colostomy and feeding bags, catheters and skin barriers; How to work the clasps on the pump's drip chamber. This list went on, so much so that even the nurse looked pale and sweaty as she requested their "sign-off" on Emma's discharge. As Kerry put her signature on the last page, she heard a familiar voice whisper:

"Don't worry, you can do this."

The nurse shook their hands and wished them *good luck.* Then Kerry pushed the stroller filled with medical supplies, and Tom proudly waved

Emma's hand as he carried her past the nurses' station, towards the elevators.

Once inside, a little old lady smiled at Tom and Kerry as she admired Emma's pink seersucker dress and delicate white sweater. "Congratulations," she said. Emma's parents smiled back at the lady, and then at each other. Moments later the elevator doors opened and Tom turned to Kerry. Emma was outstretched in his hands. "Here," he said, "I think you've earned the right to carry her out of here." Kerry tearfully accepted; cradling her nine pound, eight ounce daughter tightly in her arms as they walked through the lobby and out the revolving front door. It was hard not to notice all the cars pulling up, filled with new patients, ready to take Emma's place inside. Her day had finally come. Emma's beautiful, glorious, frightening, long-awaited day had arrived. On May 17, 2008, after one hundred and eleven days in the hospital, Emma Sheeran headed home.

"Thank you, God," Kerry whispered.

Chapter 13

HEARTBREAK HILL

GRACIE'S RED CURLS bounced in unison with her father's footsteps as he conquered Commonwealth Avenue's second of three hills. Tom perked up at the sight; it was just the thing he needed to convince his legs to keep climbing. With Mile 19 behind him and Heartbreak Hill dead ahead, his calves needed a distraction to keep them from spontaneously combusting. Tom knew if he could just saddle up alongside Joe for the next eight minutes, he'd have a chance at breaking through the wall he was hitting. His ankle throbbed; his thighs quivered; his shoulders ached. Tom's body begged him to stop, but his soul wouldn't allow it. The mental vs. physical debate was intense and yet all the while he still ran. He summoned as much force as he could and powered past his friend just as the hill leveled out. Then he looked over his shoulder to catch a glimpse of Needham Joe behind him.

"Hey! No passing on the right!" Joe yelled.

"Oh, is that you? I didn't realize I was passing you," Tom said. "How's my dust taste?"

"Don't even try, bro. You know it's only gonna be a matter of minutes before I'm serving you a big plate of my own," Joe laughed. "Enjoy this limited time we have together!" He was huffing and puffing a little more then usual. So was Tom. "What kind of inspiration have you got in store for me?" Joe asked, pointing to Tom's note. Tom hesitated as he looked at the sweaty, worn paper in his hand. Perhaps this was a good place to end the story. He couldn't imagine dragging a near stranger through the next chapter. Even more, he couldn't fathom having enough breath to speak while trudging up Heartbreak Hill.

"I finished the letter already," Tom said, stuffing it into his shorts. "Her esophagus was connected and she was able to come home two weeks later."

"Wow," Joe said, "I can't believe I missed the ending! Way to go, Mighty Emma!"

"Yeah," Tom smiled, "but what about Gracie? What kind of valve problems was she born with? I still don't know much about what she's been through."

Tom was excited to let Joe do the talking for once. He preserved his oxygen and listened as his new friend from Needham explained that Gracie was born with pulmonary atresia, a defect by which the valve that lets blood flow from her heart to her lungs had formed incorrectly. In Gracie's case, a solid sheet of tissue had blocked the blood that came from the right side of her heart from going back to her lungs to get oxygen. Joe told him that at birth, Gracie underwent immediate open-heart surgery to place a shunt between her aorta and the pulmonary artery in order to keep blood flowing to her lungs. "This saved her life," Joe said. He went on to explain that she did well with the shunt for the first three years, but soon enough, the effects of her underdeveloped heart's right ventricle played a part in several follow-up surgeries. These were attempts to correct the area where blood exited to her pulmonary artery. "She would get out of breath pretty easily," Joe explained, "But that never kept her from dancing!"

"So, it took five surgeries to fix it?" Tom asked.

"They tried, but they were never able to actually fix it," Joe said.

"Oh, when you said that Children's saved her life five times, I assumed they fixed it," Tom said.

"They did save her five times," Joe explained, "but the sixth time, they just couldn't pull off another miracle." Tom looked at Joe, unable to process the last thing he had said.

"But I thought you said...she was here today?" Tom questioned.

"She's with me every day, brother," Joe smiled. "Now, if you'll excuse me, I feel the wind at my back." In a heartbeat, Joe took off, unapologetically leaving Tom in his wake as he seized every step of Commonwealth's third of three summits. His feet seemed to barely touch the ground, gliding past every other runner as if he were riding on the wings of an angel. Disappearing suddenly, Tom had to wonder if Joe were ever really there to begin with. He tried, but it was impossible to spot him amongst the twenty-six thousand other marathoners, all running through Boston with their own stories. Some fueled with glory and inspiration, others simply trying to heal their broken hearts. Either way, they were doing it together. Mothers, fathers, daughters, sons, sisters and brothers...hoping for a gust of wind...just trying to make it up the hill.

* * *

"Tommy! There he is! Oh, my God, give me my camera, Tom! Come on, he's coming! Do you see him? He's coming! He's right there...give me my damn camera, please!" Jane screamed. Tom and Jane Sheeran were perched on a sidewalk with hundreds of other fans, waving their arms uncontrollably like a couple of wild air traffic controllers. It was impossible for Tom not to see them as he slowly approached, but that didn't stop Jane from bellowing his name at the loudest possible octave known to man.

"TOMMY!!!!!" they screamed. Even Tom's father couldn't help himself, belting out cheers for his boy. This was one of those moments that deserved a little pomp and circumstance. Here Tom was, once again making his parents burst with pride.

His whole life, Tom had always approached everything through an optimist's eyes. His generous spirit had granted him a special place in their family. If anyone needed help, Tom would come running. If they needed a problem solved, Tom would solve it. If they needed to settle a fight, Tom would be their referee. This past year, however, the tables had been turned. Their dear son was now the one in need. It was heartbreaking to watch him in this role, to see him suffer. But his beautiful grace throughout everything had been remarkable. His strength went beyond measure. Today was just another reminder of that.

Tom waved to let them know he had spotted them. A sudden burst of emotion pummeled through him as he made eye contact. These two fans, in particular, were the very reason he was capable of doing what he was doing. Jane and Tom Sr. were the kind of parents every child wants. Sure, Jane was loud and easily excited, but that never bothered Tom. She spent his whole life encouraging him to reach further then he thought he could, never missing an opportunity to tell him how special he was. Tom Sr. led by example. His devotion to God had rubbed of on Tom and played a big part in his faith. Most importantly, however, Jane and Tom Sr. were always there for him. Today and everyday before, his parents were the kind of people who would run into a burning building without hesitation. This past year, especially, they had reminded Tom of the true gifts that make up a family: generosity; unconditional love and support; unwavering compassion. Tom and Jane had given all of these in abundance to their son and his wife. They had pulled Tom and Kerry through some of their most difficult days.

"How are you feeling, honey? You look good. Are you thirsty? I think I have some water in my bag. Hold on, Tom…hand me my bag. I gotta get Tommy some water," Jane barked.

"I'm fine, Ma. There's a water station right there. I'll get some there," Tom said.

"Lookin' good, kid," Tom Sr. said. "Only six more to go and you'll have earned that medal, son."

"Thanks, Pop," Tom grinned. Suddenly, a flood of emotion poured out from within him. He was embarrassed to be crying in front of so many people, but he couldn't control himself. "Thanks so much for coming today," Tom wept.

"We wouldn't have missed it for the world," Jane said, handing him her water. Not surprisingly, she was choking up too. "Oh, Tommy! You've come so far. We're so proud of you, honey."

"So proud," Tom Sr. concurred. Jane convinced an innocent bystander to take a few pictures of the three of them, then she snapped nine or ten more before they kissed him goodbye. "That's MY son!" Jane screamed as Tom turned around to wave one last time.

Continuing up the second half of Heartbreak, Tom's legs couldn't believe what his heart was asking him to do. The sixty seconds he'd spent with his parents had been a tease. He feared it would be impossible to shift into second gear. The crowd was dense and intimidating. He wondered what he must look like to these spectators. *Do they think I'm running out of gas? Do they know how badly I wish the race would end?* he wondered. Fearing this was written all over his face, Tom did his best to look down and take small but meaningful strides. His legs fought him. *What kind of sadomasochist designed this freaking course?* he wondered. *Why would anyone put three big freaking hills at mile 20 of a marathon? There's got to be a better way to Kenmore Square!* Suddenly, his angry mental rant was interrupted by another excited fan.

"Yeah, Tom! Yeah, Buddy! Alright, Tom!" Mike yelled. It was Tom's college roommate, Mike McGourty. He'd forgotten Mike had planned to camp out at this mile, too. The sound of his friend's voice was just the medicine he needed. "Yeah Tom! Kick Haatbreak Hill's ahhss, Buddy! Kick it haad!" he yelled.

Tom lovingly referred to Mike as a "Native Masshole". Their bond went back sixteen years, beginning in Browning Dorm at the University of Rhode Island. Their mutual hatred for each other's sports teams had kept the fire alive in their relationship. Tom had seen Mike through a difficult end to Mike's first marriage, and Mike had seen Tom through every minute of Emma's ups and downs. Tom had practically lived with him and his wife throughout the ordeal. Mike was the first person to call Tom every morning, and the last one Tom dialed every night. Kerry referred to Mike as Tom's *boyfriend* and teased them about being "*worse then two hens in a henhouse*". They were great friends.

"I'm hitting the wall, man!" Tom yelled, as he got closer.

"Nah! You're fine, dude! The towp of the hill's right there! You gowt this!" Mike yelled back.

"It's my legs, they're screaming at me," Tom wailed.

"Tell your legs to shut the fuck up and keep running. You're almost done!" Mike commanded. Mothers covered their young children's ears and seethed at the exchange going on between Tom and his buddy. It wasn't right for two balding men in their thirties to be speaking in such a manner.

"I don't think I can stop to say *hi*. I'm sorry, dude," Tom apologized. He felt guilty knowing how much effort it had taken for Mike to be there, cheering him on.

"Don't stowp, buddy. Just keep goin'! Do it feh her! Finish this feh Emma." Mike insisted. Tom reached his hand out and slapped Mike a big, fat high-five as he passed by. *What timing*, Tom thought, considering Mike was the call he would have made if he had his phone at that moment. As usual, his friend had said exactly what he needed to hear. Following Mike's advice, Tom reached inside the part of his heart that was decorated with big brown eyes and innocent smiles. It was all he needed to do for a quick recharge. In less then a minute, his feet touched the crest of the summit and felt the flat ground beneath them. The crowd sounded as delirious as he felt. Tom had done it. He had put Heartbreak behind him. Looking down at Kerry's note, he acknowledged the need to do this, now, figuratively. And so Tom read:

MILE 21: Trouble on the Highway....

THE BIG WHITE stork holding a baby girl on the Sheeran's front lawn had started to brown. Withered rhododendron flowers hung from its metal stakes in the ground. Green and yellow balloons were tied to the mailbox next to their driveway. Shrieks and giggles could be heard coming from the backyard. Glimpses of monkeys blowing bubbles and hanging from the swing set could be seen from the road.

Ryan's birthday party was well underway. This year's theme was Curious George. Kerry beamed as she placed Ryan's monkey cake in front of him, candles blazing. She crossed her fingers as he and Thomas blew them out, hoping their wishes were the same as hers. The proud two-year-old wore a bathing suit and a golden crown, and giggled as he watched Thomas stick his finger in the icing. He checked to make sure his mom wasn't watching, then quickly did the same. Tom did his best to manage the kids on the Slip 'N Slide. It killed him to see the beating it was giving his grass. All around the party, children's faces were hidden under monkey masks. Even the littlest guest wore one, fast asleep, snuggled in her grandmother's arms.

Emma had been home for two weeks, and boy had she made an entrance. The kitchen was filled with medications, charts and scales. The living room had been swallowed by her gear: a pack n play, breast pump, baby swings, bouncy seats, IV poles and feeding bags. The nursery was piled with boxes of catheters, colostomy bags and countless other supplies. A chart was taped to the wall next to the changing table, listing every diaper's weight and colostomy poop cleanse. Thomas and Ryan enjoyed placing the wet diapers on the scale. Casa Sheeran had transformed into it's own version of a NICU. The only difference was, half the staff members were three and under.

The boys had to be constantly reminded not to yank on Emma's g-tube, especially while a feeding was in process. This was a daily event. Tom took pleasure in pointing out the insanity of his life, every morning, as he playfully kicked Emma's IV pole across the kitchen—one arm holding Emma, the other Ryan, two spoons clenched in his teeth and two cereal bowls on his head. Thomas LOVED it when Tom did this. Luckily for Kerry, Donna had come back to Rhode Island just before Emma was discharged. Jane, too, was a solid fixture within their four walls. They had set up Emma's equipment, tracking systems, feeding/care schedules and nursing visits, and had gotten most of it down to a science. They were figuring out their new life together and it was working. It was stressful and exhausting, but it worked. They called themselves "Team Emma."

One thing they did not have down to a science, however, was Emma's bottle-feedings. This had proved to be their greatest challenge. Her suck and swallow ability had been stunted during her time in the hospital. When they tried to feed her, the nipple would just rest in Emma's mouth, un-sucked, until enough milk had pooled in the back of her throat to send her into a coughing fit. Emma hated bottle feedings. She was more then happy to receive her mother's milk the old-fashioned way: through the hole in her stomach. Once in a while she'd get the hang of it for a few seconds, but drinking as much as half an ounce from the bottle would often take up to two hours to achieve. Tom, Donna and Jane each took turns trying, but their patience always seemed to wear thin around the sixty-minute mark. Kerry, on the other hand, refused to give up.

Two weeks earlier, the voice in Kerry's head had started up again. It was while she and Donna were watching a "how to" video for the feeding pump. The instructional went through all the pump's functions and settings, and taught the viewer everything they needed to know in order to set the amount/rate per hour for each feeding. It touted this specific pump as being discreet and handy, showing how it could be carried in a little backpack and fished through the child's shirt, almost unnoticeably. The video had shown a little boy who was about six years old, running around a playground with the little backpack on. He would stop periodically to check his g-tube, then continue on with his fun.

"That's not going to be Emma."

The voice told Kerry this as she stood behind her mother at the computer and watched.

"Not saying there's anything wrong with what you're seeing, but I just thought you should know—that won't be Emma."

Kerry was conflicted by what she had heard. She'd grown fond of the tube that had allowed her baby to thrive. Their little miracle weighed ten healthy pounds. Quite frankly, Kerry had started to dislike the bottles almost as much as Emma. But the voice seemed so insistent:

"You're her mother. Help her learn. She'll never have a chance if you don't help her."

So from that moment on, Kerry had vowed to do whatever it took to help Emma figure out her new body. Her connected esophagus needed to be put to good use. The voice had said so.

The kitchen timer went off as Ryan splashed around in a grassy puddle at the base of the Slip 'N Slide. Thomas waited for his mom to head inside for a bottle, then snatched another brownie off the picnic table. Scoping the scene from her Adirondack chair, Donna shook her head. When Kerry arrived back on the deck, she handed Emma to her and started cleaning.

"I can't even believe you're having a birthday party right now," Donna said. "You are a total glutton for punishment!"

"What are you talking about?" Kerry asked.

"And you wanted four kids? Ha! This house is absolute chaos!" Donna laughed.

"It's Ry-Ry's birthday!" Kerry countered. "Plus, we have A LOT to celebrate."

"You have A LOT going on, my dear," Donna said. "How are you going to continue functioning at this rate?" Donna was genuinely concerned.

Kerry and Tom had been moving on all cylinders from sun up to sun down. Donna had been working the night shift with Emma, but that wasn't going to continue, considering she was heading back to New Jersey in a couple of days. Tom had been waking up to go running before work almost four times a week. He was putting in long hours at the office, now that the deal in Singapore was official. When Tom was home, he would jump right in wherever he was needed. Kerry would mostly assign him to Thomas and Ryan, having learned that too many hands on deck with Emma could lead to potential mistakes with medications and such. That left Kerry in charge of a mountainous daily routine from 7 a.m. to 6 p.m.: mealtimes, play dates, naptime, cleaning, cooking, laundry, birthday parties, pre-school events, taking care of Emma and her medical needs, and of course, helping her learn how to suck, swallow and breathe all at the same time. These were *her* responsibilities. Kerry dreaded the day her mother would leave her with all of this on her own. She was thin, exhausted and completely overwhelmed. But Emma's mother was never going to admit it.

"We'll figure something out," Kerry said, working the nipple into Emma's mouth. "The important thing is, she's home and we're all together." Kerry kissed Emma's head, then went back to work on the nipple. "Sure would be a lot easier if Missy Moo would start sucking these down!" she quipped.

Tom limped into the kitchen, gnashing his teeth and growling at the back yard. Thomas was behind him, whimpering about the Slip 'N Slide. "I rolled my ankle on that stupid thing!" Tom yelled. "It's over now. I turned the water off! It's not safe!" In all honestly, Tom wasn't as angry as he appeared. *This twisted ankle*, he thought, *might be just the excuse I've been looking for.* Running had been more difficult then he'd anticipated. Not only had he been sacrificing sleep for exercise, but surprisingly his thirty-four-year-old body was rebelling against him. Tom's knees hurt. His back hurt. And now, his ankle. Running two miles without stopping had been a giant feat that left him heaving to catch his breath. *Two miles! How the hell am I ever going to make it to twenty-six point two?* he had wondered. His two weeks of training had him wondering if perhaps he *did* jump the gun on the whole "marathon" thing. Luckily, he hadn't officially signed up with the Boston Children's Hospital team, so there was still time to back out if he needed to. "This is gonna mess up my training," Tom said, loud enough for everyone to hear. He reached into the freezer for a cold pack, then plopped on the couch. "Does it look swollen to you?" he asked. But Kerry was too busy trying to get Emma to drink. "Come on Em, you can do it. Keep trying, peewee," she begged. Donna dried off the boys and brought them upstairs for their afternoon nap. "There's no way I'm going to be able to run on this," Tom announced.

A few weeks later, Kerry was straightening up in their bedroom when she pulled one of Tom's new running sneakers out from the dusty floor under their bed. She placed it on the shelf in the closet alongside its match and gazed at the pair for a moment, shaking her head.

"Mommy!" Thomas yelled, "Emma's coughing again!" Kerry jumped and ran downstairs to find Emma covered in vomit. It was the third time in two days she'd gotten sick. And it wasn't just a little vomit. It was a lot. This was especially aggravating for Kerry, considering how long it had taken Emma to drink the bottle. She'd come so far over the past twenty-one days, learning to swallow. More then half of Emma's feedings were now by mouth, which was impressive. Kerry would even try to nurse her now and then. She hadn't been very successful, but they were trying, nonetheless. So to see it all come up, after Emma had worked so hard to swallow it down, was downright frustrating.

Kerry picked Emma up and cleaned her off, then grabbed the phone to call the hospital. She explained what was going on to the on-call surgeon: the coughing, the runny nose, the vomiting. Having been to Emma's pediatrician the day before, Kerry hoped it was just a little bug. But the possibility of a stricture weighed heavily on her mind. Before leaving the hospital back in May, Dr. Buchmiller had explained that strictures can be common post-esophageal repair. Like an hourglass, the esophagus can tighten to the point where food and liquids no longer fit down. Dilation under anesthesia is required in these cases, to open the esophagus back up. One of the most obvious signs of a stricture, Dr. Buchmiller had said, is excessive vomiting. Kerry was fearful that this was happening to Emma, as was the on-call surgeon. He suggested she bring Emma up to Boston for an immediate assessment.

"I'm taking her to Boston in twenty minutes, Mom," Kerry said.

"I'm so sorry I'm not there to help you right now," Donna bemoaned. "Who's going to watch the boys?"

"My sitter gets her at 2:30, then Jane will relieve her around 4:30. It's fine. I've got it all under control," Kerry asserted.

"Of course this has to happen the first time Tom's traveling for work," Donna said.

"I know, but this is just the kind of thing I'm going to need to handle on my own. He travels all the time, Mom. I can do this. I can get her to Boston. It's fine," Kerry said.

"Can't Jane-Marie go with you? Is there anyone that can go with you?" Donna asked.

"Mom, I can't call the entire world to help me every time I need to take Emma to the doctor," Kerry said. "I can do this myself." The truth was, Kerry didn't *want* to do this on her own, but felt she *had* to. Kids like Emma weren't going to breeze through life. Her daughter would be seeing doctors and surgeons a lot, especially during her first few years. Kerry already knew this. So it seemed to her, the sooner she learned how to handle these kinds of situations, the better. Today was probably just the first of many. "I'll call you when I know something," Kerry said. Then she hung up the phone and packed Emma's diaper bag with enough supplies to last three days.

Driving past the Providence Place mall, Kerry glanced at the clock on the dashboard. *Ten minutes to get to Providence*, she thought, *not bad.* She knew that if she could make it past North Attleboro by 3:15 p.m., she'd have a good chance at beating all the after school traffic on 95 North. The car was quiet and Kerry was determined. She glanced at the back seat. Although she couldn't see her, she knew Emma was sleeping quietly in her car seat, as she had been since they'd left home. *Dammit*, Kerry thought, *I wish I had installed that little mirror I used with Thomas and Ry.* It was just one of the many things in the middle of hers and Tom's to-do list, but right now it seemed like it should have been at the top. Under the law, a newborn's car seat had to face backwards for the first year of a baby's life. Therefore, without a mirror, it was impossible to actually see a child while driving, aside from the occasional leg kick or arm wave.

Tom called from the airport to let Kerry know he was about to take off. The sound of the phone woke Emma, but she happily cooed at her toys and stretched her legs. Heading out of Savannah with a layover in Charlotte, Tom planned on driving up to Boston as soon as he landed. His plan was going to work as long as rush hour traffic didn't hold him up. When Kerry hung up her phone, she realized the battery was low, and turned it off in order to preserve its power. Emma whimpered softly, so Kerry sang her a lullaby. This calmed her down nicely, transforming her cries back into coos.

Traffic moved, and signs for Walpole appeared. Kerry checked the rear view mirror for traces of tranquility, but Emma's legs and arms seemed frustrated. Her whimpers started up again, this time with a little more force. Kerry thought about stopping to settle Emma, but the on-call surgeon's voice played back in her head: "*If she has a stricture, we need to see her immediately.*" *Stopping to settle her might delay us just enough to get us stuck in traffic*, Kerry thought. That wasn't going to work. Emma needed to get to Boston as soon as possible, and if it meant Kerry were going to have to sing songs the whole way, then that was what she was going to do.

At first, Emma really took to the "Alphabet Song". Kerry's animation was impressive, her voice calming. But by the fourth or fifth time, Emma's cries had become more distressed. Switching to "*Row, Row, Row Your Boat*", Kerry noticed another lull in Emma's whimpers. Continuing to sing, she glanced in the rear-view mirror and was surprised to see Emma's legs still kicking. *She's probably trying to settle herself back to sleep*, Kerry thought. Emma quieted down. It seemed Kerry's lullabies were working. Looking at her clock, she realized they had made their way past Walpole. Signs for Norwood appeared, which meant they'd almost made it to the 95/93 split. *We did it!* she thought. *We beat the after-school rush!* She glanced back at Emma's legs. They were still moving. Carefully, Kerry faded out her song: "Merrily, merrily, merrily, merrily, life is but a dream."

As Kerry's ears adjusted to the quiet, they heard a noise coming from the back seat. At first, it sounded like her air conditioner was failing, but when she turned it off, the noise persisted. It was only a few seconds before Kerry realized it was Emma who was making this noise. But it wasn't the whimper she had been making earlier. It was a faint grunt. So faint, she listened for a few more seconds before deciding the noise was real. "Emma?! Honey?" she called. The grunting continued. Something wasn't right. *Time to pull over*, Kerry thought. *But where?* She was in the left lane and there was no breakdown lane on the left. She threw on her blinker and tried to move towards the right, but two SUVs in the middle lane wouldn't let her in. "Are you okay, Em? Are you okay, peewee?" she yelled. Kerry's heart was beating so fast it caused her voice to quiver. "COME ON! LET ME CROSS!" she screamed at the SUVs. Up ahead, she noticed a large grassy spot on the right side of the road, so she stepped on the gas and blew past the two unaccommodating cars at warp speed. "You're okay, right honey?" Kerry asked. *Everything's fine*, she thought. *I'm going to pull over and check her, just to be safe, but everything's fine.* She made it to the big patch of grass and had her seatbelt undone before the car was even in park. In a split second, she sprinted around the car and opened the rear door. Emma's eyes bulged in terror. Her entire body was blue.

"Oh, God!" Kerry screamed, tugging at the straps on the car seat. "Oh, my God, Emma!" She pulled her daughter from their Honda Pilot and into the sunlight. Cars on 95 North were whizzing by them. The bright afternoon sun reflected off their windshields and into Kerry's eyes. She flipped Emma over and patted her back, but when she turned her back around Emma was even bluer, her eyes even more terrified. "Oh, my God! What's wrong?!" Kerry screamed. Holding Emma over her shoulder, she ripped open the passenger side door and reached for her phone. Flipping it open, she quickly realized she'd turned it off minutes earlier. The twenty seconds it took to power on seemed like an eternity, but once it did, Kerry desperately began to dial. She managed to get 9-1 dialed, but as she pressed the last "1" her phone lost power. Emma's grunts were getting shorter. Her chest pulled to breathe. Hardly any air was getting through to her lungs. Kerry's mind raced faster then the cars and trucks on 95 North. *How can this be happening?* she wondered. *I don't understand how this could be happening right now!* She threw the phone on the front seat and ran around to the side of the road. "HELP!" she screamed over and over, waving her right arm in a fury and holding Emma in her left. "HELP ME!" Flashes of Emma's short life played out in her head as the traffic drove past them: her birth; her first operation; the day she left the hospital. *How can this be happening?* Kerry's mind repeated.

Two cars pulled over in front of the Pilot and from them emerged two men: one was older, in his early sixties with a mustache and grey hair; the other was in his thirties with light brown hair. Never having met, these two good Samaritans wore identical expressions of desperation as they approached Emma and Kerry. "Call 911!" Kerry yelled to them. "She can't breathe! My phone's dead! She can't breathe! I don't know why!"

The older man reached into his pocket and frantically dialed 911 on his flip phone. Kerry listened to his shaky voice trying to explain where exactly they were on 95 North. *Thank God he's here*, Kerry thought, *I don't even know where we're standing right now!*

Kerry lay Emma on the grass and tilted her head back. She pried Emma's jaw open and looked in her mouth, then felt around with her finger, but nothing was inside. Maria's voice played in her head: *"ABCs, baby! Airway, Breathing, Circulation."* She frantically placed her mouth over Emma's nose and mouth and began blowing rescue breaths into her. Emma looked fatigued and grey. Kerry picked her back up and patted her on the back. Looking to the young man for help, she was immediately crushed by his fearful eyes, his complete uncertainty. Two more cars pulled over, and two more men arrived on the scene. But none of them knew how to help the grunting, blue baby. *Should I begin chest compressions?* Kerry asked herself. *Is it time?* Visions of Emma's fluoroscopy code zipped through her head. "Keep her awake!" Kerry yelled as she handed Emma to the young man. "I'm going to get my suction!"

Dumping the entire contents of her diaper bag on the front seat, Kerry spotted the green bulb syringe almost immediately. She grabbed it and ran back to Emma and the men. The young man had handed her to another man, who was bouncing Emma in his arms. "Come on, sweetie, you've got to breathe," he begged. Emma's eyes started to roll back, and no amount of yelling, bouncing or patting was helping to convince them not to. "Rescue's on their way! They should be here any minute now!" the man with the mustache announced. He looked like Wilfred Brimley, only with more hair.

Kerry opened Emma's mouth and began suctioning liquid from the back of her throat. It didn't help her tremendously, but it wasn't hurting her either. And since no one else had any ideas on how to go about saving Emma's life, she figured she would try to do what she'd seen the doctors and nurses do one hundred times over. For five excruciating minutes, Kerry suctioned Emma's throat and blew breaths into her, all the while wondering how on earth any of this was possible. The idea that Emma's journey could end in this horrifying situation, after all she'd accomplished, was inconceivable. Suddenly life, in general, felt meaningless. *People can spend their whole lives, reaching for something...and then...in an instant...it's over? Why? What's the point?* she wondered.

Traffic continued to whiz by. Kerry looked out onto the highway. *If she dies right now, I can always walk out into the road. All it would take is one car*, she thought, *and this could all be over.* It seemed more than reasonable, considering the circumstances. "WHERE'S THE AMBULANCE?!" Kerry screamed, in between breaths. "WHAT'S TAKING SO LONG?!"

"Here they come!" Wilfred Brimley's look-alike yelled, waving his arms in the air. The flashing red lights and siren were more of a relief to the their eyes and ears then anything they'd ever seen or heard. Kerry ran towards the rescue team with Emma in her arms. "She can't breathe! She needs oxygen!" Kerry shrieked, handing her baby to a competent looking man. "HELP HER!" she begged. Placing a mask over her face, the team began to work tirelessly on Emma. Kerry did her best to explain her daughter's history to an EMT, but the more she spoke, the crazier her story sounded. The team's original confidence soon crumbled into confusion. "I'm sorry, say that again…a tracheal esophagus what? And you think she might have what?" asked a tall man with a pen and note pad. "A stricture…in her esophagus…from the surgery…" Kerry cried. "She also has bowel atresia, a colostomy, g-tube, and two little holes in her heart," she rattled. It was as if Kerry were vomiting information at them.

The man with the note pad ran back to the ambulance where Emma was being treated. Seconds later he pointed to the front seat and yelled "Get in!" to Kerry. Closing the passenger door, Emma's mother looked out at the four men standing on the side of the road. A collective look of dismay was painted across each of their faces. Wilfred Brimley's look-alike had his hands on his hips as he shook his head in bewilderment. Looking directly at Kerry, he made the sign of the cross. The back doors to the ambulance slammed shut and the siren howled. Kerry mouthed the words "thank you" to all of them as the ambulance sped off.

"How is she?" Kerry yelled. A voice from the back of the ambulance said they were having some success in getting her oxygen up, but that's all they would say. Kerry's body shook. She didn't know what to do with herself. "Where do you live?" the driver asked. It was the same man who had been jotting down notes.

"East Greenwich, Rhode Island," Kerry answered.

"Then why were you driving to Boston?" he asked.

"That's where she had all of her surgeries," Kerry said. She turned around, but all she could see were three people hovering over Emma.

"When someone's in trouble, you call 911 or you take them to the nearest hospital," he continued. "You don't drive them to a hospital that's an hour or more away." His tone was borderline disgusted.

"She wasn't in trouble when I left to…." Kerry began.

"You take them to the nearest hospital or you call 911," he commanded. Kerry fell silent. Shame circulated throughout her veins. He was right. This was all her fault. If she had driven straight to Providence, she'd have been there in ten minutes and none of this would have happened. Emma would have been sleeping, and she wouldn't have woken up and started to cry. Her mother had been right, too. Kerry should have asked Jane-Marie to come with her. If Jane-Marie had been sitting in the back seat, she would have seen Emma and known she was in trouble. None of this would have happened if Kerry hadn't been so stubborn. Now Emma was clinging to life, because her mother didn't want to ask anyone for help. Kerry despised herself.

The doors to Norwood Hospital swung open and Emma arrived to the emergency room in a threatening fuss. The medical staff scampered around her, attaching monitor probes, IVs, and collecting as much medical history on their five-month old patient as they could. It was hard for them to hide their astonishment as they tore off Emma's clothes and unveiled everything Kerry was describing. The nurse who was writing it down had a hard time getting all of Emma's medications straight.

Aside from what was going on with Kerry's daughter, the hospital was quiet. Emma's coloring returned to a pale pink, which was slightly encouraging. But her numbers on the monitor were scarily inconsistent and she could barely open her eyes. The grunting sound continued to emerge from her tiny mouth. Emma did not look good. The nurse pressed Kerry to give her a rough estimate of how long Emma had been "blue" for, but it was impossible for her to guess. Maybe because the whole experience seemed to have taken place in a time warp. Maybe because nine or ten minutes was five minutes too many. For whatever reason, Kerry couldn't say. But she did her best to answer all of the nurses other questions. All one hundred and nineteen of them. And it didn't bother Kerry in the least that it took forty-five minutes to do so. Because she knew when she was finished, she would have to call Tom and tell him what she had done.

"Tom? Can you hear me?" Kerry asked.

"What number are you calling from?" Tom said.

"Tom, Emma had a problem on the way…." Kerry started.

"Hello? Ker? I can't hear you. You're all broken up…." Tom said.

"I said, Emma had a problem…." Kerry began again.

"Emma what? I can't hear you! What phone are you calling from?" Tom quipped.

"NORWOOD HOSPITAL!" Kerry yelled. She covered her face to hide from all the heads that had turned in her direction. "EMMA'S IN THE EMERGENCY ROOM IN NORWOOD… SHE COULDN'T BREATHE WHILE I WAS DRIVING. WE DON'T KNOW WHAT'S WRONG."

"Emma's in Norwood Hospital?" Tom asked. His words were panicked. "Is she okay? I couldn't hear the last thing you said! What happened?" The same nurse who was taking notes tapped Kerry on the shoulder. She needed to clarify more of Emma's history.

"She's alive, Tom, but she's not in good shape. If you can hear me, please come to Norwood Hospital as soon as you can," Kerry finished. She hated to hang up, knowing how terrified she'd just made her husband. She pictured him sitting in the airplane on the tarmac in Charlotte, North Carolina, and could only imagine how trapped and unhinged he felt. She wondered if he were going to hate her for letting this happen. After all they'd been through, it seemed logical that he would. Kerry walked over to the top of the bed and gently stroked Emma's head. The nurse continued to fire off question after question, until the sound of Emma's alarms interrupted them.

"She's dropping!" A blonde nurse in pink scrubs yelled.

"Get respiratory!" A young male doctor ordered.

"Turn her on her right side!" Kerry demanded. "Her left lung gets better air." The entire room froze for a second, until the doctor shook his head at the blonde nurse. "Mom knows best, lets get her on her right side," he said. "And get respiratory!"

Twenty minutes later, the initial hysteria of Emma's arrival had settled, when a woman peeked her head into the room and announced that a visitor had arrived. Kerry lifted her head from Emma's pillow, unable to imagine whom it was. "Sean Sheeran?" The woman said as she stepped aside to let Tom's brother through. "I was on a train home from work...and Danielle called me...and said Tommy had called saying Emma was in Norwood Hospital," Sean explained. "Norwood was literally the next stop when she called." Kerry was confused. *Does this mean Tom heard everything I said?* she wondered. *Does he know how bad things are?* "He didn't want you to be here alone," Sean explained. Kerry looked down at Emma. Her little body was weak, her breaths shallow. The muscles that covered her stomach and ribs were wrenching in and out. "I don't know what happened," Kerry said. It was hard for her to look up. Blotches resurfaced all over her face, tears filled her eyes. Sean put his arms around her and gently squeezed. "I was just trying to get her to Boston," Kerry cried. "I don't know what happened."

By the time Tom got to the hospital, the doctors were preparing to put Emma on a respirator. Her lungs had collapsed; her body was losing its fight to keep breathing. Arrangements had been made for transport to Children's Hospital Boston and the folks at Norwood were more then anxious to hand her over. Tom ran straight to his little girl's side and kissed her unconscious head. "Come on, honey," he begged, "hold on, we're gonna get you back to Children's and you're gonna be okay. Hold on for me, Emma. Hold on for Daddy, please." Kerry stood on the other side of the bed with her eyes glued on Emma's chest. It seemed impossible for such a tiny human to go on tugging and working for each breath. She welcomed the relief the respirator would give her baby. But when the anesthesiologist arrived, ready to stick the tube down Emma's airway, panic once again took ahold.

"She just underwent an eight-hour operation to connect her esophagus...please be *so* careful not to tear anything," Kerry said to the stranger in the surgical mask.

"I'm not planning on going down her esophagus, but I will be as careful as I can," he replied.

"I know, but her trachea had a fistula at birth. She's had that repaired too," Kerry said.

"Ma'am, I'm going to be extremely cautious," he snarled. "Trust me, we would really have preferred the team at Children's to do this, but she can't wait any longer. I'm going to have to ask you to stand back while I try to intubate her." Kerry took a couple steps back, but her trembling hands reached out, attempting to capture the thoughts that were tearing through her head.

"She's so delicate," Kerry cried. "Please be careful!" Tom walked around the bed and tried his best to shield Kerry from watching as the stranger fed the tube into Emma's trachea. They both covered their mouths, praying their baby be spared of any further trauma. In a matter of moments, the man in the mask had visual confirmation that the intubation was successful. It took Emma a few minutes to settle into the machine which had taken over for her lungs. Minutes later the ambulance from Children's arrived.

The Norwood ER team watched with piteous eyes as Emma was wheeled away. "Is she your only daughter?" the blonde nurse in the pink scrubs asked. Kerry nodded her head *yes*. "Daughters have a way of bringing a lot of drama into their parents' lives," she smiled. Kerry shook her head and wiped her tears. "Just wait until she's seventeen, like mine, and getting her driver's license. They keep you worrying your whole life," the nurse finished. Kerry pulled a tissue out of her pocket and blew her nose. "Seventeen and getting her license?" Kerry asked. "That sounds like a dream come true."

Tom drove behind the ambulance the entire way to Boston, relying on Kerry's constant thumbs up from the ambulance's passenger seat to let him know how Emma was doing. Having a dead cell phone continued to haunt them, even though it was only a thirty-minute ride. The ambulance driver didn't speak much, other then to assure Kerry he was aware Emma was intubated, and that he would be careful to avoid any sudden jolts or stops along the way.

The NICU team at Children's was ready to receive Emma immediately, already having scheduled an X-ray to determine if she did, indeed, have a stricture in her esophagus. Tom embraced the head night nurse the moment he saw her, but Kerry couldn't lift her head to look into the familiar face. After all these people had done to save Emma's life—keeping her alive for three-and-a-half months so that the surgeons could fix her—here she was, back in their NICU in worse shape then ever. All because of her thoughtless mother, whom they never should have trusted to take care of her. Kerry kept her head down all the way past Bay 6 and into the isolation room at the end of the hall on the right hand side. The same room Caitlin nearly lost her fight in.

Once they had her settled in the room, the respiratory team suctioned Emma's lungs via the breathing vent. They were shocked at the amount of white liquid they were pulling up. "Aspiration," Kerry and Tom heard one of them say. "Look at all this liquid," the woman continued. "This is a complete aspiration." The doctor who was overseeing everything turned to Tom and Kerry. "Was she drinking when this happened?" he asked.

"No," Kerry replied shaking her head. "We were in the car. I was driving and she was in her car seat."

"It must be vomit, then," the doctor said. "She must have vomited and inhaled it." Kerry looked at Tom, suddenly enlightened by what she was hearing. *Of course that was what had happened*, she thought, *just as Emma had vomited back at the house*. It seemed so logical; she wondered why they hadn't already thought of it. *This is good*, Kerry thought. *Now all they have to do is vacuum all the vomit out of her lungs and she is going to be just fine*. She looked at Tom with a twinkle of hope. He was thinking the same exact thought.

"Once they get all the liquid out, she'll be able to breath again?" Tom asked.

"I wish it were that easy," the doctor replied. "We still have to figure out if a stricture in her esophagus caused this, or if something else is going on with our Emma. Either way, her lungs have taken a pretty bad beating. We're just going to have to wait and see." *Wait and see*, Kerry thought. It was as if those words were hammering them back into the ditch they had just climbed out of five weeks earlier.

"Something else?" Kerry asked.

"Lets not get ahead of ourselves. First things first, we get her an X-ray," the doctor said.

Waiting for Emma to return from radiology, Tom and Kerry paced around silently in her isolation room. Tom had tried talking to her, resolute to find out exactly what had happened on their car ride. But every time she had tried to describe it, Kerry's chest tightened and she lost her ability to speak. *What else does he want me to tell him?* she wondered. *I already told him everything.* Giving Tom all the gory details wasn't going to help her push the entire scenario into the back of her head, where she wanted it. It was bad enough she was experiencing the vivid recurrence of every terrifying moment. Every grunt, every wheeze, the second she opened the car door to find her blue baby—it all played over and over in her head. The looks on the good Samaritans' faces; the look on Emma's face. Kerry wasn't sure if she'd ever be able to escape the vision of her baby's panic-stricken eyes. She heard the words of the Norwood ambulance driver, like someone kept pressing rewind, only with every lecture, he was angrier and more disgusted then the last.

And there was certainly no reason to tell Tom that each time this scene ran through her head, it always ended with Kerry walking out onto the busy highway. These were the things neither Tom nor anyone else ever needed to know. All she had to do was just wait for the visions to stop, and then she could start digging a hole. She'd bury all of it deep down, far away where it could never be found.

"She doesn't have a stricture," the doctor announced as they wheeled Emma's crib back into the room. "This is good and bad, sort of," he added.

"I don't understand," Tom said.

"Well, if it were a stricture, we'd know exactly how to treat it. We'd just dilate her esophagus. But something else is making Emma sick. You said she's had a runny nose and was vomiting and coughing a lot? She might have a virus, and viruses we cannot cure. They have to run their course. We'll culture her immediately to see if we can determine if, in fact, she does. If it turns out to be RSV or something of the sort, it could be a difficult fight, considering the shape her lungs are already in," the doctor warned.

RSV was something Tom and Kerry had been educated about, prior to

Emma's discharge. The literature the hospital had provided warned that Respiratory Syncytial Virus was much more serious then a common cold, affecting mostly children under the age of two. Pre-mature babies born thirty-five weeks and under and those with additional respiratory/health complications, they'd learned, are at the greatest risk of falling victim to the dangerous lung infections that can result from this virus. Complications, they knew, could be deadly. Once again, Tom and Kerry knew too much. Waiting to see how this would all play out was easier said then done. It would be a couple days before they even got the results of Emma's cultures. Looking at her, that very moment, neither her mother nor father felt certain of what two whole days might bring Emma.

* * *

A familiar voice whispered in Kerry's ear and woke her. "I thought I heard a rumor my Missy Moo was back," Jackie said with a sad pout. Kerry rubbed her eyes and sat up. *Is it morning already?* she wondered. Four days had passed. It was hard to tell the time from inside a room with no windows. Even the shades on the glass wall were drawn. Kerry had to wonder, *Are they trying to keep the rest of the world away from Emma? Or keep Emma away from the rest of the world?* It had already occurred to her that there was a reason the sickest children were stationed in the back of the NICU. Despair can be contagious in such a place.

"What happened?" Jackie asked, checking Emma's IV pump.

"She's got RSV," Kerry said.

"I heard," Jackie answered, "but I'm talking about everything else."

"It was terrible, Jackie" Kerry said. Her lip quivered, so she covered her mouth with her hands. It seemed unlikely she was going to be able to say anything else, so Jackie stepped in:

"That's okay, honey. I already know what happened, you don't have to talk about it. I just can't believe it. I'm so sorry," she said. Kerry got up from the chair she'd been sleeping in. The shorts and T-shirt she'd been wearing since Emma's arrival were stuck to her body. Peeking over the side of the crib, Kerry was disappointed to see that the dream she'd just dreamt hadn't come true. Emma was still unconscious on the ventilator, and looked even more swollen then she did three hours earlier. There were no pretty little bows in her hair, no cute clothes. Tubes and wires had made a comeback all over Emma's body. The alarms on her monitors worked over time, to the point where Kerry had trained herself to sleep through their noise. "Good morning, peewee," Kerry whispered through the slats of the crib. "It's time to wake up."

Jackie pulled the shades up on the glass wall to unveil a bustling NICU, chock full of new babies and parents. No Shawna and Tim, no Liz and Cheryl, not one familiar face aside from the staff walked the floor. "Is it okay with you if we keep these up?" Jackie asked, wrapping the cords tight. "It's so bloody dark in here." Kerry nodded her head *yes*, although she hated being exposed. It felt like they were in a fish bowl. The looks the doctors and nurses gave her every time they walked past were excruciating. Their expressions were different this time around. Shorter glances; sad, pitiful eyes. It was obvious the entire staff knew what had happened on the side of 95 North. Their faces said so. Kerry turned her back to the glass wall and picked up Emma's hand. "Come back to me, please," she whispered.

Jackie offered Emma's care basin to Kerry, but was met with refusal. Oblivious to the fact that Kerry no longer trusted her ability to properly tend to Emma, Jackie frowned, then opened a Q-tip and cleaned around her patient's g-tube. "When's the last time you saw daylight?" Jackie asked. Kerry's eyes were still trying to adjust to the hint of morning sun creeping in from across the floor.

"I don't know," Kerry said.

"Well, I do… I just talked to Tom. He says you haven't left the room, other then to use the w.c. and pump, since you got here," Jackie admonished. "You need to go home and get yourself together."

"I can't," Kerry said. "I won't leave her."

"You can come back tonight. Tom's coming up, and I promise I'll take good care of her while you're gone," Jackie said. "Plus, your boys could probably use a little dose of their mum." Kerry had tried to pretend that Thomas and Ryan were leading a perfectly normal life at home with Jane. She wanted to believe that none of the stress she and Tom were feeling had leaked into their world, although the rational part of her brain knew that was impossible. Kerry wanted to hold them, cradle them and tell them everything was going to be okay. And yet she couldn't, because she wasn't sure it would. It wasn't fair. Thomas and Ryan were just settling into life as it should be—together with their baby sister and parents. And now, in an instant, all of that had changed.

Kerry was afraid to hear their questions, perhaps even more scared to have to answer them. *I'm so pathetic,* she thought, *I don't even know how to take care of my children. And here, I thought I always wanted four.* It was hard for Kerry to know what the right thing to do was. If she were to leave Emma, and something should happen, she wouldn't be there to help her. And if she never left her side, and Emma stayed like this for days, weeks or even months, then Thomas and Ryan would be wondering why their mother and sister disappeared for so long without saying goodbye. *Where's the voice when I really need it?* Kerry wondered. *I need someone to tell me what I'm supposed to do!*

"I have to pump," Kerry said, feeling the fullness in her breasts. She grabbed her supplies and left the NICU with her head down. As she walked out the door, Sr. Carlotta walked in, but Kerry kept her downward stare all the way to the pumping room. As she set up her bottles, Kerry thought about how she couldn't drive home even if she wanted to. Her brother-in-law had picked up her Pilot on the side of 95 and returned it to her house. Plus, the idea of getting behind the wheel and driving past the Norwood exit made her sick to her stomach. *Someone would have to drive all the way to Boston to get me, then four or five hours later they'd have to drive me back,* she thought. It seemed ridiculous to ask that of anyone, yet Kerry knew if she called either of her two dearest friends, they'd do it without question.

The rush of her breast milk started to fill the bottles. Kerry gazed at the poster on the wall. She'd seen it so many times, the image was etched in her brain: a beautiful young mother holding a dark-haired baby to her bosom, with the words "BREASTMILK IS LIQUID GOLD FOR YOUR NEWBORN INFANT" written above it. It sickened Kerry to be back in this room. She had everything set up so nicely in her upstairs bathroom at home, but here she was back inside the cinderblock walls, staring at the happy mother who was smiling at the baby in her arms, reminding Kerry of a bond she'd never feel with Emma. A minute or two went by, before she was suddenly distracted by the words her pump was echoing: *GO HOME, GO HOME, GO HOME, GO HOME.* Thomas' big blue eyes appeared, along with Ryan's smile. A vision of Kerry holding both her sons, pressed to her heart, filled her head. *But how,* she wondered. *It's not that easy!* To which her pump replied: *CALL THEM, CALL THEM, CALL THEM, CALL THEM.*

Annie and Jen waved their arms furiously when they spotted Kerry from across Longwood Avenue. Getting closer, Kerry squinted her eyes to make sure these two women were indeed her friends. Annie looked like Annie, but Jen was sporting a new look. As soon as she reached them, they simultaneously wrapped their arms around her. Kerry was already crying.

"I'm so sorry, Ker," Jen said.

"How is she?" Annie asked.

"The same," Kerry said. "Thank you for getting me." She looked at both her friends, then took a step back and wiped away her tears so as to fully scan Jen. Her blonde hair stood out, more then ever, considering how dark her skin had become. Songs from *Willy Wonka & the Chocolate Factory* rang through Kerry's head. Suddenly she felt like smiling a little.

"What's with the umpalumpa?" Kerry asked Annie.

"Very funny," Jen quipped.

"No seriously, have you seen what you look like?" Kerry asked.

"It keeps getting worse," Annie said.

"You literally called me a minute after I got a spray tan," Jen explained.

"She's telling the truth," Annie insisted.

"Oh, I believe you," Kerry said, grinning at Jen.

"I can't wash it off for six hours," Jen explained.

"We'll have you back to Emma before she even showers," Annie promised.

"You look like a Florida sunset," Kerry laughed.

"Shut up and get in the car," Jen barked. "People are starting to stare."

With that, Kerry hopped into the front seat. It felt good to laugh at the orange imprint Jen had left on her driver's seat. It was nice to feel the sun on her arm as it hung out of the window, and the breeze on her face as they drove towards Rhode Island. Safe in the company of two friends who would shield her from that horrible patch of grass on Route 95. On her way home, to be a mother to her baby boys for the afternoon.

When Kerry returned around 5 p.m., she paused for a minute before walking through the door to Emma's isolation room. Through the glass wall, she saw Tom with his face pressed against Emma's. His back was to Kerry, but she could tell he was upset. His shoulders shook, he rubbed his eyes. Every once in a while he'd turn sideways, and Kerry could see him whispering in Emma's ear. Looking at Emma's monitor, she was disappointed to see her respiratory rate was much higher than it had been that morning: over one hundred breaths a minute. For a baby her age, thirty-five to forty would have been an acceptable rate, but Emma's lungs were combating an infection that was seizing every lobe, branch by branch.

Kerry glanced at Emma's heart rate, which was pushing two hundred. Her blood pressure was scarily high. During the last six hours, it appeared, her baby had taken a bad turn. Standing outside the door, Kerry wasn't sure she was ready to face the reality of what was going on inside the glass wall. Her rock...her optimist...her husband looked defeated. Every tear he wiped sank Kerry deeper, further from the scrap of hope she was holding onto. Watching him speak into her little ear, Kerry could only imagine the words he was saying, the sound of his voice. *Why is this happening, God? How could you take Emma after all this?* she wondered. *Why?* Acceptance wasn't realistic at this particular moment. And as far as perspectives go, it would have taken a magician to make a new one appear. Agony's vicious grip was taking ahold, leaving them to wait and see if their daughter's body was going to give up its fight. And there was no way around it.

One of the respiratory therapists pushed a high frequency respirator down the hall and stopped in front of Emma's door. Kerry reluctantly pulled the handle and held the door open, bowing her head as she shuffled in behind the machine. Aware that his private conversation with Emma was being interrupted, Tom whispered, "I promise," into her ear. Then he kissed her head three times and got out of the way as Jackie and the therapist hooked Emma up to the last possible chance she had at surviving in the NICU.

No words needed to be spoken; it was frighteningly clear what the next steps would be. Tom turned to Kerry and buried his head in her chest. "Come on, babe. This is just a little setback," Kerry said, kissing his head. "Maybe she just needs a little more rest, so that she can fight some more." Kerry wasn't even sure she believed the words she was saying. Tom shook his head, then finished wiping his tears and excused himself to the bathroom. Reaching for Emma's hand, Kerry silently vowed to stay by her side for as long as she needed. "Mommy's back, Emma," she said. "I'm so sorry, honey. Mommy's so, so sorry. I'm back, now."

Flashbacks of the Norwood ambulance driver replayed in Kerry's mind as she watched the ventilator push breath after breath into Emma's chest. *None of this should be happening right now,* she thought. *What kind of an idiot am I? She's a delicate baby who's been through two major surgeries. Why didn't I just call an ambulance?* With Tom gone, it seemed like a good time to break down. So Kerry turned to Jackie and unloaded:

"This is all my fault, Jack," she said, biting her lower lip.

"Come on, Kerry. You know that's not true at all," Jackie said.

"It *is* true. I failed her. It's my job to protect her and I failed my most important job as her mother," Kerry said.

"You were told to bring her to Boston, Kerry. You thought she had a stricture," Jackie reminded her.

"I should have known she was getting sick," Kerry continued. "I should have brought her back to the doctor, or called an ambulance, or at least asked my sister-in-law to drive up with me. Anything would have been better then what I did," Kerry said.

"You were doing the right thing!" Jackie insisted. "Stop this, immediately! She could have vomited in the ambulance...or at the doctor's office...or with your sister-in-law sitting right next to her...and nothing could have prevented it! She breathed in her own vomit, Kerry. It was a horrible accident, but YOU didn't do this to her! So STOP feeling sorry for yourself because that's not helping anything." Jackie wiped her tears and pointed to Emma. "That little girl needs her mummy to be as strong as she can be right now, so just stop!"

Kerry stood up straight and lifted her head. She wasn't sure she'd be able to convince herself of what Jackie had just said, but it didn't sound entirely crazy. Jackie walked over and opened her arms. Accepting her embrace, Kerry held on tight in a desperate attempt to absorb every single one of Jackie's words. "I'm sorry I yelled at you," Jackie said, "but there's just not room for any nonsense in here, not with all these machines." Hints of a smile formed on both their faces. Jackie looked at the door. "Looks like Emma has some visitors," she said, winking at Sister Carlotta and Tom as they walked in.

Sister Carlotta Gilarde's wrinkled hands dripped with white rosary beads. She wore a simple black dress and a gold cross, which hung down the front of her four-foot, ten-inch body. Her short grey hair was swept back, revealing a face that was weathered with compassion. Kerry greeted her with caution, unsure if she were ready to discuss Emma's recent decline. Tom reached for a chair but Sister Carlotta suggested they stand and hold hands around Emma's crib while she offer up a special prayer. Even Jackie joined in, making a perfect circle around Emma. Sister Carlotta began:

> "Dear Father, we stand here in your presence, surrounding someone so very dear to us, our Emma. We pray that her body stays strong and continue to fight the terrible infection in her lungs. We pray that the medicine she's been given will help her, and that all the doctors and nurses who are caring for her continue to help her through this fight. We don't know what your will is, dear Father, but we pray that Emma stays on this earth and grows up to be a strong young lady, encompassed in her loving family, eager to spread the word that your son, Jesus Christ, so beautifully taught us. We pray that throughout this and all of life's struggles, we continue to have undying strength and faith in you, God. Through Christ, our Lord, Amen."

"Amen" Jackie, Tom and Kerry answered. Jackie walked over to Emma's IV and silenced an alarm which had started to beep.

"Thank you," Tom softly smiled.

"Of course," Sister Carlotta said.

"I don't get it," Kerry said.

"What do you mean?" Sister Carlotta asked.

"I just don't get the whole *faith in God* thing." Kerry shrugged her shoulders. "I've come to terms with a lot, as far as Emma's struggles are concerned. I've even figured out how God reveals Himself to me. I really have. But the whole "faith" thing doesn't make any sense. How can I trust that all I need to do is have faith in God, and everything will be okay with Emma? I've seen how things go around here. I've seen way too much to believe that *faith* will save the day. What about all the kids in this hospital that don't make it? Terminally ill? Riddled with cancer? Born, so that they can die? Did their parents not have enough faith? It just doesn't make any sense," Kerry sighed.

"It *doesn't* make any sense when you put it that way," Sister Carlotta answered. "And wouldn't it be just wonderful if that's how simple it were. I'd be out of a job, my dear." She wrapped the rosary around her wrist and reached for Kerry's hands. "Our lives are constantly facing challenges, some folks more then others. Do you think I can walk up to all the patients we have in this hospital, and all their parents, and just tell them everything's going to be fine as long as they believe? That as long as they pray and have faith, that God will heal them? You know I can't do that. Nobody can make that kind of a promise. The *faith* I'm talking about is one of durability, of perseverance. We have to have faith that, no matter how bad things get, God will guide us through it and give us the strength to handle it. Just like the old "Footsteps in the Sand" prayer. We have to have faith God will carry us when we need him the most."

Kerry sat down. She looked at Emma, then back at Sister Carlotta. "So you mean God's *not* going to make her better?" Kerry asked with a smile. It seemed silly, now that she understood faith's true meaning, to have even posed the question in the first place. "It took me thirty-three years, but I think I get it," Kerry said. Flashbacks of the scene on the side of Route 95 ran through her mind: the man who looked like Wilfred Brimley, the ambulance's siren, the green suction bulb. Kerry thought about Dr. Wilkins-Haug's second opinion, the song on the radio, the phone call to Jean. All of these things had directed her and Tom throughout their journey with Emma. All had given them the strength to handle every difficult step. All had helped to keep Emma alive. *Who am I to doubt there's plenty more where that came from?* she wondered. "I get it," Kerry cried, squeezing Sister Carlotta's hands. "Thank you."

Jackie reached for a tissue and quietly blew her nose in the corner of the room. Dabbing her tears, she turned back around to see three sets of eyes staring at her. "What?" Jackie asked. "You're all making me cry, it's not good." She blew her nose again. "I think you should probably leave now, Sister Carlotta, before you get us any more soggy in here!" Jackie insisted. "I'm going, I'm going. Not to worry, I have plenty more stops to make before bed," Sister Carlotta assured her. Tom escorted the little nun outside of the room, while Kerry grabbed a basin and prepared to do Emma's cares. Jackie smiled. "It's about time you started earning Missy Moo's keep around here," she jabbed.

The following morning, Emma's vent settings had been tweaked up. Kerry and Tom wore the same clothes as the day before. Their doleful expressions were blinding. Emma's alarms were constantly sounding, her tiny organs exhausted from all the work being asked of them. The neonatologists could barely look up as they rounded on their dire patient. They bowed their heads and scuttled out the door as unnoticeably fast as they could. Jackie worked quietly, making notes in the computer and sipping the Starbucks coffee Tom had brought her. Tom paced around the room. His eyes were locked on Emma's monitor. The numbers on the screen had him in a never-ending frenzy. Anguish flowed through his veins and strangled his heart.

Kerry's eyes could no longer face the computer screens that told her daughter's saga. She had turned her back to them somewhere around 3 a.m. Thoughts of tragedy and despair filled her head. She thought about the mothers she had seen in the NICU, the ones who never went home with their babies. She thought about everyone she knew who had lost a loved one way before they were ready to say goodbye. She thought about her own father, Joe, whose story was rarely discussed, yet heart-breaking nonetheless.

In 1967, Joe lost his first wife under terrible circumstances. Kerry's two oldest sisters were only one and three years old at the time. One day Anne was there, the next she was gone. Their lives were flipped upside down faster then they knew what had hit them, and yet Joe continued on. He took care of his girls, fell in love again a couple years later and went on to have four more children, of which Kerry was the youngest. Joe was able to be happy again. *How?* She wondered. *How did he do it?* The thought of being happy some day without Emma was inconceivable to her. *How,* Kerry wondered, *do people get through this shit?*

"I'll be right back," she said, touching Tom's arm. Grabbing her purse, she took off down the hall and out the front door of the NICU. She headed straight into the pumping room and locked the door, then took out her phone and dialed home. When her father answered, she wasted no time getting straight to the point:

"Dad? It's me. I need help," Kerry said. "Emma's bad. She's really bad. I'm really worried, Dad."

"Oh, Kerry...my sweetheart...we'll be there as soon as we can," Joe said.

"How am I supposed to do this, Dad? How did you do it when Anne died?" she asked.

"Kerry, don't go there right now," Joe insisted.

"Dad, I need your help!" Kerry implored.

"Sweetheart," Joe sighed. "It was different. When Anne died, it was a terrible shock. Our lives completely changed. Of course the devastation lasted, but her actual passing was immediate. It happened and it was over. Everything with Emma, all these things that keep happening...the tragedy...the suffering...it just keeps going on and on. And just when you think it can't get any more difficult, it continues. It's different for you. I *can't* tell you how to get through this. I wouldn't know where to begin." Kerry tried to compose herself, but her voice had already begun to crack.

"Why? Why do these things keep happening?" she cried.

"You can ask yourself that question for the rest of your life, sweetheart, and you'll never get an answer," Joe said with certainty. "This, I know." Kerry blew her nose. She could hear Joe doing the same. *Huh*, she thought, scratching at her hive-ridden chest, *he's right*. Turning to her right, she stared at the woman on the poster, nuzzling her black-haired baby. The voice in her head spoke:

"Why aren't you with your baby, right now?"

Kerry stood up. It was selfish for her to stay in the room, crying on the phone and trying to figure out her own problems, while Emma held on for her life three doors away. Suddenly, it was all a big waste of time.

"Thanks, Dad. I've got to go," Kerry said. Then she hung up the phone and anxiously returned to the place where she belonged, at Emma's side.

Over the course of the next seven hours, Emma was inundated with visitors. Family members peeked over the side rails of her crib, looking for signs of the "Mighty Emma" they had grown to adore. Deb and Nancy held her little hands and played soft music on a cd player they had brought with them. Kate gave Emma a little stuffed bunny, and snuggled it next to her. Maria treated Tom and Kerry to Starbucks coffee. She scolded Emma for being so dramatic, and ragged on Tom for not keeping up with his running. Before she left, Maria made sure to tell Tom how ugly his Yankees hat was. The Haitian woman offered prayers as she mopped around Emma's crib. Liz and Cheryl, who had brought Matthew home two weeks before, returned with dinner and two bottles of wine. They tried to get Jackie to allow Emma's parents a glass or two of pinot noir, bedside. Dr. Borer, Dr. Buchmiller and Dr. Wilkins-Haug stopped in to see the baby they had so heroically saved, facing the unimaginable. Social workers, doctors, nurses, and friends flooded her hospital room. They crowded around Emma and her parents, hoping for a miracle. Wishing things were different.

When the last of Emma's visitors had left, Tom collapsed into Kerry's arms and wept. "It's too much to take! I can't talk to anyone else," he cried. Kerry rubbed his head. "Me neither," she said. Although there was one more person she was still hoping to speak to. One person she'd counted on many times before. Someone who, no matter how bad things had gotten, was always attainable. Always available. So as the doctor ordered Jackie to switch Emma's ventilator to maximum support, Kerry closed her eyes, held Tom's hand and called upon the last person she knew who could possibly understand what they were going through.

"Hail Mary, full of grace," she began.

Chapter 14

THE STUFF DREAMS ARE MADE OF

THE BACKSIDE OF Heartbreak Hill had eaten at Tom's quadriceps. His shins felt like they'd been whacked with a two-by-four. Unfortunately, the relief he'd been hoping for, was still yet to come. With the hills behind him, the race was transforming from a physical challenge into a mental one. It was hard to decide which was more difficult, but since the mental was all that was left, he chose to believe he'd already conquered the worst of it.

"Born to Run" blared from an old school boom box outside some Boston College apartments. Students joyfully serenaded every runner who passed them. Tom pulled his earphones out and soaked in the largest display of drunken karaoke he'd ever seen. Fifteen years ago, he'd probably be standing right alongside these kids—chugging beers with Mike and all his college buddies. He'd be hanging around, having fun without a care in the world...hardly any responsibilities. That was the stuff dreams were made of, back then. Hell, it was the stuff dreams were made of even now. Only today, those days were few and far between, especially the "not a care in the world" ones. Nonetheless they were awesome memories. Memories Tom would tap into anytime he needed to remind himself that life, as tough as it could be, was really fun sometimes. If he had any energy to spare, he might have screamed at the top of his lungs: *"Enjoy it kids! It's not gonna last!"* But such honesty was not appropriate, and so instead he flashed them a jealous smile and continued down Commonwealth Avenue.

Salty sweat burned his eyeballs. He longed for a water stop. Even dumping Gatorade all over his face sounded good. Squinting as he rounded the Chestnut Hill Reservoir, Tom contemplated jumping off to the side and submerging his head. He knew, however, that off-roading at this point would cost him the race. So he suffered through the fire that had been lit under his eyelids and prayed that Mile 23 would greet him with a cold cup of water.

To his right, a fellow runner squirted himself with a plastic bottle he had unhooked from his belt. *Lucky Bastard!* Tom thought. The clear refreshing water shot out with force all over his cleanly shaven head and washed down his face. *Oh, my God, it's like he's rubbing it in!* Tom thought. He wondered, if he were to explain to this man just how badly he was hurting, if the guy might lend him some water. *Bald guys are supposed to help each other out,* Tom thought. *He looks nice enough.* Falling behind a few steps, he feared he might lose his chance. He watched as the man tucked the bottle back into his belt, trying to see how much water was actually left.

Suddenly something shiny caught Tom's eye. He looked about a foot and a half down and noticed a metal rod with joints descending from the man's shorts. His prosthetic leg alternated perfectly with his other muscular limb, making it hard to discern which one was, in fact, his *"good leg"*. Awestruck, Tom studied his long, symmetrical stride. Nothing was off balance. The man advanced even further ahead, but Tom refused to lose complete sight of him and made it his mission to stay within fifteen feet of this new inspiration for at least another mile. He held true to this promise all the way past a water stop, Cleveland Circle, and through the end of Mile 23, keeping his eyes, which magically were no longer burning, on the two most impressive legs he'd seen all day.

Refusing to get ahead of himself, Tom peeked down Beacon Street with great excitement and anticipation. The smells from the restaurants, the distant skyscrapers beckoned him and he found them hard to resist. *It's time,* he thought, *to finish.* Opening the torn, wet piece of paper for the last time, Tom scanned the remaining lines Kerry had written to him. It took him a good minute to read what was left, but he did. And when he was done, he inhaled the biggest breath he could before setting off to conquer the last two and a half miles of the marathon.

At Coolidge Corner, he could almost envision a beautiful little brunette princess waving to him from a large Tudor-style building on his left. His mind began to wander. Images played out in his head, of a dream he had dreamt:

He pictured a little baby, surrounded with the tallest, greenest trees. She had all the oxygen a child could ever ask for. The baby was breathing quietly as she leaned against her father's chest. Her wispy hair danced in the light breeze, and her delicate hands pulled gently at the hair on his arms. Her brothers galloped in circles around them, stealing her attention and giggles whenever they could. The smell of her head was celestial; a scent only the heavens could have cooked up. Her dress was pink and covered in tiny white flowers. Behind them, red, orange and yellow balloons bounced in the wind. Tons of them, tied to every white rail of the deck they were sitting on. People were smiling in the background. Familiar faces...eating, drinking and laughing with each other. Music was playing. A huge white tent sprawled the length of the yard. Little kids were chasing big ones out of a giant inflatable house, demanding their God-given right to bounce. Others were flying on swings, then jumping off at the highest possible point while their mothers and grandmothers watched, worriedly. Grandparents, aunts, uncles, cousins, neighbors and friends gathered around the beautiful baby as her father held her in his lap. Her mother fed her a spoonful of cake. The guests roared as the baby gleefully licked white icing from her mother's finger.

CITGO Hill glared back at Tom as he began his summit. It was hard to believe he was actually looking at the historical, iconic, neon sign he'd been picturing since his first step in Hopkinton. He greeted it with a smile and compelled his legs to continue running up towards Kenmore Square. Each step was more painful then the last, causing him to wonder if he might have to limp, rather then run across the finish line. As he got closer, he realized he was approaching another icon on his right: the home of the big green monster. He would have been lying had he said the sight of Fenway Park didn't excite him, but that was a secret he would carry to his grave. In fact, in an effort to shake the unexpected mushy feeling, Tom commanded his legs to go even faster so that he could put it all behind him. Just then, his heart was occupied by something much more important then a stadium that housed a bunch of Red Sox players:

Inside the house, a long white christening dress hung from the doorway. The neck of the hanger was adorned with a delicate gold cross, given to the baby by her godparents: two of the guardian angels whom God had assigned her. The kitchen was clean and clutter-free. No pump, no machines, just a dining table with a high chair pushed next to it. Pictures covered the shelves and counter tops, of three siblings crawling all over each other, dripping in love. Photos of them digging holes on the beach, sitting on Santa's lap, taking their first bites of food, and sleeping in their parents' arms. The walls were decorated with colorful drawings and art projects. Not one medical chart was in sight.

"Tom!! Tom Sheeran!! GO TOM!" a woman screamed from the sidewalk. Recognizing the British accent that could only belong to one Bostonian, Tom looked over to see a semi-intoxicated Jackie jumping around more excited then he could have ever thought possible. Her ample bosom jumped right along with her, and he imagined his wife making a crack about her possibly knocking someone out if she didn't stop. "You're AMAZING, Tom!" Jackie screamed. It was an honest sentiment that ran much deeper then that moment in particular. In her line of work, it was rare to come across a man of such magnitude. Packed with so much love and dedication, she sometimes wondered should she stick him with a pin, if he would burst. Tom was the father every child should be lucky enough to have. He *was* amazing. "KEEP GOING!" Jackie added, as if there were any other choice.

Taking her advice and another deep breath, Tom continued picturing his dream:

Reluctant to let her go, the father handed the baby to her mother and watched as they disappeared into the house. The two of them snuck past the white dress and up the stairs into the pink and yellow nursery. The mother undid the baby's diaper and ran a warm washcloth across her torso. Her little body was pink, smooth, and etched with scars that told a beautiful story of triumph. With a new diaper in place, the mother scooped the baby into her arms and sat, comfortably in the glider. Then she unbuttoned her shirt and offered her breast to the hungry little baby who latched on immediately and swallowed every drop without the slightest little cough. The mother rocked back and forth in the chair, nuzzling her little dark-haired baby and singing the sweet lullabies she had written in her head. When her belly was full, the baby closed her eyes and continued to gently suck until her mouth could no longer stay awake. The mother kissed her head and lay her daughter in a wooden crib. On her way out the door, she paused to look at the four pink letters that spelled out her daughter's name across the wall. Looking gratefully upwards, she insisted it was the most beautiful name in the whole world.

"One Mile To Go" was painted in the street as Tom passed The Hotel Commonwealth. Suddenly, his body became infused with a unique energy he had only ever felt a fraction of before. Chills ran up his back and darted down his arms. "FINISH STRONG!" fans yelled from outside a pub. *Yes, I believe I will*, Tom thought. His stride picked up, faster then it had been in the last three hours. Barely touching the flat pavement, his feet swept the ground like a horse on its final lap in the Kentucky Derby. Guttural cheers from some fellow runners fueled his ambition, and he let out a few of his own, so as to repay them.

Leaving Kenmore Square, Tom ran under an overpass and past a statue of Leif Ericson, the explorer. Another jolt of energy surged through him and suddenly he was passing runner after runner in full confidence they would never catch him. Turning right on Hereford, Tom was barely aware his legs were once again heading uphill. "We're almost there!" a man in front of him screamed, sending a wave of smiles and emotion throughout all the marathoners within listening distance.

Passing the sign for Newbury Street, Tom was finally able to turn off the GPS that had been running through his brain since he'd woken up that morning. He knew he had only one more street to go before wrapping up one of the greatest personal achievements of his entire life. The fans refused to let any of the runners miss their left turn onto Boylston Street, pointing and welcoming him in a frenzy of excitement. Tom's eyes grew wide. What he saw up ahead was magnificent, and he *had* to have it. Passing the Prudential Center, he heard two men screaming his name. He looked up to see his twin brother, Timmy, and his friend, Brad. Sunglasses couldn't hide the euphoria in their eyes as they cheered Tom on through his threshold of accomplishment. With less then fifty feet to go, tears streamed down Tom's face as he pictured one last dream:

It was a conversation between the father and his daughter. The daughter was in the hospital, deathly ill. She was fading away. The father was losing hope. Pressing his face against hers, he made a secret pact with his baby. For if only she would reach deep down to gather every drop of strength and will inside her little body, refusing to give in—then he would do the same. Knowing it was a lot to ask of such a small person, he added a bonus to his end of the bargain. He would run a marathon in her honor, through the city she was born in. He vowed that no matter how difficult it was, he would run all the way to the town that had saved her life on more then one occasion. The father made this promise amongst the chirping machines and vital alarms. He sealed it with three kisses on her forehead and promised to keep it a secret between them.

Crossing the finish line, Tom made sure to lead with his right leg. Reaching for his watch, he pressed the STOP button just as the numbers read four hours, four minutes and seven seconds.

Adorned in a huge smile and heavy blue and yellow medal, he scanned the sea of faces around him. The crowds of people in Copley Square greeted him with intense exhilaration, but none were quite so radiant as the dark-haired woman and the fifteen-month-old girl sitting upon her shoulders. The toddler's pink high-top sneakers kicked jubilantly the moment her brown eyes caught sight of her daddy. "You made it," Tom smiled. Kerry kissed his salty lips before handing Emma over. "We've been waiting here for hours," she smiled.

"You did it!" Kerry wept. "*We* did it!" he yelled, tossing their daughter into the brisk Boston air. The three of them embraced, dancing around in a sea of emotion. "What happened to your ankle?" Kerry asked, pointing to the ace bandage pulled tightly around his food. "Oh nothing," he answered. "I rolled it back in Wellesley." Emma squealed with happiness. "Come on, peewee. Let's show Daddy the cake we made him," Kerry smiled. A ray of sunlight broke through the clouds, catching reflections in the pavement underneath their feet. Looking up to heaven, Tom had to wonder what he had done to deserve everything. *After all*, he thought, *not everyone gets to see so many of their wildest dreams come true.*

Chapter 15

SERIOUSLY, GOD?

THE RED AND blue lights reflected off Tom's sunglasses as he turned around to assess his predicament. After slamming the police car door shut, it seemed to take an eternity for the officer to finally reach Tom's window. The only two people speaking in the car were Dora and Boots. It seemed Swiper had swiped some of Dora's things. Kerry viciously handed Tom the folder containing the car's registration and insurance information. "What's happen? Why we stopping?" asked a squeaky voice in the back seat. Kerry turned around to address Emma's question directly. "Daddy's getting into trouble right now because he chose to break the rules of the road," she explained. She kept her body facing Emma's so as to avoid any eye contact with the repeat offender to her left. "Daddy break rules?" Emma asked. The officer had gotten dangerously close to the window, at this point. "Alright, enough already. Daddy's not in trouble, I just need to talk to this nice man for a minute. It's no big deal," Tom insisted.

"License and registration?" the policeman asked.

"Here you go, Officer," Tom said. Kerry turned forwards and stared straight ahead. She folded her arms over the bump in her stomach.

"Sir, do you know why I pulled you over?" the policeman asked.

"Officer, I'm sorry if I was going a little fast. It's just…that…my wife is pregnant…and we're late getting to a very important doctor's appointment in Boston," Tom explained.

"Sir, this is a forty-five mile per hour zone and I just clocked you doing sixty-five. That's quite a penalty, you understand?" the policeman said, glancing at Kerry.

"Officer, I promise I don't usually speed. We've been stuck in traffic the whole way up from Rhode Island. Turning onto 128 was the first time in the last two hours where we haven't been sitting bumper to bumper. I think I just got a little excited," Tom explained. The officer excused himself for a moment, taking all of Tom's information back to the police car.

"*I think I just got a little excited?*" Kerry laughed. "I don't know which was worse: that—or blaming it on my eleven-week pregnancy!"

"Mommy? Daddy in trouble?" Emma asked.

"No, honey. Daddy has a good feeling about this nice policeman. Everything's fine. Just watch your show," Tom said.

"This is making us even later!" Kerry barked.

Stress was the last thing any of them needed at this particular moment. It had been seven weeks since Kerry had taken the pregnancy test, and every single day since they had anxiously awaited *this* doctor's appointment. To say they were nervous was an understatement. Coming to the decision to try for another child had been a long journey....

Several things had to be considered:

1. Were the geneticists certain there was no genetic link to any of Emma's complications at birth?
2. What if their next child were born with problems? Could they handle that? Was it fair to take that risk?
3. Would they be able to give all their children the attention they required should they welcome another?
4. Would they be able to deal with the stress that would come with a pregnancy?
5. Was adding another person the right decision for their family?

These questions ran through their minds constantly.

Early on, when Emma had come home for good, there was no way in hell Tom and Kerry would ever entertain the idea of expanding their brood. Life was anything but easy that first year and a half. Three toddlers with high energy, busy schedules and temper tantrums ruled their world. It was one thing to deal with a kid who didn't want to wear a diaper. It's was another to have one hand them her colostomy bag when she was sick of it. Kerry was convinced Ryan had potty trained himself in record time because he was worried poop might start shooting out of his belly if he didn't get to the toilet in time. Some days Thomas would beg to be put down for a nap, given the craziness that constantly ensued around him. The Sheeran's house had been a revolving door of early intervention specialists, lactation consultants and visiting nurses. Emma spent a lot of time visiting her pediatrician and keeping up with all her appointments in Boston. She got sick a lot. She was hospitalized a lot. Even the family cat had run away, unable to handle the chaos within their four walls. Another baby was impossible. It would never happen.

Family vacations sounded like a great idea, in theory. But when the Sheerans found themselves in the middle of the Adirondacks, four hours from the nearest major hospital, they realized they probably should have thought things through a little more. With Thomas covered in hand, foot and mouth disease and Emma's g-tube having popped out, they had to make their escape in the middle of the night. It was a nice five-hour drive home, with nothing but saran wrap and a bathing suit to keep the contents of Emma's stomach in place. During their trip home, Tom and Kerry passed the time joking about a fourth kid and how utterly ridiculous it sounded. Like maybe the silliest idea since thinking a far away lakeside retreat was going to help them all to decompress.

It took a village to keep Team Sheeran running those first couple of years after Emma's birth, but they kept running, nonetheless. Their pace was fast, and their supporters kept up right alongside them. It seemed an even exchange, considering Emma was the biggest miracle any of them had ever witnessed. They were there to help care for the boys, make dinners and carpool. They were there to wipe tears and fuel laughter. Relationships had grown; friendships had become stronger—all because of a little girl who had taught the world about perspective. A little girl who had taught people about themselves. Kerry found it harder to be put off by Jane's intensity, since that fuel had helped steer her through some of their roughest nights with Emma. Jane tried not to view Kerry as stubborn, and instead praised her to be *"one of the most devoted mothers in the world."* Donna's strict rules had become less of a burden and more of a reminder that, no matter what happened in life, certain things were *always* expected of them.

When Emma was six months old, she learned how to breastfeed, exclusively. It took many hours of trying, and some very patient lactation consultants to help both Kerry and Emma connect in this way. Once they did, however, there was no stopping them. It was as if all the stars in the sky had aligned that moment in July 2008 when Emma latched on to Kerry's breast and began to suck, swallow and breath, all at the same time. Four months later, when Dr. Buchmiller was confident Emma no longer needed it, the g-tube came out and the hole in Emma's stomach was stitched shut. The feeding pump, IV pole, backpack and instructional CD were all packed up and returned. Life had become a little easier. Another baby wasn't completely out of the question.

In December of 2009, after having had surgeries to successfully fix her urinary and bowel systems, potty training was the next mountain for Emma to climb. No longer having to be catheterized daily, Emma was on the road to figuring out the sensations necessary in order to become completely continent. Her kidneys grew perfectly in sync, her bladder functioned beautifully and her bowels were finally in tact. None of this was ever a guarantee for Emma. Tom and Kerry were told it was common for kids born with these types of complications to face many obstacles. Yet in true form, their daughter refused to fall within the norm.

At two years old, her colostomy was reversed. During her recovery, as Kerry was strolling her in Prouty Garden at Children's Hospital, Emma pooped for the first time into a diaper. Other patients and their family members snickered as Kerry practically did back flips to celebrate the eruption coming from her daughter's bum. She still, today, shows pictures of the soiled Pamper to anyone willing to look.

In May of 2010, Thomas had graduated preschool, Ryan had turned four, and Emma had seven surgeries behind her. Even the two little holes in her heart had closed, eliminating the need to be followed by a cardiologist. Life was sweet and Team Sheeran was running like a well-oiled machine. Once again, Kerry and Tom approached the idea of expanding their brood. The five questions bounced around them incessantly, until one day when Kerry had a conversation with her friend Susan, a mother of four:

"Tom and I always wanted four kids, but we're afraid," Kerry had explained.

"Afraid of what? Nothing was genetic with Emma. Her doctors told you there was nothing you had done to cause any of her complications. Right?" Susan had asked.

"They said it's unexplainable—a fluke during her fourth week of development. Something midline that happened during cell division." Kerry had answered.

"Didn't they say that while they can't pinpoint why it happened, there's no specific reason it should happen again?" Susan had asked.

"But it could happen. Anything can happen," Kerry had said.

"Of course it can, but those are the chances you face anytime you have a child," Susan had said.

"I guess, but now we know too much! Every other time I got pregnant, it was ignorant bliss about the future," Kerry had said.

"You have to put it in God's hands, Kerry. That's what I did. It's my only advice for you. If you decide to go for it, just put it in God's hands," Susan had advised.

Of course, what Susan had said, Kerry already knew. But it didn't hurt to be reminded that life, like a marathon, would turn where it wanted to. Keeping up with its winding, unheralded course was always going to be the challenge, but that was the beauty of it. And God was going to be there, no matter what happened. Tom agreed with this viewpoint, hence Kerry's subsequent pregnancy and their *nearly* ticketed, nerve-wracking drive up to Boston.

THE TRAFFIC LIGHT turned green and Tom finally pulled up in front of Brigham and Women's hospital. "Just park the car and meet me up there. I'm already twenty minutes late!" Kerry yelled as she slammed the car door. It was surreal to walk through the same doors she had entered two and a half years earlier, in search of a second opinion. Everything looked exactly the same as she passed through security and rode the elevator to the second floor of the Connors Center, where Dr. Wilkins-Haug and the Maternal Fetal Medicine department were still stationed. Opening the door to the waiting room, Kerry's hands shook and a hive or two popped out on her chest.

She pulled a piece of paper out of her pocket and scanned the list of questions she had written down. *I can't forget to ask the doctor about a VBAC,* Kerry thought. *And natural birth—these are the two important things, assuming everything's okay.* Her heart raced, and she longed for Emma and Tom to keep her company. Looking around, she saw the chairs she had sat in so many times before, waiting to hear the next piece of bad news about Emma. She shook her head at the pile of magazines in the corner, disgusted by their attempt to distract mothers from the reality of the ultrasound machines just beyond the waiting room's door. Kerry's legs trembled uncontrollably. She felt sick. Acid bubbled up the back of her throat. She scanned the room for the nearest garbage can, in case she had to make a run for it. Suddenly, it felt as though they had made a questionable decision.

Minutes later, the door to the waiting room swung open and a friendly brunette called: "Kerry Sheeran?" Realizing she was forced to answer, being the only person in the room, Kerry stood up and walked towards the woman in the white coat. "I wasn't expecting you to take me so fast," Kerry explained. "My husband is still parking the car!"

"That's okay, we can get started and he can join us when he gets here," she assured Kerry. "By the way, my name is Julie and I'll be doing your ultrasound today," she smiled. Kerry gulped as they walked through the doorway into the dark familiar room. Lying on the table, she lifted her shirt to reveal the biggest example of *faith* she could ever imagine existed. As Julie squirted surgilube on Kerry's abdomen, the voice reminded the expectant mother:

"It's all in God's hands"

Kerry's body trembled with the first roll of the ultrasound wand. "Are you okay?" Julie asked.

"I'm just really nauseous. Really, really nauseous…and nervous," Kerry explained. "I've had a lot of scary moments in these ultrasound rooms."

"I'm sure you have. I was just reading your chart," Julie said, rolling the wand back and forth.

"I know certain things don't show up this early in pregnancy," Kerry continued, "I guess I'm just nervous about a heartbeat at this point. As long as I know there's a heartbeat, then I can wait until the next ultrasound to worry about the next thing, right?" Kerry asked. Julie nodded her head but was silent, squinting at the screen. She was pausing to type things, then rolling the wand in several different directions and squinting some more. Another few hives popped up on Kerry's chest before she spoke again. "You're being really quiet...that's making me nervous. Is everything okay?" Kerry asked. Julie turned the screen in Kerry's direction and finally spoke.

"Do you see what I see?" she asked. Kerry looked up to see two babies, head to head on the monitor.

"Oh, my God, I cannot believe it. Twins! What?! I can't believe this happened on our fourth try! Twins run in my family...so I always knew it was a possibility...but I thought I had a deal with God! I thought if I were going to get twins, that it would happen on the first or second try, not the fourth!" Kerry had her hands on her head, trying to keep it from exploding. She looked to Julie for sympathy. "You don't understand... I have three *really* young kids! My oldest is only five! I don't know how this is even going to be possible! My daughter just had her seventh surgery four months ago!" Kerry cried.

"Uhhh...boy...uhhh, then I...uhhh...don't know if you're going to like what I have to say next," Julie mumbled.

"Oh my God, are their hearts beating? Please tell me their hearts are beating!" Kerry begged.

"There's three," Julie declared.

Kerry sat up, reached over and grabbed Julie's arm in a tight grip.

"Are you kidding me right now? Are you messing with me?" Kerry asked.

"You mean this wasn't in vitro? No fertility meds? You didn't know?" Julie asked, frightened. Her mouth gaping open, Kerry shook her head *no*. "Oh...uhhh...this doesn't usually happen...I mean, it's never happened...while I was scanning someone," Julie sputtered.

"Are you kidding me?" Kerry asked. "Are YOU kidding me?" she squalled, beaming her eyes through the ceiling. Hives were everywhere. "Are all three hearts beating?" she asked.

"Yes, three heartbeats. Two are identical. I can tell by the way they're connected to the same placenta." Julie said.

"Oh…. I'm gonna kill Susan," Kerry snarled.

"Who's Susan?" Julie inquired.

"SERIOUSLY?" Kerry yelled, once again looking towards the sky. Suddenly the door opened, and Tom pushed Emma's stroller into the room. He could tell by the two wide-eyed women and strong smell of panic that something was going down.

"Uh oh, what's wrong?" he asked.

"Nothing's wrong," Kerry answered. Her eyes twitched; her face was covered in blotches.

"Do you want to tell him or should I?" Julie asked.

"Tell me what?" Tom snapped. His white knuckles had a death grip on Emma's stroller.

Kerry took a deep breath in, then closed her eyes and slowly exhaled. When she opened her eyes again, Emma was smiling and waving to her. Looking at Tom, she gathered as much nerve as she could muster before opening her mouth and catapulting their lives into the next unimaginable chapter.

"Sit down, babe," she advised. "Save your legs. You're probably gonna want to go for a long run later…."

The End

GOD IS GOOD

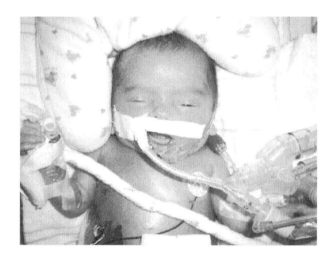

Emma, 2 days old

Emma, 5 years old

GOD IS LOVE

Kerry with Louise Wilkins-Haug, MD

2nd from left, Nurse Jackie; far right, Nurse Nancy,
in front, Nurse Maria

GOD IS LOVE

Sister Carlotta with Emma

Kerry Kangarooing with Emma

GOD IS LOVE

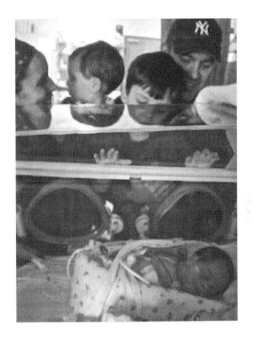

Team Sheeran together for the first time

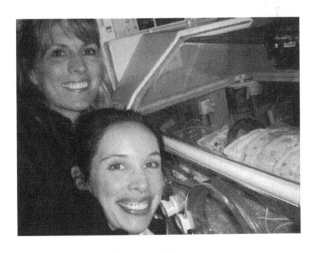

Jean and Kerry

GOD IS LOVE

Joe and Donna Sullivan

Jane and Tom Sheeran

GOD IS LOVE

Nurse Kate

From left: Tom, Nurse Nancy, Nurse Jessica & Nurse Deb

GOD IS LOVE

Kerry and Dr. Buchmiller (post Emma's esophageal repair)

Lis, Cheryl, Isabel & Matthew

MIRACLES

Emma and Caitlin, 2 years old

NICU Soul Mates: Emma and Matthew (5 years old)

THE 2009 BOSTON MARATHON

Kerry and Emma

From left: Brad, Timmy, Emma, Tom, Bella & Sean in Copley Square

Tom Sheeran, Official Marathon Runner

EPILOGUE

Shining Light
Your Average Joe
Why Some Mistakes Are Good
and
Boston Strong

Almost every time Emma has a check-up at Boston Children's Hospital, Tom and I make it a point to stop over to the NICU and say hello to the doctors and nurses who happen to be working that day. Inevitably we will see five to ten folks whom we know personally, and the moment they lay eyes on their former patient—emotion ensues. Seeing Emma today and knowing her story from the beginning, it's impossible not to gasp or tear up when they're in her presence. It's always our favorite part of the day.

We do this not just simply because we owe our daughter's life to these people, but because *they* deserve it. After everything they do, day after day and year after year, sick baby after sick baby, they deserve to see just how much their hard work and dedication pays off. It's only fair that they know how meaningful their efforts are, how families are kept together and children go on to thrive, living beautiful lives because of their care. We do this because not every story ends as Emma's did, and many times they are faced with the ultimate "bad day at work." We bring Emma to see the people who were responsible for saving her life, because we know that most people seek meaning in their lives at one point or another. Because it's only fair, that since they revealed God to us, that we should attempt to do the same for them.

We also keep in touch with Cheryl and Liz, Shawna and Tim, and a couple other families we met at Boston Children's Hospital. Their journeys inspired us throughout our ordeal with Emma, and have forever left an imprint on our hearts. Our story is theirs, and vice-versa. When asked why I decided to tell ours in the form of a novel, my answer was simple: I wanted to show other parents that there are ways of getting through the most difficult days of a child's illness. Staying strong requires support, endurance, love, and a lot of faith—both in God and in our own parental instincts. What Emma overcame was medically miraculous. What I overcame was life changing all around. Discovering this kind of strength can be a beautiful experience for both the parents and the child.

THE MARATHON is a story of survival, revealed through a series of conversations with a character who represents many: Needham Joe. As Tom makes his way through the actual Marathon, his conversations with Needham Joe become the way by which Tom is able to tell his true story. Joe listens to Tom sporadically throughout his journey from Hopkinton to Boston, becoming invested in Emma. He also tells Tom about his own daughter, and the struggles his family endured as a result of her congenital heart-defect. Towards the end of the race, Joe reveals that his daughter, who had survived five open heart surgeries, didn't make it through her sixth. After breaking this news to Tom, he takes off into the sea of runners—disappearing so suddenly that Tom has to wonder "if he were ever really there to begin with." Joe, fictional only by the circumstance he is written in, represents the 26,000 other runners—all with their own stories of desperation and triumph. He is the true story of a dear friend/NICU nurse who lost her own daughter to a congenital heart defect, but continued to work in Boston Children's NICU to help save Emma and so many others. He is Tom, himself, reliving the harrowing story that brought him to Boston that day. He represents the countless parents who have endured heartache or suffered the loss of a child. Joe is a combination of so many people we know—continuing to move forward despite the crippling grief they have had to bear. He is the ultimate example of strength.

Never forgetting how close we were to being in Joe's shoes, we are forever grateful for the path Emma's life has taken from the very beginning. What will always fascinate me is the fact that a *placenta previa* note (written by mistake on my chart) led to the 27-week ultrasound, which told us that "something" was not right with Emma. Without that ultrasound, Emma's ascites would have gone undetected—causing her to eventually fill with so much amniotic fluid that she would have perished in utero. The series of mistakes and eventual misdiagnosis in Rhode Island were all part of the path that led to Emma's life being saved in Boston. It does not, in any way, represent the norm for the thousands of life-saving, hard-working, medical miracle workers in our beloved community. Emma has been rescued ten times over by some of the finest doctors in the Ocean State. Her pediatrician has become an honorary member of our family. Here's the thing about medicine: it is anything *but* an exact science. This is something a parent of a sick child must learn, and learn fast. Nobody is perfect, which is why it is the parents' responsibility to seek second opinions, proper care and advocacy for their children. Neglect is one thing. But mistakes can happen to anyone at any time. By arming ourselves with as much knowledge as possible, and attaining multiple opinions from specialists, we parents have the ability to seek the best possible medical treatment for our children. My advice is simple, effective, and comes from experience: speak up, ask questions, take part in "rounds," do lots of research, and, perhaps most importantly, follow your gut. Parents, by nature, are connected to their children in a way science will never be able to explain.

Ironically, while I was wrapping up my final chapters of this book, the bombings occurred in the 2013 Boston Marathon. Never will I forget, as I was typing away on my computer, the moment a text came through from a dear friend with news of chaos and destruction at the very finish line I had been describing just moments prior. I watched in horror, along with the rest of America, as stories of unimaginable carnage were revealed: families and human bodies having been torn apart. I watched this all with the same sadness and anger that stays with me today, leaving me to ask the same question repeatedly: *How dare they?*

Violence and murder are atrocious to begin with. But unleashing these at an event, specifically designed to inspire and demonstrate the power of the human body and spirit? Well, that's a whole other level of evil, which many of us will never comprehend. How dare anyone try to destroy such a beautiful example of good in our world?

Lives were mangled and lost. Innocent lives. Many of us cannot begin to imagine the kind of pain these families have suffered. The only solace on that dreadful day came from the people on the streets of Boston. As it turned out, the power of the human body and spirit was demonstrated, after all. Heroes emerged from the wreckage, victims fought for their lives, help came running.

In 2014, 36,000 participants (including Tom, Mike, Cheryl and Dr. Buchmiller) will take part in the Boston Marathon. 9,000 more then average. Collectively, most of these marathoners will be raising millions of dollars across thirty-five charities. Reminding us that LOVE is indestructible. That GOD is good. That WE are strong.

Boston Strong.

REFERENCES:

"Wheelchair Racing in the Boston Marathon" by, Mike Siviki – www.disaboom.com

http://www.marathonguide.com/Features/Articles/2010RecapOvervie w.cfm

boston.cbslocal.com/guide/mile-by-mile-guide-to-the-boston-marathon/

"26 Miles To Boston" by Michael Connelly

"The Boston Marathon—A Century of Blood, Sweat, and Cheers" by Tom Derderian

www.teamhoyt.com

www.50statesmarathonclub.com

ABOUT THE AUTHOR

(Back row: Kerry, Thomas, Tom.
Front row: Emma, Catie, Ryan, Charlotte, Erin)

Author, **Kerry Sullivan Sheeran** was born and raised in Wyckoff, New Jersey. She is a graduate of Villanova University with a BA in English, and a former marketing/sales executive at *Money Magazine* and *The Wall Street Journal* International. Now married and the mother of six, her life experiences have allowed her to connect with many parents who have suffered the illness of a child. Patient advocacy and supporting advances in prenatal & neonatal care are her passions. Although she's written several children's books, THE MARATHON is her first novel. A stay-at-home mother, Kerry lives with her family in East Greenwich, Rhode Island. For more information go to **www.kerrysheeran.com**.

Made in the USA
Charleston, SC
03 April 2014